Contents

BERLITZ®

ARABIC for travellers

By the staff of Berlitz Guides

How best to use this phrase book

Colloquial Arabic rather than the classical, written form is used throughout. However, when a word differs from country to country, we give either the classical or the Egyptian version. If you are not understood the first time, try the alternative in brackets [ ].

• Start with the **Guide to pronunciation** (pp. 6–10), then go on to **Some basic expressions** (pp. 11–16). This gives you a minimum vocabulary and helps you to pronounce the language.

• Consult the **Contents** pages (3–5) for the section you need. In each chapter you'll find facts, hints and information. Simple phrases are followed by a list of words applicable to the situation.

• Separate, detailed contents lists are included at the beginning of the extensive **Eating out** and **Shopping guide** sections (Menus, p. 40, Shops and services, p. 97).

• If you want to find out how to say something in Arabic, use the **Dictionary** section (pp. 162–189). This will give you the word cross-referenced to its use in a phrase on a specific page.

• If you wish to learn more about constructing sentences, check the **Basic grammar** (pp. 158–161).

• Note the **colour margins** are indexed in Arabic and English to help both listener and speaker. And, in addition, there is also an **index in Arabic** for the use of your listener.

• The symbol ☛ suggests phrases your listener can use to help you. Hand this phrase book to the Arabic-speaker to encourage pointing to an appropriate answer.

Library of Congress Catalog Card No. 86-70987.

Revised edition—1st printing Printed in Switzerland

Acknowledgments
We are particularly grateful to Yehya Chahin and Christina Jackson for their invaluable help in the preparation of this book, and to Dr. T.J.A. Bennett for his advice concerning the phonetic transcription. We also wish to thank Adam Bahaa-el-Din for assistance.

Guide to pronunciation

The traditional Arabic script is composed of consonants only and is written from right to left. A system of vowel signs (small marks above or below the characters), used mainly in the Koran, in poetry and in texts for beginners ensures proper pronunciation.

Written Arabic is fairly uniform. The spoken language, however, can differ considerably from one country to another or even among regions of the same country. We have based our transcription on the dialect used in most parts of Lower Egypt and especially in Cairo. This dialect is widely understood throughout the Middle East thanks to Egyptian films, radio and the recordings of popular artists. In addition, the Egyptian dialect is easier to learn than the others because some difficult sounds have been replaced by simpler ones, so that several letters of the alphabet are pronounced alike.

You'll find the pronunciation of the Arabic letters and sounds explained below, as well as the symbols we use for them in the transcriptions. Of course, the sounds of any two languages are never exactly the same; but if you follow carefully the indications supplied here, you'll have no difficulty in reading our transcriptions in such a way as to make yourself understood. This and the following section are intended to make you familiar with our transcription and to help you get used to the sounds of Arabic.

As a minimum vocabulary for your trip, we've selected a number of basic words and phrases under the title "Some Basic Expressions" (pages 11–16).

Letters written **bold** should be stressed (pronounced louder).

Consonants

Letter	Approximate pronunciation	Symbol	Example	
ء	glottal stop*	'	رأى	**ra**'ā
ب	like **b** in **b**oy	b	باب	bǣb
ت	like **t** in **t**en	t	تاج	tǣg
ث	in classical Arabic, like **th** in **th**in; in spoken Arabic: 1) like **s** in **s**it	s	ثوره	**saw**ra
	2) like **t** in **t**en	t	ثور	tōr
ج	1) like **g** in **g**et (Egypt)	g	جميل	gæ**mīl**
	2) like **s** in plea**s**ure (most other countries)	zh	جميل	zhæ**mīl**
ح	like **h** in **h**oot, but more "emphatic" and with slight friction in throat	ḥ	حديد	ḥæ**dīd**
خ	like **ch** in Scottish lo**ch**	kh	خرج	**kha**ragæ
د	like **d** in **d**ay	d	دب	dibb
ذ	in classical Arabic, like **th** in **th**en; in spoken Arabic: 1) like **z** in **z**ebra	z	ذكى	**zæ**kī
	2) like **d** in **d**ay	d	دهب	**dæ**hæb
ر	like **r** in rolled Scottish **r**	r	رجل	**ra**gol
ز	like **z** in **z**ebra	z	زيت	zēt
س	like **s** in **s**it	s	سبب	**sæ**bæb
ش	like **sh** in **sh**ine	sh	شمس	shæms
ص	like **s** in **s**un, pronounced with considerable "emphasis"	ṣ	صبر	ṣabr

* This corresponds, in English, to the initial blocking of the throat before a vowel, as before the second o in "cooperate". It is also heard in the Cockney pronunciation of t in "water" (wa'er). In Arabic, the glottal stop can occur before a vowel *or* a consonant and even at the end of a word.

ض	like **d** in **d**uck, pronounced with "emphasis"	ḍ	ضيف **dē**f
ط	like **t** in **t**ough, pronounced with "emphasis"	ṭ	طياره ṭay**yā**ra
ظ	like **th** in **th**en, pronounced with emphasis	ẓ	ظريف ẓarīf
ع	similar to glottal stop (see above)	ʼ	رفيع rafīʼ
غ	like a soft version of **ch** in Scottish lo**ch** (or like French pronunciation of **r** in "**r**ue")	g̱	غالى **g̱æ**lī
ف	like **f** in **f**eed	f	فانوس fæ**nūs**
ق	a guttural **k**, pronounced deep in the throat	q	قلب qalb
ك	like **k** in **k**ite	k	كتاب ki**tæb**
ل	like **l** in **l**et	l	لطيف laṭīf
م	like **m** in **m**eet	m	ملبن **mæl**bæn
ن	like **n** in **n**eat	n	نرجس **nær**gis
هـ	like **h** in **h**ear, whatever its position in the word	h	هرم **ha**ram
و	like **w** in **w**ell	w	ورد wærd
ى	like **y** in **y**ell	y	يكتب **yæk**tob

Note: The letter **v** does not exist in the Arabic alphabet. However, in certain cases it is used when a foreign word has been assimilated into the Arabic language, e.g. **vīd**yō.

Certain letters of the Arabic alphabet are known as the "sun" letters: **t**, **d**, **r**, **z**, **s**, **sh**, **ṣ**, **ḍ**, **ṭ**, **ẓ**, **l** and **n**. When a noun or adjective preceded by the article الـ (æl) begins with one of these letters, the l of the æl takes on the sound of the initial letter of the word, e.g. æl-**ra**gol becomes ær-**ra**gol, æl-ṭa**yā**ra becomes aṭ-ṭa**yā**ra.

Vowels

The letters ا , و and ى in the list above can also serve as vowels. In addition, Arabic has three vowel signs (َ , ُ , ِ); they occur either above or below the letter and are pronounced after the letter that carries the sign. In contemporary written Arabic—as in this book—the vowel signs are generally omitted. The context shows the reader which is the appropriate vowel he has to supply.

ا َ	1) like **a** in northern English h**a**t or in American wh**a**t (short)	a	صبر	ṣabr
	2) like **a** in c**a**r (long)	ā	طار	ṭār
	3) like **a** in c**a**n (short)	æ	كتب	**kæ**tæbæ
	4) like **a** in c**a**n, but long	ǣ	كتاب	ki**tǣb**
و ُ	1) like **aw** in r**aw**, but with the lips more tightly rounded; it sounds quite reminiscent of **oo** in f**oo**t (short)	o	بن	bonn
	2) like **ou** in f**ou**r (long)	ō	يوم	yōm
	3) like **oo** in b**oo**t (long)	ū	نور	nūr
ى ِ	1) like **i** in s**i**t (short)	i	من	min
	2) like **ee** in m**ee**t (long)	ī	جميل	gæ**mīl**
	3) like **ay** in d**ay**, but a pure vowel, not a diphthong (long)	ē	بيت	bēt

Note. Each symbol in our transcriptions should be pronounced as shown above, regardless of its position in the word; e.g., **s** always has—even between two vowels or at the end of a word—to be pronounced as in sit, not as in houses.

Any consonants written double must be pronounced long; e.g., **kk** should be pronounced as in thi**ck c**oat, **ss** as in ma**ss s**urvey, etc.

The Arabic alphabet

Here are the 28 characters which comprise the Arabic alphabet. A character may have different forms, depending on whether it's used by itself or comes at the end, in the middle or at the beginning of a word.

Isolated	Final	Median	Initial	Name
ا	ـا			ælif
ب	ـب	ـبـ	بـ	be'
ت	ـت	ـتـ	تـ	te'
ث	ـث	ـثـ	ثـ	se'
ج	ـج	ـجـ	جـ	gīm
ح	ـح	ـحـ	حـ	ḥa'
خ	ـخ	ـخـ	خـ	kha'
د	ـد			dæl
ذ	ـذ			zæl
ر	ـر			re'
ز	ـز			zēn
س	ـس	ـسـ	سـ	sīn
ش	ـش	ـشـ	شـ	shīn
ص	ـص	ـصـ	صـ	ṣād
ض	ـض	ـضـ	ضـ	ḍād
ط	ـط	ـطـ	ط	ṭa'
ظ	ـظ	ـظـ	ظ	za'
ع	ـع	ـعـ	عـ	'ēn
غ	ـغ	ـغـ	غـ	gēn
ف	ـف	ـفـ	فـ	fe'
ق	ـق	ـقـ	قـ	qāf
ك	ـك	ـكـ	كـ	kæf
ل	ـل	ـلـ	لـ	læm
م	ـم	ـمـ	مـ	mīm
ن	ـن	ـنـ	نـ	nūn
ه ة	ـه ـة	ـهـ	هـ	he'
و	ـو			wāw
ى	ـى	ـيـ	يـ	ye'

Some basic expressions

Yes.	**næ**'æm	نعم.
No.	læ	لا.
Please.	min **faḍ**lak (**faḍ**lik)	من فضلَك (فضلِك).
Thank you.	**shok**ran	شكراً.
Thank you very much.	**shok**ran gæ**zī**læn	شكراً جزيلاً.
You're welcome.	**'æf**wæn	عفواً.
I beg your pardon?	**'æf**wæn	عفواً.
Excuse me. (May I get past?)	es**mæḥ**lī (esmæ**ḥī**lī)	إسمح لي (إسمحي لي).
Excuse me.	**'æf**wæn	عفواً.
Sorry!	**æ**sef (**æs**fæ)	أسف (أسفة).

Greetings التحيات

Good morning.	ṣa**bāḥ** æl-**khēr**	صباح الخير.
Good evening.	mæ**sǣ**' æl-**khēr**	مساء الخير.
Good night.	**tiṣ**baḥ **'æ**læ khēr	تصبح على خير.
Hello.	**æh**læn	أهلاً.
Come in, make yourself at home.	it**faḍ**ḍal (itfaḍ**ḍa**lī)	إتفضّل (إتفضّلي).
This is Mr./Mrs./Miss...	o**qad**dim æs-**sæy**yid/ æs-sæy**yi**dæ/æl-**æ**nisæ	أقدّم السيد / السيدة / الآنسة..

Words in Arabic have different forms, depending whether the person in question is a man or a woman. In this section both versions are given; the feminine form is in parentheses. When only one version is given, the phrase does not change. Arabs appreciate foreigners making an effort to express themselves in Arabic. No one will expect you to speak it perfectly, and even if you just use the masculine form, everyone will understand.

How do you do? (Pleased to meet you.)	tæshær**rafna**	تشرّفنا.
How are you?	**kæy**fæ **ḥǣ**lak (**ḥǣ**lik)	كيف حالك (حالكِ)؟
Very well, thanks.	**kwæy**yis (kwæy**yi**sæ) æl-**ḥæm**du lil**lǣh**	كويس (كويسه) الحمدلله.
And you?	wæ **in**tæ (**in**ti)	وأنتَ (أنتِ)؟
Fine.	**kwæy**yis (kwæy**yi**sæ)	كويس (كويسه).
Good-bye.	mæ'æs sæ**lǣ**mæ	مع السلامة.
See you later.	ilæl **liqā'**	إلى اللقاء.
Have a good day.	na**hā**rak (na**hā**rik) sæ**'id**	نهارك (نهارك) سعيد.

Questions أسئلة

Where?	**æy**næ	أين؟
How?	**kæy**fæ	كيف؟
When?	**mæ**tæ	متى؟
What?	mǣ/**mǣ**zæ	ما/ ماذا؟
Why?	li**mǣ**zæ	لماذا؟
Who?	mæn	من؟
Which?	æyy	أي؟
Where is/are...?	**æy**næ	أين...؟
Where can I find/ Where can I get...?	**æy**næ **æ**gid	أين أجد...؟
How far?	kæm æl-mæ**sǣ**fæ	كم المسافة؟
How long?	kæm min æl-**waqt**	كم من الوقت؟
How much/How many?	kæm	كم؟
How much does this cost?	bi**kæm hǣ**zæ	بكم هذا؟
When does... open/ close?	**mæ**tæ **yæf**tæḥ/**yaq**fil	متى يفتح/ يقفل...؟

What do you call this/that in Arabic?	mǣ ism **hǣ**zæ bil **'ara**bī	ما اسم هذا بالعربي؟
What does this/that mean?	mǣ **mæ**'nǣ **hǣ**zæ	ما معنى هذا؟

Do you speak...? هل تتكلّم...؟

Do you speak English?	hæl tætæ**kæl**læm (tætækæl**læ**mi) ingi**lī**zī	هل تتكلم (تتكلمين) إنجليزي؟
Does anyone here speak English?	hæl **yū**gæd **æ**ḥæd yætæ**kæl**læm ingi**lī**zī	هل يوجد أحد يتكلم إنجليزي؟
I don't speak Arabic.	ænæ lǣ ætæ**kæl**læm æl-**'ara**bī	أنا لا أتكلم العربي.
Could you speak more slowly?	**mom**kin tætæ**kal**læm (tætækæl**læ**mi) bi**boṭ'**	ممكن تتكلم (تتكلمِ) ببطء؟
Could you repeat that?	**mom**kin ti**kar**rar (tikar**ra**ri) **hǣ**zæ	ممكن تكرّر (تكررِ) هذا؟
Can you translate this for me?	**mom**kin titær**gim**lī (titærgi**mi**lī) **hǣ**zæ	ممكن تترجم لي (تترجمِ لي) هذا؟
Can you translate this for us?	**mom**kin titærgim**li**nǣ (titærgi**mil**nǣ) **hǣ**zæ	ممكن تترجم لنا (تترجمِ لنا) هذا؟
Please point to the... in the book.	min **faḍ**lak **ḥæd**did æl-... fil ki**tǣb**	من فضلك حدد ال... في الكتاب.
answer	gæ**wǣb**	جواب.
phrase/sentence	**gom**læ	جملة.
word	**kel**mæ	كلمة.
Just a moment.	**laḥ**za min **faḍ**lak (**faḍ**lik)	لحظة من فضلك (فضلِك).
I'll see if I can find it in this book.	sæ'**æb**ḥæs **'æn**hǣ fī **hǣ**zæl ki**tǣb**	سأبحث عنها في هذا الكتاب.
I understand.	**æ**næ **æf**hæm	أنا أفهم.
I don't understand.	ænæ lǣ **æf**hæm	أنا لا أفهم.
Do you understand?	hæl **tæf**hæm (tæf**hæ**mi)	هل تفهم (تفهمِ)؟

Can/May...? ممكن...؟

Can I have...? (I'd like..., please.)	o**rīd**... min **faḍ**lak (**faḍ**lik)	أريد... من فضلك (فضلِك).
Can we have...? (We'd like..., please.)	no**rīd**... min **faḍ**lak (**faḍ**lik)	نريد... من فضلك (فضلِك).
Can you show me...?	**mom**kin to**rī**nī	ممكن ترين...؟
I can't.	læ yom**ki**nonī	لا يمكنني.
Can you tell me...?	**mom**kin tæ**qol**lī (tæ**qo**lilī)	ممكن تقول لي (تقولي لي)...؟
Can you help me?	**mom**kin tisæ'**id**nī (tisæ'**idi**nī)	ممكن تساعدني (تساعديني)؟
Can I help you?	**mom**kin æ**sæ**'dæk	ممكن أساعدك؟
Can you direct me to...?	**mom**kin ta**ṣif** lī aṭ-ṭarīq ilæ	ممكن تصف لي الطريق إلى...؟

Wanting... أريد... من فضلك

I'd like...	orīd min **faḍ**lak (**faḍ**lik)	أريد من فضلك (فضلِك)...
We'd like...	no**rīd** min **faḍ**lak (**faḍ**lik)	نريد من فضلك (فضلِك)...
What do you want?	**mæ**zæ to**rīd** (torīdi)	ماذا تريد (تريدِ)؟
Give me...	a'aṭīnī	أعطني...
Give it to me.	a'aṭīho lī	أعطيه لي.
Bring me...	a**ḥ**ḍir (aḥ**ḍi**ri) lī	أحضر (أحضِر) لي...
Bring it to me.	aḥ**ḍir**ho (aḥḍi**rī**ho) lī	أحضرة (أحضِرية) لي.
Show me...	ærīnī	أريني...
Show it to me.	**mom**kin to**rī**ho lī	ممكن تريه لي.
I'm looking for...	æb**ḥ**æs 'æn	أبحث عن...
I'm hungry.	ænæ gæ'**æn** (gæ'ænæ)	أنا جعان (جعانة).
I'm thirsty.	ænæ 'aṭ**shæn** ('aṭshænæ)	أنا عطشان (عطشانة).
I'm tired.	ænæ tæ'**bæn** (tæ'**bæ**næ)	أنا تعبان (تعبانة).
I'm lost.	ænæ toht	أنا تهت.
It's important.	innæho mo**himm**	إنه مهم.
It's urgent.	innæho '**æ**gil	إنه عاجل.

It is/There is... إنه/ يوجد...

It is...	innæho	إنه...
Is it...?	hæl **ho**wæ	هل هو...؟
It isn't...	in**næ**ho **læy**sæ	إنه ليس...
Here it is.	hǣ **ho**wæ (**hi**yæ)	ها هو (هي).
Here they are.	hǣ hom	ها هم.
There it is.	hǣ **ho**wæ ho**nǣk**	ها هو هناك.
There they are.	hǣ hom ho**nǣk**	ها هم هناك.
There is/are...	**yū**gæd	يوجد...
Is/Are there...?	hæl **yū**gæd	هل يوجد...؟
There isn't/aren't...	lǣ **yū**gæd	لا يوجد...
There isn't/aren't any.	lǣ **yū**gæd **min**ho	لا يوجد منه.

It's... إنه...

big/small	kæ**bīr**/ṣa**gīr**	كبير/ صغير
quick/slow	sæ**rī'**/ba**ṭī'**	سريع/ بطيء
hot/cold	**sǣ**khin/**bǣ**rid	ساخن/ بارد.
full/empty	mæl**yǣn**/**fā**ḍī	مليان/ فاضي
easy/difficult	sæhl/ṣa'b	سهل/ صعب
heavy/light	tæ**qīl**/khæ**fīf**	ثقيل/ خفيف
open/shut	mæf**tūḥ**/mæq**fūl**	مفتوح/ مقفول
right/wrong	ṣaḥḥ/**ga**laṭ	صح/ غلط
old/new	qa**dīm**/gæ**dīd**	قديم/ جديد
old/young	'æ**gūz**/shǣbb	عجوز/ شاب
next/last	**qā**dim/æ**khīr**	قادم/ أخير
beautiful/ugly	gæ**mīl**/qa**bīḥ**	جميل/ قبيح
free (vacant)/occupied	**khǣ**līy/mæsh**gūl**	خالي/ مشغول
good/bad	**kwæy**yis/**sæy**yi'	كويس/ سيىء
better/worse	**æḥ**sæn/**æs**wæ'	أحسن/ أسوأ
early/late	mo**bæk**kir/mit'**akh**khar	مبكر/ متاخر
cheap/expensive	ra**khīṣ**/**gǣ**lī	رخيص/ غالي

16

| near/far | qaŕib/bæ'īd | قريب / بعيد |
| here/there | honæ/honǣk | هنا / هناك |

Quantities كميات

a little/a lot	shwæyæ [qalīl]/kitīr	شويه [قليل] / كثير
few/a few	qalīl/ba'ḍ	قليل / بعض
much/many	kitīr	كثير
more/less	aktar/aqall	أكثر / أقل
more than/less than	aktar min/aqall min	أكثر من / أقل من
enough/too	yækfī/kitīr	يكفي / كثير
some/any	min æl/æyy	من الـ / أي

A few more useful words بعض الكلمات المفيدة

at	'indæ	عند	under	tæḥt	تحت
on	'ælæ	على	inside	fiddǣkhil	في الداخل
in	fī	في	outside	fil khǣrig	في الخارج
to	ilæ	إلى	up(stairs)	foq	فوق
after	bæ'd	بعد	down(stairs)	tæḥt	تحت
before	qabl	قبل	and	wæ	و
for	li	لـ	or	æw	أو
from	min	من	but	lækin	لكن
with	mæ'æ/bi	مع / بـ	not	læysæ	ليس
without	bidūn	بدون	never	æbædæn	أبداً
through	min khilǣl	من خلال	nothing	lǣ she'	لا شيء
towards	ilæ	إلى	none	wælæ wǣḥid	ولا واحد
until	ḥættæ	حتى	very	giddæn	جداً
during	æsnǣ'	أثناء	too (also)	aydan	أيضاً
next to	bigǣnib	بجانب	only	faqat	فقط
behind	warā'	وراء	yet	bæ'd	بعد
between	bēn	بين	soon	qaŕibæn	قريباً
since	monzo	منذ	now	æl'æn	الآن
above	foq	فوق	then	bæ'dēn	بعدين
below	tæḥt	تحت	perhaps	robbæmæ	ربما

عبارات أساسية

Arrival

Passport control—Customs مراقبة جوازات السفر ـ الجمرك

Here's my passport.	hǣ **how**æ gæ**wǣz** **safarī**	ها هو جواز سفري.
I'll be staying...	sæ'**æb**qā	سأبقى...
a few days	ba'ḍ æl-æyy**ǣm**	بعض الأيام
a week	os**bū'**	أسبوع
2 weeks	osbū'**ēn**	أسبوعين
a month	shahr	شهر
I don't know yet.	lǣ æ'**æ**rif bæ'd	لا أعرف بعد.
I'm here on holiday.	**æ**næ **ho**næ fī æ**gǣ**zæ	أنا هنا في إجازة.
I'm here on business.	**æ**næ **ho**næ li shogl	أنا هنا لشغل.
I'm just passing through.	**æ**næ **ho**næ fī mu**rūr**	أنا هنا في مرور.

جواز سفرك من فضلك.	Your passport, please.
هل عندك شيء للإعلان عنه؟	Do you have anything to declare?
من فضلك أفتح هذه الحقيبة.	Please open this suitcase.
يجب دفع رسوم على هذا.	You'll have to pay duty on this.
هل معك حقائب أخرى؟	Do you have any more luggage?

It's for my personal use.	h**ǣ**zæ listi'**mǣ**lī æsh-**shakh**ṣī	هذا لاستعمالي الشخصي.
This is a gift.	h**ǣ**zihi hi**dey**yæ	هذه هدية.

بضائع للإعلان عنها
goods to declare

المسموحات
nothing to declare

NUMBERS, see page 146

I've nothing to declare.	**læy**sæ **'in**dī she' li o'**o**lin **'æn**ho	ليس عندي شيء لأعلن عنه.
I've...	**'in**dī	عندي...
a carton of cigarettes	khar**ṭū**shit sæ**gæ**yir	خرطوشة سجاير
a bottle of...	zo**gæ**git	زجاجة...

Baggage—Porter الحقائب ـ الشيال (عتال)

Porter!	shæy**yæl** ['æt**tæl**]	شيال [عتال]!
Please take this...	min **faḍ**lak khod **hæ**zæ	من فضلك خذ هذا...
suitcase/travelling bag	æl-ḥa**qī**bæ/ash-**shan**ṭa	الحقيبة/ الشنطة
That's mine.	**hæ**zihi lī	هذه لي.
Take this luggage to the...	khod hæ**zi**hil ḥa**qā**'ib ilæ	خذ هذه الحقائب إلى...
bus/taxi	æl-oto**bīs**/æt-**tæk**sī	الأوتوبيس/ التاكسي
left luggage office (baggage check)	**mæk**tæb æl-æmæ**næt**	مكتب الأمانات
One piece is missing.	**nā**qiṣ **qiṭ**'a **wæḥ**dæ	ناقص قطعة واحدة.
Where are the luggage trolleys (carts)?	**æy**næ **'a**rabit æl-ḥa**qā**'ib	أين عربة الحقائب؟

Changing money تحويل النقود

Where's the currency exchange office?	**æy**næ **mæk**tæb æt-tæḥ**wīl**	أين مكتب التحويل؟
Can you change...?	**mom**kin ti**ḥaw**wil	ممكن تحوّل...؟
traveller's cheques (checks)	shī**kæt** si**yæ**ḥiyyæ	شيكات سياحية
some dollars/pounds	dō**lā**rāt/gonē**hæt**	دولارات/ جنيهات
this into dinars/ Egyptian pounds	**hæ**zæ ilæ dina**rāt**/ gonē**hæt** maṣ**rey**yæ	هذا إلى دينارات/ جنيهات مصرية
What's the exchange rate?	**mæ** si'r æt-tæḥ**wīl**	ما سعر التحويل؟

BANK—CURRENCY, see page 129

Where is...? أين...؟

Where is the...?	**æy**næ	أين...؟
booking office	**mæk**tæb æl-**ḥægz**	مكتب الحجز
car hire (rental)	**mæk**tæb tæ'**gīr** æs-sæyy**ārāt**	مكتب تأجير السيارات
duty-free shop	æs-**sūq** æl-**ḥorra**	السوق الحرة
newsstand	koshk æl-gar**ā**'id	كشك الجرائد
restaurant	æl-**maṭ**'am	المطعم
How do I get to...?	**kæy**fæ **æd**hæb **ilæ**	كيف أذهب إلى...؟
Is there a bus into town?	hæl **yū**gæd oto**bīs** lil **bæ**læd	هل يوجد أوتوبيس للبلد؟
Where can I get a taxi?	**æy**næ **æ**gid **tæk**sī	أين أجد تاكسي؟
Where can I hire (rent) a car?	**æy**næ **æst**'ægir sæy**yā**ra	أين أستأجر سيارة؟

Hotel reservation حجز الفندق

Do you have a hotel guide?	hæl '**in**dæk dæ**līl** fæ**nǣ**diq	هل عندك دليل فنادق؟
Could you reserve a hotel room for me?	**mom**kin taḥ**giz**lī **gor**fa fī **fon**doq	ممكن تحجز لي غرفة في فندق؟
in the centre	fī wasṭ æl-**bæ**læd	في وسط البلد
near the railway station	qa**rīb** min ma**ḥaṭ**ṭit æl-qi**ṭār**	قريب من محطة القطار
a single room	**gor**fa li shakhṣ	غرفة لشخص
a double room	**gor**fa li shakh**ṣēn**	غرفة لشخصين
not too expensive	**læy**sæt **gæl**yæ ki**tīr**	ليست غالية كثير
Where is the hotel/ boarding house?	**æy**næ æl-**fon**doq/ æl-bæn**syōn**	أين الفندق / البنسيون؟
Do you have a street map?	hæl '**in**dæk kha**rī**ṭa lil **bæ**læd	هل عندك خريطة للبلد؟

HOTEL/ACCOMMODATION, see page 22

Car hire (rental) تأجير السيارات

Car rental agencies operate in most larger centres. To hire a car you must produce an international driving licence and be at least 25 years old. However, driving in the Middle East is not easy, and it might be more convenient to hire a chauffeur-driven car.

I'd like to hire (rent)...	o**rīd** tæ'**gīr**	أريد تأجير...
a small car	sæy**yā**ra ṣa**gī**ra	سيارة صغيرة
a medium-sized car	sæy**yā**ra mutæ**wæs**siṭa	سيارة متوسطة
a large car	sæy**yā**ra kæ**bī**ra	سيارة كبيرة
an automatic car	sæy**yā**ra oto**mæ**tik	سيارة أوتوماتيك
a chauffeur-driven car	sæy**yā**ra bi **sæ**'iq	سيارة بسائق
I'd like it for a day/ a week.	o**rī**dohæ li yōm/ li os**bū'**	أريدها ليوم/ لأسبوع.
Are there any week-end arrangements?	hæl **tū**gæd æs'**ār khāṣ**ṣa li ni**hæ**yæt æl-osbū'	هل توجد أسعار خاصة لنهاية الأسبوع؟
Do you have any special rates?	hæl '**in**dæk æs'**ār khāṣ**ṣa	هل عندك أسعار خاصة؟
What's the charge per day/week?	kæm æl-ḥi**sæb** fil yōm/ os**bū'**	كم الحساب في اليوم/ الأسبوع؟
Is mileage included?	hæl æl-kīlome**trāt** mæḥ**sū**bæ	هل الكيلومترات محسوبة؟
What's the charge per kilometre?	bi**kæm** æl-kīlo**metr**	بكم الكيلومتر؟
I want to leave the car in...	o**rīd** tark æs-sæy**yā**ra fī	أريد ترك السيارة في...
I want full insurance.	o**rīd** tæ'**mīn** **shæ**mil	أريد تأمين شامل.
What's the deposit?	kæm aḍ-ḍa**mān**	كم الضمان؟
I've a credit card.	'**in**dī kært maṣ**ra**fī	عندي كارت مصرفي.
Here's my driving licence.	**hæ**zihi **rokh**ṣit qiyæ**dæ**tī	هذه رخصة قيادتي.

CAR, see page 75

Taxi التاكسي

The normal procedure is to stop a taxi in the street. It's advisable to ask the fare beforehand. In addition to taxis, you'll find a collective-taxi service. This is a group taxi which follows a fixed route, picking up and letting passengers off along the way.

Where can I get a collective taxi?	**æ**ynæ **æ**gid **tæk**sī moshtarak	أين أجد تاكسي مشترك؟
Please get me a taxi.	**mom**kin **tæ**gid lī **tæk**sī	ممكن تجد لي تاكسي؟
What's the fare to...?	kæm **æd**fæ' ilæ	كم أدفع إلى...؟
How far is it to...?	kæm æl-mæ**sǣ**fæ ilæ	كم المسافة إلى...؟
Take me to...	**khod**nī ilæ	خذني إلى...
this address	**hǣ**zæl 'in**wǣn**	هذا العنوان
the airport	æl-ma**ṭār**	المطار
the town centre	wasṭ æl-**bæ**læd	وسط البلد
the... Hotel	æl-**fon**doq	الفندق ...
the railway station	ma**ḥaṭ**ṭit æl-qi**ṭār**	محطة القطار
Turn... at the next corner.	it**tæ**gih ilæ... **'æ**læ æn-**nā**ṣiya æl-qā**di**mæ	إتجه إلى... على الناصية القادمة.
left	æsh-shi**mǣl**	الشمال
right	æl-yæ**mīn**	اليمين
Go straight ahead.	**'æ**læ ṭūl	على طول.
Please stop here.	qeff **ho**næ min **faḍ**lak	قف هنا من فضلك.
I'm in a hurry.	ænæ mos**tæ'**gil	أنا مستعجل.
Could you drive more slowly?	min **faḍ**lak sūq bi**boṭ'**	من فضلك سوق ببطء؟
Could you help me carry my luggage?	**mom**kin tisǣ'**id**nī fī ḥæml ḥaqā'**i**bī	ممكن تساعدني في حمل حقائبي؟
Could you wait for me?	**mom**kin tanta**ẓir**nī	ممكن تنتظرني؟
I'll be back in 10 minutes.	ænæ sæ'ærgæ' bæ'd 10 da**qā**'iq	أنا سأرجع بعد ١٠ دقائق.

TIPPING, see inside back-cover

Hotel—Other accommodation

Early reservation (and confirmation) is essential in most major tourist centres during the high season. You may have to pay a supplementary charge on Islamic high holidays.

فندق
(fondoq) Hotel. There's no official classification of hotels in the Middle East, but you'll find those of the highest international standards as well as others which seem to have no standards at all! You'd be well advised to choose a hotel with care, thus avoiding any unpleasant surprise. Your travel agent or the local tourist office usually has a list of hotels in three or more price categories.

بنسيون
(bæn**syōn**) Boarding house. Generally occupying a floor of an apartment block, boarding houses are found in most towns. Prices are reasonable, and service is good. If you plan to stay a week or so, ask the manager for a reduction.

شقق مفروشه
(**sho**qaq mæf**rū**shæ) Furnished flats (apartments). Found particularly in Cairo and Beirut, such accommodation is cheap and practical for longer stays (several weeks).

بيت شباب
(bēt shæ**bæb**) Youth hostel. These are found in most Middle Eastern countries. Inquire at the local tourist office or at the Youth Hostels Association in your own country before leaving home.

Can you recommend a hotel/boarding house?	**mom**kin tin**ṣaḥ**nī bi **fon**doq/bæn**syōn**	ممكن تنصحني بفندق / بنسيون؟
Are there any flats (apartments) vacant?	hæl **yū**gæd **sho**qaq mæf**rū**shæ **khæ**lyæ	هل يوجد شقق مفروشة خالية؟

Checking-in—Reception في الاستقبال

My name is...	**is**mī	أسمي...
I've a reservation.	**'in**dī ḥægz	عندي حجز.
We've reserved 2 rooms.	ḥæ**gæz**næ gorfa**tēn**	حجزنا غرفتين.
Here's the confirmation.	**hǣ**zæ tæ'**kīd** æl-**ḥægz**	هذا تأكيد الحجز.
Do you have any vacancies?	hæl **'in**dæk **gor**fa **khæl**yæ	هل عندك غرفة خالية؟
I'd like a...	o**rīd**	أريد....
single room	**gor**fa li shakhṣ	غرفة لشخص
double room	**gor**fa li shakh**ṣēn**	غرفة لشخصين
room with twin beds	**gor**fa bi sirī**rēn**	غرفة بسريرين
room with a double bed	**gor**fa bi si**rīr** kæ**bīr**	غرفة بسرير كبير
room with a bath	**gor**fa bi ḥæm**mǣm**	غرفة بحمام
room with a shower	**gor**fa bi dōsh	غرفة بدش
room with a balcony	**gor**fa bi bæl**kō**næ	غرفة ببلكونة
room with a view	**gor**fa bi **man**ẓar gæ**mīl**	غرفة بمنظر جميل
We'd like a room...	no**rīd** **gor**fa	نريد غرفة...
at the front	tæ**ṭoll** 'ælæ **shǣ**ri'	تطل على الشارع
at the back	tæ**ṭoll** 'ælæ æd-**dǣ**khil	تطل على الداخل
It must be quiet.	lǣ bodd æn tæ**kūn** **hǣd**yæ	لا بد أن تكون هادئة.
Is there...?	hæl **yū**gæd	هل يوجد...؟
air conditioning	tæk**yīf** **hæ**wæ'	تكييف هواء
heating	tæd**fi'**æ	تدفئة
a radio/television in the room	**rad**yō/tilivis**yōn** fil **gor**fa	راديو/ تلفزيون في الغرفة
a laundry service	**khid**mit gæ**sīl** wæ **mæk**wæ	خدمة غسيل ومكوه
room service	**khid**mæ fil **gor**fa	خدمة في الغرفة
hot water	mǣ' **sǣ**khin	ماء ساخن

CHECKING OUT, see page 31

running water	mǣ' gǣrī	ماء جاري
a private toilet	tæwǣlīt khāṣṣ	تواليت خاص
Could you put... in the room?	momkin waḍ'... fil gorfa	ممكن وضع... في الغرفة؟
an extra bed	sirīr ziyǣdæ	سرير زيادة
a cot (crib)	sirīr aṭfāl	سرير أطفال

How much? كم؟

What's the price...?	kæm æt-tæmæn	كم الثمن...؟
per night/per week	fil læylæ/fil osbū'	في الليلة / في الأسبوع
for bed and breakfast	bil nōm wæl fiṭār	بالنوم والفطار
excluding meals	bidūn wægbǣt	بدون وجبات
for full board (A.P.)	lil iqāmæ æl-kǣmilæ	للإقامة الكاملة
for half board (M.A.P.)	li niṣf iqāmæ	لنصف إقامة
Does that include...?	hæl mæḥsūb	هل محسوب...؟
breakfast	æl-fiṭār	الفطار
service	æl-khidmæ	الخدمة
tourist tax	ær-risūm æs-siyǣḥiyyæ	الرسوم السياحية
Is there any reduction for children?	hæl yūgæd takhfīḍ lil aṭfāl	هل يوجد تخفيض للأطفال؟
Do you charge for the baby?	hæl toḥǣsib 'ælæl ṭifl	هل تحاسب على الطفل؟
That's too expensive.	hǣzæ gǣlī kitīr	هذا غالي كثير.
Don't you have anything cheaper?	hæl 'indæk she' arkhaṣ	هل عندك شيء أرخص؟

How long? كم من الوقت؟

We'll be staying...	sænæbqā	سنبقى...
overnight only	æl-læylæ faqaṭ	الليلة فقط
a few days	ba'ḍ æl-æyyǣm	بعض الأيام
a week (at least)	osbū' ('ælæl aqall)	أسبوع (على الأقل)
I don't know yet.	lǣ æ'ærif bæ'd	لا أعرف بعد.

NUMBERS, see page 146

Decision القرار

May I see the room?	**mom**kin **ara** æl-**gor**fa	ممكن أرى الغرفة؟
That's fine. I'll take it.	**kwæy**yis. sæ'æ**khodh**hǣ	كويس. سأخذها.
No. I don't like it.	læ. lǣ to'**gib**nī	لا. لا تعجبني.
It's too...	**hi**yæ... ki**tīr**	هي... كثير
cold/hot	**bær**dæ/**sokh**næ	باردة/ ساخنة
dark/small	ḍ**al**ma/ṣa**gī**ra	ضلمه / صغيرة
noisy	**dæw**shæ	دوشة
I asked for a room with a bath.	**æ**næ ṭ**alabt gor**fa bi ḥæm**mǣm**	أنا طلبت غرفة بحمام.
Do you have anything...?	hæl **'in**dæk she'	هل عندك شيء...؟
better/bigger	**æḥ**sæn/**æk**bar	أحسن/ أكبر
cheaper/quieter	**ar**khaṣ/**æh**dæ'	أرخص/ أهدأ
Do you have a room with a better view?	hæl **'in**dæk **gor**fa ta**ṭoll** '**æ**læ **man**ẓar gæ**mīl**	هل عندك غرفة تطل على منظر جميل؟

Registration التسجيل

Upon arrival at a hotel or boarding house you'll be asked to fill in a registration form *æl-istimāra*.

اللقب/ الاسم	Name/First name
عنوان السكن/ الشارع/ الرقم	Home address/Street/Number
الجنسية/ المهنة	Nationality/Profession
تاريخ/ مكان الميلاد	Date/Place of birth
أتى من.../ ذاهب إلى...	Coming from.../Going to...
رقم جواز السفر	Passport number
المكان/ التاريخ	Place/Date
التوقيع	Signature

What does this mean? mǣ **mæ**'nǣ **hǣ**zæ ما معنى هذا؟

جواز سفرك، من فضلك؟	May I see your passport, please?
ممكن تملأ هذه الاستمارة؟	Would you mind filling in this registration form?
وقّع هنا من فضلك.	Please sign here.
كم من الوقت ستمكث هنا؟	How long will you be staying?

What's my room number?	mǣ **ra**qam gor**fa**tī	ما رقم غرفتي؟
Will you have our luggage sent up?	**mom**kin **tir**sil **læ**næ æl-ḥa**qā**'ib foq	ممكن ترسل لنا الحقائب فوق؟
Where can I park my car?	**æy**næ **ær**kin [a**ṣoff**] sæyyā**ra**tī	أين أركن [أصف] سيارتي؟
Does the hotel have a garage?	hæl **yū**gæd gæ**rāzh** lil **fon**doq	هل يوجد جراج للفندق؟
I'd like to leave this in the safe.	o**rīd** æn **a**ḍa' **hǣ**zæ fil **khæz**næ	أريد أن أضع هذا في الخزنة.

Hotel staff موظفين الفندق

hall porter	'**ǣ**mil æl-**fon**doq	عامل الفندق
maid	**khǣ**dimæt æl-**gor**fa	خادمة الغرفة
manager	æl-mo**dīr**	المدير
page (bellboy)	**khǣ**dim æl-**fon**doq	خادم الفندق
porter	æsh-shæy**yǣl** [æl-'æt**tǣl**]	الشيال [العتال]
receptionist	mo**waẓ**ẓaf æl-istiq**bǣl**	موظف الاستقبال
switchboard operator	'**ǣ**mil æt-tili**fōn**	عامل التليفون
waiter/waitress	æl-gar**sōn**/æl-gar**sō**na	الجرسون / الجرسونة

To attract the attention of staff members say please: *min faḍlak* to a man, *min faḍlik* to a woman.

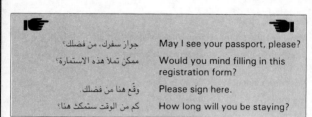

General requirements أسئلة عامة

The key to room..., please.	mof**tāḥ gor**fit... min **faḍ**lak	مفتاح غرفة... من فضلك.
Will you wake me at..., please?	æy**qiẓ**nī æs-**sǣ**'æ... min **faḍ**lak	أيقظني الساعة... من فضلك.
Is there a bathroom on this floor?	hæl **yū**gæd ḥæm**mǣm** fī **hǣ**zæl **ṭā**biq	هل يوجد حمام في هذا الطابق؟
What's the voltage?	kæm volt æl-kah**ra**ba'	كم ڤولت الكهرباء؟
Where's the socket (outlet) for the shaver?	**æy**næ fīshet æl-kah**ra**ba' li mæki**nat** æl-ḥi**lǣ**qa	أين فيشة الكهرباء لماكينة الحلاقة؟
Can you find me a...?	**mom**kin tū**gid**lī	ممكن توجد لي...؟
babysitter	**ḥǣ**risæt aṭ**fāl**	حارسة أطفال
secretary	seker**tē**ræ	سكرتيرة
typewriter	**æ**læ **kæt**bæ	آلة كاتبة
May I have a/an/some...?	min **faḍ**lak o**rīd**	من فضلك أريد...
ashtray	ṭaf**fā**yit sæ**gǣ**yir	طفاية سجاير
bath towel	**fū**ṭa lil ḥæm**mǣm**	فوطة للحمام
(extra) blanket	baṭ**ṭa**ni**yy**a (zi**yǣ**dæ)	بطانية (زيادة)
envelopes	ẓo**rūf**	ظروف
(more) hangers	'æl**lǣ**qāt (zi**yǣ**dæ)	علاقات (زيادة)
hot-water bottle	**qir**bit mǣ' **sǣ**khin	قربة ماء ساخن
ice cubes	tælg	ثلج
needle and thread	**ib**ræ wæ khēṭ	إبرة وخيط
(extra) pillow	mæ**khæd**dæ (zi**yǣ**dæ)	مخدة (زيادة)
reading lamp	**lam**ba lil qi**rā'**æ	لمبة للقراءة
soap	ṣā**būn**	صابون
writing paper	**wa**raq khi**ṭā**bāt	ورق خطابات
Where's the...?	æy**næ**	أين...؟
dining room	**ṣā**lit aṭ-ṭa'**ām**	صالة الطعام
emergency exit	**makh**rag aṭ-ṭa**wā**ri'	مخرج الطوارئ
hairdresser's	ṣa**lōn** æl-ḥi**lǣ**qa	صالون الحلاقة
lift (elevator)	æl-maṣ'**ad**	المصعد

TELLING THE TIME, see page 153

Telephone—Post (mail) التليفون ـ البريد

Can you get me Cairo 123456?	a'aṭīnī min **faḍlak** æl-qāhira 123456	أعطني من فضلك القاهرة ١٢٣٤٥٦.
Do you have stamps?	hæl **'indæk** ṭa**wābi'**	هل عندك طوابع؟
Would you post this for me, please?	**mom**kin ir**sǣl hǣ**zæ lī min **faḍ**lak	ممكن ارسال هذا لي من فضلك؟
Are there any letters for me?	hæl **tū**gæd khiṭā**bāt** lī	هل توجد خطابات لي؟
Are there any messages for me?	hæl **tū**gæd ra**sǣ**'il lī	هل توجد رسائل لي؟
How much are my telephone charges?	kæm ḥi**sǣb** æt-tili**fōn**	كم حساب التليفون؟

Difficulties الصعوبات

The... doesn't work.	... lǣ **yæ'**mæl	... لا يعمل
air conditioning	tæk**yīf** æl-**hæ**wæ'	تكييف الهواء
fan	æl-mar**wa**ḥa	المروحة
heating	æt-tæd**fī'**æ	التدفئة
light	æn-**nūr**	النور
radio	ær-**rad**yō	الراديو
television	æt-tilivis**yōn**	التليفزيون
The tap (faucet) is dripping.	æl-ḥænæ**fiy**yæ tu**sæ**rib	الحنفية تسرب.
There's no hot water.	lǣ **yū**gæd mǣ' **sǣ**khin	لا يوجد ماء ساخن.
The wash-basin is blocked.	æl-ḥōḍ mæs**dūd**	الحوض مسدود.
The window is jammed.	æsh-shib**bǣk** mæz**nūq**	الشباك مزنوق.
The curtains are stuck.	æs-sæ**tǣ**'ir mæz**nū**qa	الستاير مزنوقة.
The bulb is burned out.	**ḥu**riqat æl-**lam**ba	حرقت اللمبة.
My room hasn't been made up.	gorfatī læm to**gæh**hæz	غرفتي لم تجهز.

POST OFFICE AND TELEPHONE, see page 132

The... is broken.	æl-... mak**sūr**	الـ... مكسور.
blind	sitāra mæ'dæ**niyy**æ	ستارة معدنية
lamp	miṣ**bāḥ**	مصباح
plug	kobs	كوبس
shutter	shīsh	شيش
switch	mof**tāḥ** æn-**nūr**	مفتاح النور
Can you get it repaired?	**mom**kin tu**ṣal**liḥ **hǣ**zæ	ممكن تصلح هذا؟

Laundry—Dry cleaner's الغسيل ـ التنظيف

I want these clothes...	o**rīd**... hǣ**zi**hil mæ**lǣ**bis	أريد... هذه الملابس.
cleaned	tan**ẓīf**	تنظيف
ironed/pressed	**mæk**wit	مكوة
washed	gæ**sīl**	غسيل
I need them...	æh**tǣg** i**læy**hǣ	أحتاج إليها...
today	æl-**yōm**	اليوم
tomorrow	**gæ**dæn	غداً
before Friday	qabl yōm æl-**gom**'æ	قبل يوم الجمعة
Can you... this?	**mom**kin... **hǣ**zæ	ممكن... هذا؟
mend/patch/stitch	**ræf**fit/tær**qī**'/khi**yā**ṭit	رفة / ترقيع / خياطة
Can you sew on this button?	**mom**kin to**khay**yiṭ **hǣ**zæl zo**rār**	ممكن تخيط هذا الزرار؟
Can you get this stain out?	**mom**kin i**zǣ**lit hǣ**zi**hil **boq**'a	ممكن إزالة هذه البقعة؟
Is my laundry ready?	hæl gæ**sī**lī **gǣ**hiz	هل غسيلي جاهز؟
This isn't mine.	**hǣ**zæ **læy**sæ lī	هذا ليس لي.
There's something missing.	**nā**qiṣ she'	ناقص شيء.
There's a hole in this.	**yū**gæd soqb fī **hǣ**zæ	يوجد ثقب في هذا.
It's shrunk.	**ho**wæ kæsh	هو كش.

Hairdresser—Barber		الحلاق
Is there a hairdresser/ beauty salon in the hotel?	hæl **yūgæd** ṣalōn ḥilæqa/ ṣalōn tægmīl fil **fondoq**	هل يوجد صالون حلاقة / صالون تجميل في الفندق؟
Can I make an appointment for Thursday?	**momkin** a**khod** **mæw**'id li yōm æl-khæ**mīs**	ممكن أخذ موعد ليوم الخميس؟
I'd like it cut and shaped.	o**rīd** qaṣṣ wæ taṣ**līḥ**	أريد قص وتصليح.
I want a haircut, please.	o**rīd** qaṣṣ æsh-**sha'r** min **faḍ**lak	أريد قص الشعر من فضلك.
bleach	i**zæ**lit æl-**lōn**	إزالة اللون
blow-dry	tæn**shīf**	تنشيف
colour rinse	**ṣab**ga khæ**fī**fæ	صبغة خفيفة
dye	**ṣab**ga	صبغة
face pack	shædd lil wægh	شد للوجه
manicure	mæni**kūr**	مانيكير
permanent wave	barma**nant**	برماننت
setting lotion	**sæ**'il li tæs**bīt** æsh-**sha'r**	سائل لتثبيت الشعر
shampoo and set	**sham**bo wæ taṣ**līḥ**	شامبو وتصليح
with a fringe (bangs)	bi **qoṣ**ṣa	بقصه
I'd like a shampoo for... hair.	o**rīd** **sham**bo li sha'r	أريد شامبو لشعر...
normal/dry/greasy (oily)	'**æ**dī/gæf/**doh**nī	عادي / جاف / دهني
Do you have a colour chart?	hæl '**in**dæk **daf**tar lil æl**wæn**	هل عندك دفتر للألوان؟
Don't cut it too short.	**læy**sæ qa**ṣīr** ki**tīr**	ليس قصير كثير.
A little more off the...	qoṣṣ qa**līl** min	قص قليل من...
back/neck	æl-**khælf**/æl-qa**fæ**	الخلف / القفا
sides/top	æl-gæ**wæ**nib/foq	الجوانب / فوق
I don't want any hairspray.	**læ** o**rīd** sbray lil sha'r	لا أريد أسبراي للشعر.

DAYS OF THE WEEK, see page 152

I'd like a shave.	o**rīd** æn **æḥ**laq **zæq**nī	أريد أن أحلق ذقني.
Would you trim my..., please?	**mom**kin taṣ**līḥ** æl-... min **faḍ**lak	ممكن تصليح الـ... من فضلك؟
beard	zæqn	ذقن
moustache	shæ**næb**	شنب
sideboards (sideburns)	sæ**wǣ**lif	سوالف

Checking out الرحيل

May I have my bill please?	o**rīd** ḥi**sǣ**bī min **faḍ**lak	أريد حسابي من فضلك.
I'm leaving early in the morning.	sæ'**ar**ḥal mo**bæk**kiran fil ṣa**bāḥ**	سأرحل مبكراً في الصباح.
Please have my bill ready.	min **faḍ**lak gæh**hiz** lī æl-ḥi**sǣb**	من فضلك جهز لي الحساب.
We'll be checking out around noon.	sæ**nar**ḥæl ḥæ**wǣ**lī aẓ-**ẓohr**	سنرحل حوالى الظهر.
I must leave at once.	lǣ bodd æn **ar**ḥal **faw**ran	لا بد أن أرحل فوراً.
Is everything included?	hæl koll she' mæḥ**sūb**	هل كل شيء محسوب؟
Can I pay by credit card?	**mom**kin **æd**fæ' bi kært maṣ**ra**fī	ممكن أدفع بكارت مصرفي؟
I think there's a mistake in the bill.	a**ẓonn** **yū**gæd **kha**ṭa' fil ḥi**sǣb**	أظن يوجد خطأ في الحساب.
Can you get us a taxi?	**mom**kin tægid **læ**næ **tæk**sī	ممكن تجد لنا تاكسي؟
Can you have our luggage brought down?	**mom**kin ti**naz**zil **læ**næ æl-ḥa**qā**'ib	ممكن تنزل لنا الحقائب؟
Here's the forwarding address.	**hǣ**zæ æl-'in**wǣn** æl-gæ**dīd**	هذا العنوان الجديد.
You have my home address.	**'in**dæk 'in**wǣn** mæn**zi**lī	عندك عنوان منزلي.
It's been a very enjoyable stay.	**kǣ**næt æl-iqā**mæ** mom**tī**'æ **gid**dæn	كانت الإقامة ممتعة جداً.

TIPPING, see inside back-cover

Camping المعسكر

Is there a camp site near here?	hæl **yū**gæd mo'**as**kar qa**rīb** min **ho**næ	هل يوجد معسكر قريب من هنا؟
Can we camp here?	**mom**kin no'**as**kir **ho**næ	ممكن نعسكر هنا؟
Have you room for a...?	hæl **'in**dæk mæ**kǣn** li	هل عندك مكان لـ...؟
tent	**khē**mæ	خيمة
caravan (trailer)	kara**van**	كارافان
What's the charge...?	kæm æl-ḥi**sǣb**	كم الحساب...؟
per day/per person	fil yōm/li shakhṣ	في اليوم/ لشخص
for a car/for a tent	li sæy**yā**ra/li **khē**mæ	لسيارة/ لخيمة
for a caravan (trailer)	li kara**van**	لكارافان
Is there...?	hæl **yū**gæd	هل يوجد...؟
drinking water	mǣ' shorb	ماء شرب
electricity	kah**ra**ba'	كهرباء
Where are the...?	**æy**næ	أين....؟
showers	æd-dōsh	الدش
toilets	æt-tæ**wǣ**līt	التواليت

butane gas	æn**bū**bit gǣz	أنبوبة جاز
campbed	**sirīr** **safar**	سرير سفر
(folding) chair	**korsī** (qo**mǣsh**)	كرسي (قماش)
charcoal	fæḥm	فحم
cool box	ṣan**dūq** tæl**lǣ**gæ	صندوق ثلاجة
mattress	**mær**tæbæ	مرتبة
mosquito net	nǣmū**siy**yæ	ناموسية
sleeping bag	ḥa**qī**bæ lil nōm	حقيبة للنوم
tent	**khē**mæ	خيمة
tent pegs	æw**tǣd** **khē**mæ	أوتاد خيمة
tent poles	'æwǣ**mīd** **khē**mæ	عواميد خيمة
water carrier	bær**mīl** mǣ'	برميل ماء
water flask	zæmzæ**miy**yæ	زمزمية

Eating out

There is every variety of eating place in the Middle East, from chic restaurant to street-side stall. Some restaurants specialize in certain dishes. Here are a few types you may come across:

مطعم (**maṭ**'am)	Restaurant; there's often a set menu, especially in those serving European specialities.
حاتي (**ḥǣ**tī)	Restaurant specializing in charcoal-grilled lamb.
مطعم لحم مشوي (**maṭ**'am læḥm **mæsh**wī)	Lebanese restaurant specializing in charcoal-grilled meat.
مطعم حمام (**maṭ**'am ḥæ**mǣm**)	Restaurant specializing in pigeon or squab.
مطعم سمك (**maṭ**'am **sæ**mæk)	Fish and seafood restaurant.
فول وفلافل (fūl wæ fæ**lǣ**fil)	Snackbar serving *fool* (brown-bean dish) and *falafel* (spicy bean rissoles) usually to take away. *Fool* and *falafel* may also be a filling for sandwiches.
كافيتريا (kæfi**tir**yæ)	Snackbar; you may have to eat standing up.
محل عصير (mæ**ḥæll** '**aṣīr**)	Fruit-juice bar—sometimes drive-in—features fresh fruit juice. Often you can get *shawerma* (thin slices of spit-roasted meat) and sandwiches.
قهوة (**qah**wa)	Coffee shop; often a part of a pastry shop.
حلويات شامي (ḥælæwiy**yǣt shǣ**mī)	Lebanese or Syrian pastry shop.
ملهى ليلي (**mæl**hæ **læy**lī)	Nightclub (cabaret); offers dinner and a show; in Egypt shows will probably feature the famed belly dancers.

كاس عرق ومازة
(kǣs 'araq wæ mæzzæ) Lebanese restaurant which serves salads and appetizers among other local dishes, as well as the national drink *arak*, an aniseed liqueur.

There are also neighbourhood restaurants, many of which specialize in a particular dish such as *kosharee* (rice, lentils and noodles in a hot sauce).

Meal times أوقات الوجبات

In Arab countries, meals are generally eaten later than you may be used to, both in private homes and in restaurants. If you feel hungry at an unusual hour, you'll always be able to find a restaurant or a snackbar serving hot food or snacks at any time of the day or night.

الفطار
(æl-fiṭār) Breakfast is served at hotels from 6 to 10 a.m.

الغداء
(æl-gædǣ') Lunch is generally served from 1 to 3 p.m.

العشاء
(æl-'æshǣ') Dinner is served from 8 to 11 p.m. In night-clubs you'll be able to dine even after midnight.

Eating habits عادات الأكل

Starting the day the Middle Eastern way, your breakfast would consist of *fool* (a brown-bean dish), white cheese, *halawa* (a sugary sesame-seed confection) and *falafel* (spicy bean rissoles) and fresh fruit juice.

The main meal of the day is usually eaten at lunch time. It will start with an aperitif (often nonalcoholic, as alcohol is forbidden to Muslims), and a great variety of appetizers, *mezza*. Then comes the main dish: a meat or vegetable stew or some charcoal-grilled meat (lamb, veal, poultry). Eating pork is forbidden by Muslim dietary law. The meal is rounded off with a very sweet dessert or some kind of pastry and a cup of coffee, but you may also save this for later in the afternoon. Supper is a less copious version of lunch. During Ramadan eating hours change completely, and so do many of the foods served.

What is Ramadan? ما هو رمضان؟

The month of Ramadan is one of Islam's holy periods, observed by Muslims in all Arab countries. As it's a lunar month, it has no regular corresponding date in the calendar year. This religious rite is a way of showing obedience to God and of strengthening social ties, and consists of fasting and refraining from drinking and smoking from sunrise to sunset.

The main and first meal of the day, which is eaten at sunset, is called *iftar*. It starts with a hot soup, followed by *fool* and eggs, generally mixed together. The rest of the meal is as normal, with oriental sweets to finish up with. The characteristic drink of this month (nonalcoholic, of course) is *qamar-el-din,* made of stewed apricot purée and served cold. *Iftar* is the occasion to get together with friends and relatives. It's also a time for charity, when beggars who knock at the door are given food. After *iftar,* people usually listen to music and to readings from the Koran on the radio and go to the mosque. Later on, at about 1 or 2 a.m., is the second meal of the "day", called *sohur,* which helps the Muslim to endure the long hours of fasting to come.

During Ramadan, public places are open all night and the streets are brightly lit. Restaurants and cafés stay open all night and are well patronized. Nevertheless, you should not forget that the month of Ramadan is first and foremost a religious month. In main tourist areas there are eating places open specially for non-Muslim visitors. In some places, however, you are expected not to eat, drink or smoke in public during daylight hours.

Arab Cuisine المطبخ العربي

Arab cooking is in many ways typical of what you'll find throughout the Mediterranean, but with a spicy oriental flavour. Foreign influences came from Greece, Italy and France, and many of the popular dishes of Egypt have been absorbed from the Turks or the Circassians, a Muslim people who emigrated from Russia in the last century. Important ingredients in Arab cuisine are beans, rice, cracked wheat, minced meat, sesame seed paste, oil, garlic, onions and lemon. Typical dishes are *fool* and *falafel*.

ماذا تريد؟	What would you like?
أنصحك بهذا.	I recommend this.
ماذا تريد أن تشرب؟	What would you like to drink?
ليس عندنا...	We don't have...

Hungry? جعان؟

Can you recommend a good restaurant?	**mom**kin tin**ṣaḥ**nī bi **maṭ**'am **kwæy**yis	ممكن تنصحني بمطعم كويس؟
Are there any inexpensive restaurants around here?	hæl **yū**gæd **maṭ**'am ra**khīṣ** qa**rīb** min **ho**næ	هل يوجد مطعم رخيص قريب من هنا؟
I'd like to reserve a table for 4.	o**rīd** æn **æḥ**giz tara**bē**za [**ṭaw**la] li 4	أريد أن أحجز ترابيزة [طاولة] لـ ٤.
We'll come at 8.	sæ**næ'**tī æs-**sǣ'**æ 8	سنأتي الساعة ٨.
Could we have a table...?	hæl **tū**gæd tara**bē**za [**ṭaw**la]	هل توجد ترابيزة [طاولة] ...؟
in the corner	fil rokn	في الركن
by the window	bi**gǣ**nib æsh-shib**bǣk**	بجانب الشباك
outside/on the terrace	fil **khǣ**rig/fil ti**rās**	في الخارج/ في التراس
in a non-smoking area	fī mæ**kǣn 'æ**dæm æt-tæd**khīn**	في مكان عدم التدخين

NUMBERS, see page 146

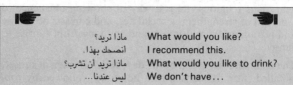

Asking and ordering النداء والطلب

Waiter/Waitress!	min **faḍ**lak/min **faḍ**lik	من فضلك/ من فضلِك!
I'd like something to eat/drink.	o**rīd** æn **æ**kol/**ashrab**	أريد أن أكل/ أشرب.
May I have the menu, please?	o**rīd** æl-**kært** min **faḍ**lak	أريد الكارت من فضلك.
Do you have a set menu/local dishes?	hæl **'in**dæk **wæg**bæ **kæm**læ/**æk**læ mæḥæl**liy**yæ	هل عندك وجبه كاملة/ وجبه محلية؟
What do you recommend?	bi **mǣ**zæ tin**ṣaḥ**nī	بماذا تنصحني؟
Do you have anything ready quickly?	hæl **'in**dæk ækl **gǣ**hiz	هل عندك أكل جاهز؟
I'm in a hurry.	**æ**næ mos**tæ'**gil	أنا مستعجل.
I'd like...	o**rīd**	أريد...
Could we have a/an..., please?	min **faḍ**lak no**rīd**	من فضلك نريد...
ashtray	ṭaf**fā**yit sæ**gǣ**yir	طفاية سجاير
cup	fin**gǣn**	فنجان
fork	**shō**kæ	شوكه
glass	kob**bǣ**yæ	كباية
knife	sik**kī**næ	سكينة
napkin (serviette)	**fū**ṭa	فوطة
plate	**ṭa**baq	طبق
spoon	mæl**'a**qa	ملعقة
May I have some...?	o**rīd**	أريد...
bread	khobz	خبز
butter	**zib**dæ	زبدة
ketchup	**ket**shob	كتشوب
lemon	læ**mūn**	لمون
mustard	mos**ṭar**da	مستردة
oil	zēt	زيت
pepper	**fil**fil	فلفل

salt	mælḥ	ملح
seasoning	bohā**rāt**	بهارات
sugar	**sok**kar	سكر
vinegar	khæll	خل

Some useful expressions for dieters and those with special requirements:

I'm on a diet.	ænæ **'ǣ**mil riz**hīm**	أنا عامل رجيم.
I don't drink alcohol.	lǣ **ash**rab koḥoli**yǣt**	لا أشرب كحوليات.
I mustn't eat food containing...	lǣ **æ**kol ækl fīh	لا آكل أكل فيه...
flour/fat	dæ**qīq**/dohn	دقيق/ دهن
salt/sugar	mælḥ/**sok**kar	ملح/ سكر
Do you have... for diabetics?	hæl **'in**dæk... li marḍa æs-**sok**kar	هل عندك... لمرض السكر؟
cakes	kēk	كيك
fruit juice	'a**ṣīr fǣ**kihæ	عصير فاكهة
a special menu	**wæg**bæ **khāṣ**ṣa	وجبة خاصة
Do you have any vegetarian dishes?	hæl **'in**dæk ækl bi**dūn** læḥm	هل عندك أكل بدون لحم؟
Could I have... instead of dessert?	o**rīd**... **bæ**ḍæl æt-tæ**ḥǣ**lī	أريد... بدل التحالي.
Can I have an artificial sweetener?	o**rīd** **sok**kar ṣi**nā'**ī	أريد سكر صناعي.

And...

I'd like some more.	o**rīd** **shwæ**yæ kæ**mǣn**	أريد شوية كمان.
Can I have more..., please?	o**rīd** kæ**mǣn** min... min **fa**ḍlak	أريد كمان من... من فضلك.
Just a small portion.	miq**dār** ṣa**gīr**	مقدار صغير.
Nothing more, thanks.	**yæk**fī **shok**ran	يكفي، شكراً.
Where are the toilets?	**æy**næ æt-tæ**wǣ**līt	أين التواليت؟

Breakfast الفطار

A Middle Eastern breakfast is described on page 34. If it doesn't suit your tastes, you may want to say:

I'd like breakfast, please.	orīd æl-fiṭār min faḍlak	أريد الفطار من فضلك.
I'll have a/an/some...	orīd	أريد....
bacon and eggs	bæykon wæ bēḍ	بيكون وبيض
boiled egg	bēḍa mæslūqa	بيضة مسلوقة
soft/hard	niṣf siwæ/gæmdæ	نصف سوى/ جامدة
cereal	ḥobūb	حبوب
fried eggs	bēḍ maqlī	بيض مقلي
fruit juice	'aṣīr fǣkihæ	عصير فاكهة
grapefruit/orange	grēb frūt/bortoqāl	جريب فروت/ برتقال
ham and eggs	zhambon wæ bēḍ	جامبون وبيض
jam	mirabba	مربى
marmalade	mirabbit bortoqāl	مربة برتقال
yoghurt	zæbǣdī	زبادى
May I have some...?	orīd... min faḍlak	أريد... من فضلك.
bread/toast	khobz/tost	خبز/ توست
butter	zibdæ	زبدة
(hot) chocolate	shokolāta (sokhnæ)	شوكولاتة (ساخنة)
coffee	qahwa	قهوة
decaffeinated	bidūn kæfæyīn	بدون كافيين
black	bidūn læbæn [ḥælīb]	بدون لبن [حليب]
honey	'æsæl	عسل
milk	læbæn [ḥælīb]	لبن [حليب]
cold/hot	bǣrid/sǣkhin	بارد/ ساخن
pepper	filfil	فلفل
roll	khobz ṣagīr	خبز صغير
salt	mælḥ	ملح
tea	shæy	شاي
with milk	bi læbæn [ḥælīb]	بلبن [حليب]
with lemon	bi læmūn	بلمون
(hot) water	mǣ' (sǣkhin)	ماء (ساخن)

What's on the menu? ماذا يوجد بالكارت؟

Most large restaurants in major cities specialize in European dishes, especially French and Italian, rather than Middle Eastern cuisine. But you'll usually find some Middle Eastern dishes on the menu. Unless you're specifically looking for European food, avoid the big restaurants and go to local eating places.

Under the headings below you'll find alphabetical lists of dishes in Arabic with their English equivalents. You can simply show the book to the waiter. If you want some fruit, for instance, let *him* point to what's available on the appropriate list. Use pages 37 and 38 for ordering in general.

Reading the menu لقراءة الكارت

طبق اليوم	ṭabaq æl-**yōm**	Dish of the day
أطباق باردة	a**ṭbāq bær**dæ	Cold dishes
أكلات فرنسية	æk**læt** fran**siyy**æ	French dishes
أكلات إيطالية	æk**læt** iṭā**liyy**æ	Italian dishes
أكلات شرقية	æk**læt** shar**qiyy**æ	Oriental dishes
أكلة محلية	**æk**læ mæḥæl**liyy**æ	Local specialities

أسماك	æs**mæk**	seafood
رز	roz	rice
بيض	bēḍ	eggs
بيرة	**bī**ra	beer
تحالي	tæ**ḥæ**lī	desserts
جبنة	**gib**næ	cheese
جيلاتي [أيس كريم]	zhi**læ**tī [æys krem]	ice cream
حلويات	ḥælæwiy**yæt**	pastries
خضروات	khoḍra**wāt**	vegetables
سلطات	sala**ṭāt**	salads
سمك	**sæ**mæk	fish
شربة	**shor**ba	soups
لحم صيد	læḥm ṣēd	game
طاجن	**ṭā**gin	stew
طيور	ṭo**yūr**	poultry
فواكه	fæ**wæ**kih	fruit
فراخ	fi**rækh**	chicken
لحم	læḥm	meat
مشروبات	mæshrū**bæt**	drinks
مشهيات [مزات]	mæshhiy**yæt** [mæz**zæt**]	starters (appetizers)
مكرونة	makar**ō**na	pasta
مشويات	mæshwiy**yæt**	grilled meat
نبيذ	ni**bīt**	wines
أكلات خفيفة	æk**læt** khæ**fī**fæ	snacks

Starters (Appetizers) مشهيات

It's customary in Arab countries to serve a variety of appetizers and salads with the aperitif. These are called *mezza* and consist of numerous small plates of hors d'œuvre—sometimes up to 40 different items. We don't have room to name them all, but here's a sampling of some popular ones.

I'd like an appetizer.	orīd **fæ**tiḥ shæ**hiy**yæ [**mæz**zæ] min **faḍ**lak	أريد فاتح شهية [مزة] من فضلك.

خرشوف	khar**shūf**	artichokes
أسبراجس	**as**paragas	asparagus tips
أنشوجه	æn**shū**gæ	anchovies
باتيه [فواجرا]	ba**tēh** [**fwa**gra]	pâté
جندفلي [محار]	gæn**do**flī [ma**ḥḥār**]	oysters
رنجه	**rin**gæ	herring
رنجة مملحة	**rin**gæ mimællæḥæ	salted herring fillets
زيتون	zæ**tūn**	olives
سجق [مقانق]	so**goq** [maqāniq]	sausages
سردين	sær**dīn**	sardines
سلامى	**sæ**lǣmī	salami
شمام	shæm**mǣm**	melon
كبد الوز	kibd æl-**wizz**	goose-liver pâté
كبد فراخ	kibd fi**rǣkh**	chopped chicken liver
كركند	kæræ**kænd**	lobster
كافيار	kav**yār**	caviar
طرش [كابيس]	**ṭor**shī [kæ**bīs**]	pickled vegetables
أنواع لحم بارد	æn**wǣ**'æ læḥm **bǣ**rid	assorted cold cuts
روز بيف	roz**bīf**	roast beef
جمبري [أرادس]	gæm**bæ**rī [a**rā**dis]	prawns/shrimps
بسطرمه	bas**ṭar**ma	cured, dried beef

باذنجان مخلل (biting**ǣn** mi**khæl**lil) aubergine (eggplant) stuffed with herbs, garlic and spices

بطارخ (baṭārikh) "Egyptian caviar", red fish roe

جبنة بيضاء بالطماطم (**gib**næ **bē**ḍa bil ṭa**mā**ṭim)	white cheese served with tomatoes, onion, parsley, oil and lemon; sometimes a hot sauce is added
عجة ('**ig**gæ)	omelet with onions, parsley and green peppers
ورق عنب محشي (**wa**raq '**i**næb **mæ**ḥshī)	vine leaves stuffed with rice and minced meat; may be served cold or hot

Typically Middle Eastern are the dips based on a paste of ground sesame seeds and eaten with flat oriental bread.

طحينة (ṭi**ḥī**na)	a paste made with ground sesame seeds and spices
بابا غنوج (bābāgæn**nūg**)	*tehina* to which mashed aubergine (eggplant) is added
حمص بالطحينة (**ḥom**moṣ bil ṭi**ḥī**na)	a spicy paste made with ground chick-peas, *tehina* and spices

Salads سلطات

What salads do you have?	mæ̅ aṣ**nāf** æs-sala**ṭāt** '**in**dæk	ما أصناف السلطات عندك؟
Can you recommend a local speciality?	**mom**kin tin**ṣaḥ**nī bi **æk**læ mæḥæl**liy**yæ	ممكن تنصحني بأكلة محلية؟
سلطة باذنجان	salaṭit biting**æ̅n**	aubergine (eggplant) salad
سلطة بطاطس	salaṭit ba**ṭā**ṭis	potato salad
سلطة بنجر	salaṭit **ban**gar	beetroot salad
سلطة تونة	salaṭit **tū**na	tunny (tuna) salad
سلطة جرجير	salaṭit gær**gīr**	rocket salad
سلطة خس	salaṭit khass	lettuce salad
سلطة خيار وطماطم [بندورة]	salaṭit khi**yār** wæ ṭa**mā**ṭim [bana**dū**ra]	cucumber and tomato salad
سلطة كرفس	salaṭit **ka**rafs	celery salad
سلطة بيض	salaṭit bēḍ	egg salad

تبولة (tæbbūlæ)	Lebanese cracked wheat salad with cucumber, onions, parsley, sweet peppers, tomatoes, mint and bread crumbs
سلطة بلدي (salaṭa bælædī)	Egyptian salad of cucumber, tomatoes, onions, rocket salad, parsley, sweet peppers, mint
سلطة زبادي (salaṭit zæbǣdī)	diced cucumber with a dressing of yoghurt, olive oil, garlic and mint

Egg dishes أطباق بيض

بيض	bēḍ	eggs
بيض بالمايونيز	bēḍ bil mæyonēz	eggs with mayonnaise
عجة	'iggæ	omelet
عجة بالبسطرمة	'iggæ bil basṭarma	omelet with cured beef
عجة بالجبنة	'iggæ bil gibnæ	cheese omelet
شكشوكة	shækshūkæ	hard boiled eggs and rice in a hot tomato sauce
عجة بكبد الفراخ	'iggæ bi kibd æl-firǣkh	chicken liver omelet
عجة باللحمة	'iggæ bil læḥmæ	omelet with minced meat

Cheese جبنة

In Arab countries, cheese is eaten with the meal, not after the main course, and is served most frequently with breakfast and supper. It also comes in various guises as an appetizer or *mezza*.

What sort of cheese do you have?	mǣ aṣnāf æl-gibæn 'indæk	ما أصناف الجبن عندك؟
جبنة رومي	gibnæ rūmī	hard cheese
جبنة قريش	gibnæ qærīsh	full, rich cheese
جبنة ريكوتا	gibnæ rikotta	type of cottage cheese

جبنة من لبن المعيز	**gib**næ min **læ**bæn æl-mi'**īz**	goat's milk cheese
جبنة ملحة	**gib**næ **mæl**ḥæ	salted curd cheese
لبنة	**læb**næ	curd cheese sprinkled with olive oil
مش	mesh	matured and salty cheese

Soup شوربة

You'll find many different kinds of soup in the Middle East, among them European and American favourites, as well as regional specialities. Lentil soup is the most popular of the local soups.

I'd like some soup.	or**īd shor**ba min **fa**ḍlak	أريد شوربة من فضلك.
What do you recommend?	bi **mǣ**zæ tin**ṣaḥ**nī	بماذا تنصحني؟
Has it got meat in it?	hæl **fī**hæ læḥm	هل فيها لحم؟
Is it a... soup?	hæl h**ǣ**zihi **shor**ba	هل هذه شوربة ...؟
light/rich	khæ**fī**fæ/tæ**qī**læ	خفيفة / ثقيلة

شوربة بسلة	**shor**bit bi**sil**læ	pea soup
شوربة بصل	**shor**bit **ba**ṣal	onion soup
شوربة خضروات	**shor**bit khoḍra**wāt**	vegetable soup
شوربة سمك	**shor**bit **sæ**mæk	fish soup
شوربة بالشعرية	**shor**ba bil shi'**riy**yæ	noodle soup
شوربة طماطم [بندورة]	**shor**bit ṭa**mā**ṭim [bana**dū**ra]	tomato soup
شوربة عدس	**shor**bit 'æds	lentil soup
شوربة عدس بالليمون	**shor**bit 'æds bil læ**mūn**	Lebanese lentil and lemon soup
شوربة فراخ	**shor**bit fi**rǣkh**	chicken soup
شوربة كوارع	**shor**bit kæ**wǣ**ri'	sheep's trotters (feet) soup
شوربة لحم	**shor**bit læḥm	meat soup

Fish and seafood أسماك

The coast is, of course, the ideal place to sample fish and seafood. In Cairo, you're most likely to be served fish from the Nile. Very often you'll find there is a fishmonger's attached to the restaurant, so you can be sure of having fresh fish and can even pick out the one you want for your dinner. As well as the more familiar varieties, there is a whole range of exotic species to tempt the palate.

I'd like some fish.	orīd **sæ**mæk min **faḍ**lak	أريد سمك من فضلك.
What kinds of seafood do you have?	æyy aṣ**nāf** æl-æs**māk** '**in**dæk	أي أصناف الأسماك عندك؟

كركند	kæræ**kænd**	lobster
جمبري [أرادس]	gæm**bæ**rī [a**rā**dis]	prawns/shrimps
جندفلي [محار]	gæn**dof**lī [maḥ**ḥār**]	oysters
كابوريا	kæ**bor**yæ	crab
سمك موسى	**sæ**mæk **mū**sæ	sole

كباب سمك (kæ**bāb** **sæ**mæk) charcoal-grilled chunks of fish with pieces of tomato and sweet peppers

سمك صيدية (**sæ**mæk ṣayya**diy**yæ) chunks of fish braised with fried onions and served with rice flavoured with onion sauce and lemon juice

كفتة سمك (**kof**tit **sæ**mæk) deep-fried balls of fish, rice and parsley

baked	fil forn	في الفرن
cured	mi**mæl**læḥ	مملح
fried	**maq**lī	مقلي
grilled (broiled)	**mæsh**wī	مشوي
in a sauce	bil **ṣal**ṣa	بالصلصة
marinated	mi**tæb**bil	متبل
poached	mæs**lūq**	مسلوق
smoked	mo**dækh**khæn	مدخن
steamed	bil bo**khār**	بالبخار

Meat لحم

Eating pork is forbidden by Muslim dietary law, and is thus rarely found on menus. Lamb is traditionally the favourite meat. In certain dishes, il may be replaced by beef or veal, which are gaining popularity.

What kinds of meat do you have?	æyy aṣ**nāf** æl-**læḥm** '**in**dæk	أي أصناف اللحم عندك؟
I'd like some...	o**rīd** læḥm	أريد لحم...
beef/veal/lamb	**ba**qarī/bitillo/**ḍā**nī	بقري/ بتلو/ ضاني

اسكالوب	iskæ**lob**	cutlet
كندوز	kæn**dūz**	milk-fed lamb
بوفتيك	bof**tek**	beefsteak
جامبون	**zham**bon	ham
راس	ra's	head
رقبة	**ra**qabæ	neck
روزبيف	roz**bīf**	roast beef
رياش [كستلتة] ضاني	ri**yǣsh** [kostæ**let**tæ] **ḍā**nī	lamb chops
سجق [مقانق]	so**goq** [ma**qā**niq]	sausages
صدر	ṣidr	breast
فخذة (كندوز)	**fækh**dæ (kæn**dūz**)	leg (of lamb)
فلتو	fi**lit**to	fillet
كبده	**kib**dæ	liver
كستلتة بتلو	kostæ**let**tæ bi**til**lo	veal chops
كتف	kitf	shoulder
كستلتة	kostæ**let**tæ	chops
كرشه	**ker**shæ	tripe
كفتة	**kof**tæ	meatballs
كلاوي	kæ**lǣ**wī	kidneys
كوارع بتلو	kæ**wǣ**ri' bi**til**lo	calf's trotters (feet)
لسان	li**sǣn**	tongue
لحم مفروم	læḥm maf**rūm**	minced meat
مخ	mokh	brains
موزة	**mō**zæ	shank/knuckle

Here are a few Arabic meat dishes:

شاورمة (shǣwirmæ)	chunks of meat roasted on a vertical spit from which thin slices are cut and served either in a bun or on a plate, usually with rice
فتة (fættæ)	boiled mutton and rice mixed with bread crumbs and broth, served with vinegar and garlic
رياش (riyǣsh)	spicy charcoal-grilled chops
كباب (kæbǣb)	spicy chunks of charcoal-grilled meat
كبيبة [كبه] (kobēbæ [kibbæ])	minced meat, cracked wheat and onion balls fried in butter or served raw are called *kobeiba naya*; when baked *kobeiba besseniyah*; and Lebanese style (rolled into dumplings and served in goat's milk soup) *kobeiba labniyeh*
كفتة (koftæ)	charcoal-grilled meatballs
سفيحة (sfīḥæ)	a pizza-like dough garnished with seasoned minced mutton (Lebanese)
مقلوبة (mæqlūbæ)	meat and aubergine (eggplant) served with rice

barbecued	**mæ**shwī 'ælæl fæḥm	مشوي على الفحم
fried	**maq**lī	مقلي
grilled (broiled)	**mæsh**wī	مشوي
minced	maf**rūm**	مفروم
roasted	**ros**to	روستو
stewed	mi**sæb**bik	مسبك
stuffed	**mæḥ**shī	محشي
underdone (rare)	qa**līl** æs-**si**wæ	قليل السوا
medium	niṣf **si**wæ	نصف سوا
well-done	mis**ti**wī	مستوى

Game and poultry لحم الصيد والطيور

Apart from fowl, game is not found often on the menu in Middle Eastern countries. However, poultry dishes are favourites, in particular chicken and duck garnished and flavoured in an extraordinary variety of ways, and often filled with rich stuffings.

I'd like some game.	orīd læḥm ṣēd	أريد لحم صيد.
What kinds of poultry do you have?	mǣ aṣnāf aṭ-ṭoyūr 'indæk	ما أصناف الطيور عندك؟

أرنب	ærnæb	rabbit
بط	baṭṭ	duck
بط بري	baṭṭ bærrī	wild duck
حمام	ḥæmǣm	pigeon
ديك رومي [حباش]	dīk rūmī [ḥæbǣsh]	turkey
سمان [سمون]	simmæn [sommon]	quail
فراخ [فراريج]	firǣkh [færǣrīzh]	chicken
فراخ [فراريج] مشوية	firǣkh [færǣrīzh] mæshwiyya	roast chicken
ورك/ صدر/ كبده	wirk/ṣidr/kibdæ	leg/breast/liver
وز	wizz	goose

بيرام حمام (birǣm ḥæmǣm)	pigeon baked in a casserole with rice and milk (Egyptian)
حمام محشي فريك/ رز (ḥæmǣm mæḥshī firīk/roz)	pigeon stuffed with cracked wheat or seasoned rice
فراخ بالخلطة (firǣkh bil khalṭa)	roast chicken served with rice mixed with nuts, chicken liver and giblets
فراخ شركسية (firǣkh shærkæsiyyæ)	boiled chicken served with rice and a sauce made of chopped walnuts, chilli peppers and bread crumbs
كشك بالفراخ (kishk bil firǣkh)	pieces of boiled chicken braised in a gravy made of yoghurt, chicken broth, onion and butter

Vegetables خضراوات

Plainly cooked vegetables may accompany your charcoal-grilled meat, but more emphasis is placed on braised vegetables, vegetable stews and stuffed vegetables. The most frequent fillings are rice and minced meat.

What vegetables do you recommend?	bi æyy æl-khoḍra**wāt** tin**ṣah**nī	بأي الخضراوات تنصح؟
I'd like some...	o**rīd**	اريد
بنجر	**ban**gar	beetroot
بطاطس	ba**ṭāṭ**is	potatoes
بصل أخضر	**ba**ṣal **akh**ḍar	leeks
باذنجان	bitin**gæn**	aubergine (eggplant)
باميه	**bæm**yæ	okra
بسلة	bi**sil**læ	peas
بصل	**ba**ṣal	onions
جرجير	gær**gīr**	rocket salad
جزر	**ga**zar	carrots
خرشوف	khar**shūf**	artichokes
خس	khass	lettuce
خيار	khi**yār**	cucumber
ذرة	**do**ra	sweet corn (corn)
سبانخ	sæ**bæ**nikh	spinach
طرشي [كابيس]	**ṭor**shī [kæ**bīs**]	pickled vegetables
طماطم [بندورة]	ta**mā**ṭim [bana**dū**ra]	tomatoes
فاصوليا خضراء	fæ**ṣol**yæ **kha**ḍra'	French (green) beans
فلفل حامي	**fil**fil **ḥæ**mī	pimiento
فجل	figl	radishes
فلفل أخضر	**fil**fil **akh**ḍar	sweet peppers
قرنبيط	qarna**bīt**	cauliflower
كرفس	ka**rafs**	celery
كرنب [ملفوف]	ko**romb** [mæl**fūf**]	cabbage
كوسه	**kū**sæ	marrow (squash)
ورق عنب	**wa**raq **'i**næb	vine leaves
لفت	lift	turnips

بامية بالموزة (**bæm**yæ bil **mō**zæ) okra braised in tomato sauce with beef knuckle

محشي (**mæḥ**shī) vegetables stuffed with a mixture of minced meat (usually lamb or mutton), rice, onion and herbs. The most popular *mahshi* are vine leaves, sweet peppers, cabbage leaves, marrow (squash), tomatoes or aubergine (eggplant). They can be eaten hot or cold and are sometimes served with yoghurt

طاجن باميه (**ṭā**gin **bæm**yæ) meat and okra stew with onions, garlic and tomatoes (Lebanese)

لوبيا بالزيت (**lob**yæ bil zēt) beans fried in oil, then braised in tomato sauce and served chilled with lemon (Lebanese)

ملوخية (molo**khiy**yæ) a very popular Egyptian dish, this is a spicy soup of greens flavoured with garlic. It's usually served with rice and the chicken or meat used in the stock

موساكا (mosæk**kæ**'æ) layers of fried aubergine (eggplant) and minced meat, covered in a white sauce and baked

baked	fil forn	في الفرن
boiled	mæs**lūq**	مسلوق
braised	mi**sæb**bik	مسبك
chopped	mi**khar**raṭ	مخرط
creamed	maf**rūm**	مفروم
diced	mokæ'æ**bæt**	مكعبات
fried	**maq**lī	مقلي
grilled (broiled)	**mæsh**wī	مشوي
roasted	**ros**to	روستو
stewed	mi**sæb**bik	مسبك
stuffed	**mæḥ**shī	محشي

Dried pulses, cereals and pasta   بقول وحبوب ومكرونه

Rice is the staple cereal; also frequently used in filling dishes are cracked wheat, lentils, beans and chick-peas. A whole meal in itself is *kosharee*, a typical Egyptian dish made with rice, lentils and noodles in a hot sauce.

أرز	roz	rice
حمص	**hommoṣ**	chick-peas
عدس	'æds	lentils
لوبيا	**lobyæ**	beans
فول	fūl	brown beans
فريك [برغل]	firīk [borgol]	cracked wheat
مكرونة	makarōna	pasta

As for the seasoning...

بقدونس	baqdūnis	parsley
بهار	bohār	spice
بودرة كاري	bodrit kǣrī	curry powder
توم	tōm	garlic
جوزة الطيب	gōzit aṭ-ṭīb	nutmeg
حبهان	hæbbæhǣn	cardamom
خلطة أعشاب	khalṭit æ'shǣb	mixture of herbs
ريحان	riḥǣn	basil
فلفل	filfil	pepper
زعتر	za'tar	thyme
سمسم	semsem	sesame seed
شطة [هريسة]	shaṭṭa [harīsa]	red chilli
قرفة	qirfæ	cinnamon
قرنفل	qoronfil	clove
كرات	korrāt	chives
كزبرة	kozbara	coriander
كمون	kæmūn	caraway
نعناع	næ'nǣ'	mint
ماء ورد	mǣ' wærd	orange flower water

Fool and falafel فول وفلافل

Fool, a brown-bean concoction seasoned with oil, garlic and lemon juice is doubtless the favourite dish in the Middle East; its widespread popularity and its price put it on a par with the hot-dog. It is served hot on a plate accompanied by a choice of marinated vegetables or salads and Arab bread, or put into a bun. Other specialities that can also be eaten at any time of the day are *falafel* (also called *ta'amia*) and *bisara*.

بصارة (biṣāra)	a purée made of onions, garlic and *fool*; served cold with Arab bread
فلافل (falāfil)	small balls of ground beans, mixed with greens and spices and fried in oil
فول (fūl)	cooked brown beans, seasoned with oil, garlic and lemon juice or served with butter

Couscous كسكس

This favourite North African dish is based on cracked wheat like the Lebanese salad *tabbule*. The couscous is, however, eaten hot, moistened with broth and topped with vegetables and the meat used for the stock. It is usually served with *harissa* (a very strong peppery preserve).

كسكس	kus**kus**ī	couscous

... and the Arab bread

This tasty, flat round bread is made of wheat and corn-flour. It is only slightly leavened, with an empty pocket running right through it, which makes it ideal for scooping up food right from the bowl or plate. Filled with *fool*, *falafel*, *shawerma* (thin slices of spit-roasted meat) or salad, it also makes delicious sandwiches. If you ask for fresh bread you'll get it warm.

خبز (طازة)	khobz (ṭ**ā**za)	(fresh) bread

Fruit فواكه

The mild climate permits the cultivation of most of the fruit known in Europe, as well as varieties from the tropics. Arabs like to end off their meal with fresh fruit, so you'll be able to get the fruits of the season at any restaurant. Larger establishments generally have a wide choice.

Do you have fresh fruit?	hæl 'indæk fæwǣkih ṭāza	هل عندك فواكه طازة؟
I'd like some…	orīd… min faḍlak	أريد… من فضلك.

أناناس	ænænæs	pineapple
برتقال	bortoqāl	oranges
برقوق	bærqūq	plums
بطيخ	baṭṭīkh	watermelon
بلح	bælæḥ	fresh dates
بلح أحمر	bælæḥ aḥmar	red dates
تفاح	toffǣḥ	apples
تين	tīn	figs
جريب فروت	grēb frūt	grapefruit
جوافة	gæwǣfæ	guavas
جوز هند	gōz hind	coconuts
خوخ [درة]	khōkh [darra]	peaches
رمان	rommān	pomegranates
زبيب	zibīb	raisins
شمام	shæmmǣm	melon
عنب	'inæb	grapes
أبيض/ أحمر/ بناتي	abyaḍ/aḥmar/ bænǣtī	green/blue/seedless
فراولة	farawla	strawberries
كريز	krēz	cherries
كمثرة [أجاص]	kommitræ [aggāṣ]	pears
منجه	mængæ	mangoes
مشمش	mishmish	apricots
موز	mōz	bananas
يوسفندي [أفندي]	yosæfændī [æfændī]	tangerines

Dessert—Pastries تحالي ـ حلويات

Arabs have a sweet tooth for gooey, syrupy desserts like the well-known *baklava*. Some desserts bear intriguing names such as "lady's navel" and "Ali's mother". Pastries are generally rich, sweet and often garnished with chopped nuts. They are eaten at the end of a meal, with a cup of coffee in the afternoon and on every other possible occasion.

I'd like... please.	o**rīd**... min **faḍ**lak	أريد... من فضلك.
a dessert	tæ**ḥǣ**lī	تحالي
some pastries	ḥælæwiy**yǣt**	حلويات
Something light, please.	she' khæ**fīf** min **faḍ**lak	شيء خفيف من فضلك.
What do you recommend?	bi **mǣ**zæ tinṣ**aḥ**nī	بماذا تنصحني؟
Just a small portion.	miq**dār** ṣa**gīr**	مقدار صغير.
Nothing more, thanks.	lǣ she' **shok**ran	لا شيء شكراً.
I'd like some...	o**rīd**... min **faḍ**lak	أريد... من فضلك
cake	kēk	كيك
caramel custard	krem kara**mil**	كريم كارامل
fruit salad	**sala**ṭit fæ**wǣ**kih	سلطة فواكه
ice cream	zhi**lǣ**tī [æys krem]	جيلاتي [أيس كريم]
rice pudding	roz bi **læ**bæn	رز بلبن
water-ice (sherbet)	gra**nī**ta [**bū**ẓa]	جرانيته [بوظا]

Some desserts are served automatically with cream, and you may want to say:

I'd like the dessert with...	o**rīd** æt-tæ**ḥǣ**lī bi	أريد التحالي بـ....
clotted cream	**qish**ṭa	قشطة
cream	**krē**mæ	كريمة
I prefer the dessert without cream.	a**faḍ**ḍal æt-tæ**ḥǣ**lī bi**dūn** **krē**mæ	أفضل التحالي بدون كريمة.

Here are some favourite Arabic desserts:

بسيمة (bæs**ī**mæ)	semolina pudding baked with coconut and sugar
بقلاوة (bæql**ǣ**wæ)	*baklava:* thin layers of pastry, filled with nuts, almonds and pistachios, steeped in syrup
بلح الشام (**bæ**læḥ æsh-**shǣm**)	"Syria's dates": puff pastry, fried, steeped in syrup
خشاف (kho**shǣf**)	stewed fruit
صرة الست (**ṣo**rrit æs-**sit**)	"lady's navel": a ring-shaped sweet, soaked in syrup
عيش السرايا ('æysh æs-sar**ā**y**ǣ**)	"palace bread": deep-fried sweet roll, steeped in syrup
قطايف (qaṭ**ā**yif)	a pastry filled with nuts, fried and then topped with syrup
كل واشكر (kol **wosh**kor)	"eat it and thank God": smaller version of *baklava,* with less crust and more nuts, steeped in syrup
أم علي (om '**æl**ī)	"Ali's mother", named after an Egyptian Mameluke queen; raisin cake, steeped in milk
بسبوسة (bæs**b**ū**s**æ)	semolina tart, baked with butter, covered with syrup
مهلبية (mæhællæ**biy**yæ)	rice or corn-flour pudding
ملبن (لكوم) (**mæl**bæn [lo**kūm**])	Turkish delight

After a dinner including dessert and fruit, Arabs like to drink a cup of Turkish coffee. You'll certainly want to sample this brew, which in any case will problably be the only type of coffee you'll be able to find (see page 62).

Drinks مشروبات

Islam forbids Muslims to drink alcohol, but in places catering for foreign visitors, you will be able to get all kinds of alcoholic drinks, as well as a large range of refreshing soft drinks.

Beer بيرة

Beer has been drunk in the Middle East as far back as the ancient Egyptians and Mesopotamians. Good beer is still brewed, and today in Egypt you can ask for Stella beer (**bī**ra **stil**læ), a light, lager beer, or an Aswan beer (**bī**rit as**wæn**), a dark beer; Almaza (al**mā**za) and Laziza (la**zī**za) are noted Lebanese brands.

I'd like a beer, please.	o**rīd bī**ra min **faḍ**lak	أريد بيرة من فضلك.
Do you have... beer?	hæl **'in**dæk **bī**ra	هل عندك بيرة؟
bottled	fī zo**gæ**gæ	في زجاجة
foreign	ægnæ**biy**yæ	أجنبية
light/dark	**fæ**tḥæ/**gæ**mqa	فاتحة / غامقة
Another bottle of beer, please.	zo**gæ**git **bī**ra **tæ**nyæ min **faḍ**lak	زجاجة بيرة تانية من فضلك.

Wine نبيت

The Middle East was doubtless the birthplace of wine. From biblical times to the 8th century A.D., vineyards flourished. The wine cellars of Ksara in Lebanon, founded by the Jesuits in 1857, are the largest in the Middle East. Egypt's Gianaclis vineyards on the Nile Delta at Abu Hummus are also noteworthy. Most of the wine is white, but among the reds is the full-bodied Omar Khayyam which has the curious aftertaste of dates.

Omar Khayyam (red)	**'o**mar khæy**yæm**	عمر خيام
Ptolemy (white)	ni**bīt** æl-ba**ṭāl**sæ	نبيت البطالسة

Matameer (red)	**nibīt** æl-maṭ**āmīr**	نبيت المطامير
Gianaclis (red or white)	**nibīt** zhænæ**klīs**	نبيت جناكليس
Queen Cleopatra (white)	**nibīt** kilyo**bā**tra	نبيت كليوباترة
Pharaoh's Wine (red)	**nibīt** æl-far**ā**'næ	نبيت الفراعنة
May I have the wine list, please.	**orīd listit** æn-nibīt min **faḍ**lak	أريد لستة النبيت من فضلك.
A bottle of ... wine, please.	**orīd** zog**æ**git ni**bīt**... min **faḍ**lak	أريد زجاجة نبيت من فضلك
red/white/rosé	**aḥ**mar/**ab**yaḍ/ro**zēh**	أحمر/ أبيض/ روزيه
dry/sweet	sek/**ḥil**wæ	سك/ حلوة
light/full-bodied	khæ**fīf**/tæ**qīl**	خفيف/ ثقيل
I'd like a bottle of champagne.	**orīd** zog**æ**git sham**bān**yā	أريد زجاجة شمبانيا

في صحتك

(fī ṣi**ḥ**itæk)

YOUR HEALTH!/CHEERS!

Other alcoholic drinks مشروبات كحولية أخرى

A local speciality you're likely to come across is *arak*, a Lebanese aniseed liqueur, similar to the French *pastis* or Greek *ouzo*.

I'd like to try a glass of arak.	**orīd** æn ætæ**zaw**waq kob**bæ**yit **'a**raq	أريد أن أتذوق كباية عرق.
I'd like a/(an)..., please.	**orīd**... min **faḍ**lak	أريد... من فضلك.
aperitif	**fæ**tiḥ shæ**hiy**yæ [apera**tīv**]	فاتح شهية [أبريتيف]
cognac	**kōn**yæk	كونياك
gin and tonic	zhin bil **to**nik	جين بالتونيك
liqueur	**li**qers	ليقرز

port	**bor**to	بورتو
rum	rum	روم
sherry	**sher**ī	شري
vermouth	ver**mūt**	ڤرموت
(double) whisky	**wis**kī (dobl)	ويسكي (دوبل)
neat (straight)	sek	سك
on the rocks	bil tælg	بالتلج
with water/with soda	bil mǣ'/bil ṣōda	بالماء/ بالصودا

Nonalcoholic drinks مشروبات بدون كحول

Freshly squeezed fruit juice is a very popular drink in the Middle East. Lemon, sugar-cane and mango juice are the favourites. You'll also find many kinds of bottled mineral waters and fizzy drinks. You must, however, specify the brand and not just ask for a lemonade or an orangeade.

I'd like a bottle of...	o**rīd** zo**gǣ**git	أريد زجاجة...
I'd like a/an...	o**rīd**	أريد...
apricot juice	'a**ṣīr mish**mish	عصير مشمش
carrot juice	'a**ṣīr ga**zar	عصير جزر
mixed fruit drink	**kok**til fæ**wǣ**kih	كوكتيل فواكه
grape juice	'a**ṣīr** '**in**æb	عصير عنب
guava juice	'a**ṣīr** gæ**wǣ**fæ	عصير جوافة
lemon juice	'a**ṣīr** læ**mūn**	عصير لمون
mango juice	'a**ṣīr mæn**gæ	عصير مانجه
(glass of) milk	(kob**bǣ**yit) **læ**bæn [ḥæ**līb**]	(كوباية) لبن [حليب]
mineral water	mǣ' mæ'dæ**niy**yæ	ماء معدنية
fizzy (carbonated)	gæ**ziy**yæ	غازية
still	'ǣ**diy**yæ	عادية
orange juice	'a**ṣīr** borto**qāl**	عصير برتقال
pomegranate juice	'a**ṣīr** rom**mān**	عصير رمان
strawberry juice	'a**ṣīr** fa**raw**la	عصير فراولة
sugar-cane juice	'a**ṣīr qa**ṣab	عصير قصب
tamarind juice	'a**ṣīr** tamr **hin**dī	عصير تمر هندي

Complaints شكاوى

There is a plate/glass missing.	**nā**qiṣ ṭabaq/kob**bǣ**yæ	ناقص طبق/ كباية.
I don't have a knife/ fork/spoon.	**læy**sæ '**in**dī sik**kī**næ/ **shō**kæ/mæl'**a**qa	ليس عندي سكينة/ شوكة/ ملعقة.
That's not what I ordered. I asked for...	**hǣ**zæ **læy**sæ **mǣ** ṭa**lab**to. ænæ ṭa**labt**	هذا ليس ما طلبت. أنا طلبت...
There must be a mistake.	**yū**gæd **kha**ṭa'	يوجد خطأ.
May I change this?	**mom**kin tæg̣**yīr hǣ**zæ	ممكن تغيير هذا؟
I asked for a small portion (for the child).	ænæ ṭa**labt** miq**dār** ṣa**gīr** (lil ṭifl)	أنا طلبت مقدار صغير (للطفل).
The meat is...	æl-**læḥm**	اللحم...
overdone	ki**tīr** æs-**si**wæ	كثير السوا
underdone (too rare)	qa**līl** æs-**si**wæ	قليل السوا
too tough	**nǣ**shif ki**tīr**	ناشف كثير
This is too...	**hǣ**zæ... ki**tīr**	هذا... كثير
bitter/salty/sweet	morr/**mǣ**liḥ/ḥilw	مر/ مالح/ حلو
I don't like this.	lǣ æ**ḥibb hǣ**zæ	لا أحب هذا.
The food is cold.	æl-**ækl bǣ**rid	الأكل بارد.
This isn't fresh.	**hǣ**zæ **læy**sæ **ṭā**za	هذا ليس طازة.
What's taking so long?	li**mǣ**zæ æt-tæ'**khīr**	لماذا التأخير؟
Have you forgotten our drinks?	hæl næ**sīt** æl-mæshrū**bǣt**	هل نسيت المشروبات؟
The wine doesn't taste right.	æn-ni**bīt** loh ṭa'm g̣æ**rīb**	النبيت له طعم غريب.
This isn't clean.	**hǣ**zæ **læy**sæ na**ẓīf**	هذا ليس نظيف.
Would you ask the head waiter to come over?	**o**ṭlob min æl-**mitr** æl-ḥo**ḍūr** min **fa**ḍlak	أطلب من المتر الحضور من فضلك.

The bill (check) الحساب

Though a service charge is included in restaurant bills, you should leave an additional tip for the waiter. In many restaurants you can settle your bill by credit card. Signs are posted indicating which cards are accepted.

I'd like the bill, please.	**orīd** æl-ḥ**isǣb** min **faḍ**lak	أريد الحساب من فضلك.
We'd like to pay separately.	no**rīd** æn-**næd**fæ' mon**fa**ṣilan	نريد أن تدفع منفصلاً.
I think there's a mistake in this bill.	**aẓonn yū**gæd **kha**ṭa' fil ḥ**isǣb**	أظن يوجد خطأ في الحساب.
What is this amount for?	**limǣ**zæ **hǣ**zæ æl-**mæb**læg	لماذا هذا المبلغ؟
Is service included?	hæl **hǣ**zæ **yæsh**mæl æl-**khid**mæ	هل هذا يشمل الخدمة؟
Is everything included?	hæl koll she' mæḥ**sūb**	هل كل شيء محسوب؟
Do you accept traveller's cheques?	hæl **taq**bal shī**kǣt** siyǣ**ḥiy**yæ	هل تقبل شيكات سياحية؟
Can I pay with this credit card?	**mom**kin **æd**fæ' bi kært maṣ**ra**fī	ممكن أدفع بكارت مصرفي؟
Thank you, this is for you.	**shok**ran **hǣ**zæ læk	شكراً، هذا لك.
Keep the change.	iḥ**ta**fiẓ bil **bā**qī	احتفظ بالباقي.
That was delicious.	kǣn æl-**ækl** 'a**ẓīm**	كان الأكل عظيم.
We enjoyed it, thank you.	'**ægæb**næ æl-**ækl** **gid**dæn **shok**ran	أعجبنا الأكل جداً، شكراً.

شامل الخدمة

SERVICE INCLUDED

TIPPING, see inside back-cover

Coffee house القهوة

Going to a café in an Arab country is more than just for refreshment. It's tradition. Inside or on the terrace, observing the drama of Arab street life, you bask in an atmosphere of calm and cordiality.

The coffee house is mainly patronized by men; an unaccompanied woman may feel ill at ease.

While you can also order tea, soft drinks or mineral water, you'll undoubtedly want to try Turkish coffee. You've a choice: you can order it without sugar, sweet or very sweet.

Two other important activities in a café are smoking a water pipe or *nargile* and playing backgammon and dominoes. If you decide to try the water pipe, clap your hands to attract the waiter's attention, and ask him for a *nargile.* You'll have to tell him whether you want *tamback*, a natural coarse-cut tobacco, or *ma assil*, a lighter tobacco mixed with molasses.

The waiter will prepare the pipe and the tobacco, take the first puff to see that it's well lit, and then turn it over to you.

When you're ready to leave, clap your hands and ask the waiter for the bill.

I'd like a cup of...	o**rīd** fin**gǣn**	أريد فنجان...
(Turkish) coffee	**qah**wa	قهوة
very sweet	**sok**kar ziy**ǣ**dæ	سكر زيادة
medium	maẓ**būṭ**	مظبوط
without sugar	**sǣ**dæ	سادة
instant coffee	nes**ka**fé	نسكافيه
tea	shæy	شاي
mint tea	shæy bi **næ**'nǣ'	شاي بنعناع
I'd like a water pipe.	o**rīd shī**shæ [nær**gī**læ]	أريد شيشة [نرجيلة].
Bring us a backgammon board/some dominoes, please.	no**rīd ṭaw**la/do**mī**nō min **faḍ**lak	نريد طاولة/ دومينو من فضلك.

Snacks—Picnic أكلات خفيفة

A major pastime in the Middle East seems to be cracking seeds. They're sold everywhere—near stadiums, at the cinema, on the streets and in the markets. The most common seed is from a variety of melon. Vendors also offer a choice of nuts and dried fruit.

Please give me some…	a'aṭīnī… min **faḍ**lak	أعطني… من فضلك.
almonds	lōz	لوز
chestnuts	æbū **far**wa [kæs**tæ**næ]	أبو فروه [كاستانا]
dried fruit	**fǣ**kihæ mogæ**fæ**fæ	فاكهة مجففة
dried seeds	moḥammaṣ**āt**	محمصات
hazelnuts	**bon**doq	بندق
nuts	mikassa**rāt**	مكسرات
pecans	**bik**kæn	بكان
pistachio	**fos**toq	فستق
walnuts	'æyn **gæ**mæl	عين جمل
peanuts	fūl sū**dǣ**nī	فول سوداني

If you're still feeling hungry you can at any time stop for a snack, usually *fool* (cooked brown beans), *falafel* (spicy bean rissoles) or *shawerma* (spit-roasted meat). The Arabs themselves indulge in particular after the cinema, a football game or a concert. Snackbars are open nearly all night.

I'll have one of these, please.	a'aṭīnī **wǣ**ḥid min hǣ**zi**hi min **faḍ**lak	أعطني واحد من هذه من فضلك.
Give me two of these and one of those.	a'aṭīnī it**nēn** min hǣ**zi**hi wæ **wǣ**ḥid min hǣ**zi**hi	أعطني اتنين من هذه وواحد من هذه من فضلك.
to the left	ilæ æsh-shi**mǣl**	إلى الشمال
to the right	ilæ æl-yæ**mīn**	إلى اليمين
above/below	foq/tæḥt	فوق/ تحت
I'd like…	o**rīd**	أريد…
6 falafels	6 fæ**lǣ**fil	٦ فلافل
a plate of fool	ṭabaq fūl	طبق فول
a fool sandwich	sænd**witsh** fūl	ساندوتش فول

I'd like a/an/some...	o**rīd**	أريد...
cheese sandwich	sænd**witsh gib**næ	ساندوتش جبنة
chicken sandwich	sænd**witsh** fi**rækh**	ساندوتش فراخ
sandwich with slices of spit-roasted meat	sænd**witsh** shæ**wir**mæ	ساندوتش شاورمة
baked macaroni with white sauce	maka**rō**na bil bæshæ**mil**læ	مكرونة بالبشملة
It's to take away.	sæ'æ**khod**ho **mæ'**ī	سأخذه معي.

Here's a basic list of food and drink that might come in useful when shopping for a picnic.

Please give me a/an/ some...	min **faḍ**lak a'ṭinī	من فضلك أعطني...
bananas	mōz	موز
biscuits	bæs**kōt**	باسكوت
bread	khobz	خبز
butter	**zib**dæ	زبدة
cake	kēk	كيك
cheese	**gib**næ	جبنة
chips (french fries)	ba**ṭā**ṭis mo**ḥam**mara	بطاطس محمرة
chocolate bar	**bæ**kō shoko**lā**ta	باكوشوكولاته
cookies	bitī fōr	بيتي فور
crackers	bæs**kōt mæ**liḥ	باسكوت مالح
crisps (chips)	shebs	شبس
dried beef	bas**ṭar**ma	بسطرمه
gherkins (pickles)	mi**khæl**lil	مخلل
grapes	**'i**næb	عنب
ice cream	zhi**læ**tī [æys krem]	جيلاتي [أيس كريم]
olives	zæ**tūn**	زيتون
oranges	borto**qāl**	برتقال
pastries	ḥælæwiy**yæt**	حلويات
sausage	so**goq** [ma**qā**niq]	سجق [مقانق]
soft drink	mæsh**rūb**	مشروب
yoghurt	zæ**bæ**dī	زبادي

Travelling around

Plane الطائرة

Is there a flight to Amman?	hæl **tū**gæd **riḥ**læ ilæ 'æm**mǣn**	هل توجد رحلة إلى عمان؟
Is it a direct flight?	hæl hǣ**zi**hi **riḥ**læ mo**bǣ**shira	هل هذه رحلة مباشرة؟
When's the next flight to Cairo?	mǣ **mæw**'id aṭ-ṭā'**ira** æl-qā**di**mæ lil qā**hi**ra	ما موعد الطائرة القادمة للقاهرة؟
Is there a connection to Beirut?	hæl **yū**gæd mo**wā**ṣla ilæ bæy**rūt**	هل يوجد مواصلة إلى بيروت؟
I'd like a ticket to…	o**rīd** tæz**ka**ra li	أريد تذكرة لـ…
single (one-way)	**zi**hǣb	ذهاب
return (roundtrip)	zi**hǣb** wæ **i**yǣb	ذهاب وإياب
What time do we take off?	**mæ**tæ næ**qūm**	متى نقوم؟
What time should I check in?	**mæ**tæ **yæ**gib æn æt**sæg**gil fil ma**ṭār**	متى يجب أن أتسجّل في المطار؟
Is there a bus to the airport?	hæl **yū**gæd oto**bīs** lil ma**ṭār**	هل يوجد أوتوبيس للمطار؟
What's the flight number?	mǣ **ra**qam ær-**riḥ**læ	ما رقم الرحلة؟
What time do we arrive?	**mæ**tæ **na**ṣil	متى نصل؟
I'd like to… my reservation.	o**rīd** æn… **ḥæg**zī	أريد أن… حجزي.
cancel	**æl**gī	ألغي
change	a**gay**yar	أغير
confirm	æ'**æk**kid	أأكد

الوصول ARRIVAL	الرحيل DEPARTURE

Bus—Coach (long-distance bus) أوتوبيس

Cities are linked by ordinary and express coach service. Coaches follow a set schedule. Early booking is advisable. City buses provide a regular, if crowded, service, so if possible avoid travelling by bus in the big cities during rush hour. Buses show their destination in Arabic only, the route number might also be indicated in Western figures.

Where's the bus station?	æynæ maḥaṭṭit æl-oto**bīs**	أين محطة الأوتوبيس؟
When's the next coach to...?	**mæ**tæ ya**qūm** æl-oto**bīs** æl-**qā**dim ilæ	متى يقوم الأوتوبيس القادم إلى...؟
Does the coach stop at...?	hæl **ya**qif æl-oto**bīs** fī	هل يقف الأوتوبيس في...؟
How long does the journey (trip) take?	kæm min æl-**waqt tæ**khod ær-**riḥ**læ	كم من الوقت تأخذ الرحلة؟
Which bus do I take to Abou-Kir?	æyy oto**bīs ar**kab ilæ æbū qīr	أي أوتوبيس أركب إلى أبو قير؟
Where's the bus stop?	æynæ ma**ḥaṭ**ṭit æl-oto**bīs**	أين محطة الأوتوبيس؟
When's the... bus to Amman?	**mæ**tæ ya**qūm** æl-oto**bīs** ... ilæ 'æm**mæn**	متى يقوم الأوتوبيس... إلى عمان؟
first	æl-**æw**wæl	الأول
last	æl-æ**khīr**	الأخير
next	æl-**qā**dim	القادم
Do I have to change buses?	hæl **yæ**gib æn a**gay**yar æl-oto**bīs**	هل يجب أن أغيّر الأوتوبيس؟
Which line should I take?	æyy khaṭṭ **æ**khod	أي خط أخذ؟
Which tram (streetcar) should I take to...?	æyy trām **æ**khod ilæ	أي ترام أخذ إلى...؟
What number is it?	mæ **ra**qam **hæ**zæ	ما رقم هذا؟
What's the fare to...?	kæm **tæ**mæn æt-tæz**ka**ra ilæ	كم ثمن التذكرة إلى...؟

TICKETS, see page 72

Where can I buy a ticket?	**æy**næ æsh**tæ**rī æt-tæz**ka**ra	أين أشتري التذكرة؟
I'd like a bus pass.	**orīd** ishti**rāk** oto**bīs**	أريد اشتراك أوتوبيس.

محطة أوتوبيس
BUS STOP

On the bus في الأوتوبيس

Can you tell me where to get off?	**mom**kin tæ**qol**lī **mæ**tæ **æn**zil min **fa**ḍlak	ممكن تقول لي متى أنزل من فضلك؟
I want to get off at Khan El-Khalili.	o**rīd** æn-no**zūl** '**in**dæ khææn æl-khæ**lī**lī	أريد النزول عند خان الخليلي.
Please let me off at the next stop.	min **fa**ḍlak æn**zil**nī fil ma**ḥa**ṭṭa æl-**qā**dimæ	من فضلك أنزلني في المحطة القادمة.
May I have my luggage, please?	o**rīd** haqā'ibī min **fa**ḍlak	أريد حقائبي من فضلك.

Collective taxi تاكسي مشترك

Shared taxi service is popular in the Middle East, especially for inter-city travel. These taxis follow fixed routes, picking up and letting passengers off along the way. Shared taxis depart only when full.

Where can I get a collective taxi to...?	**æy**næ æ**gid tæk**sī mosh**ta**rak ilæ	أين أجد تاكسي مشترك إلى...؟

Underground (subway) مترو

Cairo is in the process of constructing an underground network; the first line opened in 1987.

Can I get to... by underground (subway)?	**mom**kin **æz**hæb ilæ... bil **mi**tro	ممكن أذهب إلى... بالمترو؟

TAXI, see page 21

Boat service الباخرة

Boats and steamers ply up and down the Nile. A trip on one of the magnificent, luxury steamers is well worthwhile.

In the normal way, you'll fly to Luxor or Aswan (or take the overnight train) and cruise between these two towns for 5 to 8 days, stopping at major temples and ruins on the way. There are also trips from and to Cairo. Tickets are available through travel agents.

There's also a one-day excursion by hydrofoil from Aswan to the ancient temple of Abu-Simbel, with its four colossal statues of Rameses II.

In Cairo you can take a water-bus to various points in the city along the Nile.

When's the next steamer to Luxor sailing?	mætæ tæ**qūm** æl-bǣ**khira** æl-qā**dimæ** ilæ **loqsor**	متى تقوم الباخرة القادمة إلى الأقصر؟
Where's the embarkation point?	æynæ ra**ṣīf** æl-bǣ**khira**	أين رصيف الباخرة؟
How long does the crossing take?	kæm min æl-**waqt** yækhod æl-'o**būr**	كم من الوقت يأخذ العبور؟
At which ports do we stop?	fī æyy mæ**wǣ**nī na**qif**	في أي موانىء نقف؟
I'd like to take a cruise/tour of the harbour.	argab fī **'æ**mæl **gæw**læ/ **gæw**læ fil **mī**nǣ'	أرغب في عمل جولة/ جولة في الميناء.
boat	**mær**kib	مركب
cabin	kæ**bī**næ	كابينة
single/double	li shakhṣ/li shakh**ṣēn**	لشخص/ لشخصين
deck	ẓahr æl-bǣ**khira**	ظهر الباخرة
ferry	mæ'**diy**yæ	معدية
hydrofoil	hidro**fīl**	هيدروفيل
life belt/boat	ḥi**zǣm** æn-næ**gǣt**/ **mær**kib æn-næ**gǣt**	حزام النجاة/ مركب النجاة
ship	sæ**fī**næ	سفينة

Train القطار

The rail network is not very extensive in the Middle East. Egypt, however, has a modern railway system and comfortable express trains with first and second class. Trains generally have a dining car. For long trips you can reserve a berth or compartment in a sleeping car. During high season, it's advisable to reserve seats in advance.

Can I get to... by rail?	**mom**kin **æ**zhæb ilæ... bil **sik**kæ æl-ḥæ**dīd**	ممكن أذهب إلى... بالسكة الحديد؟
Where's the railway station?	**æy**næ ma**ḥaṭ**ṭit æl-qi**ṭār**	أين محطة القطار؟

دخول	ENTRANCE	
خروج	EXIT	

إلى الرصيف	TO THE PLATFORMS
استعلامات	INFORMATION

Where is the...? أين...؟

Where is/are the...?	**æy**næ	أين...؟
baggage check	**mæk**tæb æl-æmǣ**nǣt**	مكتب الأمانات
bar	æl-**bār**	البار
booking office	**mæk**tæb æl-**ḥægz**	مكتب الحجز
left-luggage office	**mæk**tæb æl-æmǣ**nǣt**	مكتب الأمانات
lost property (lost and found) office	**mæk**tæb æl-mæfqū**dǣt**	مكتب المفقودات
newsstand	koshk æl-ga**rā**'id	كشك الجرائد
platform 3	ra**ṣīf** 3	رصيف ٣
reservations office	**mæk**tæb æl-**ḥægz**	مكتب الحجز
restaurant	æl-**maṭ**'am	المطعم
snack bar	**maṭ**'am snǣk	مطعم سناك
ticket office	shib**bǣk** æt-tæ**zǣ**kir	شباك التذاكر
waiting room	**ṣa**lit æl-inti**ẓār**	صالة الانتظار
Where are the toilets?	**æy**næ æt-tæwǣ**līt**	أين التواليت؟

TAXI, see page 21

Inquiries الاستعلامات

When is the ... train to Aswan?	**mætæ** yæ**qūm** æl-qi**ṭār** ... ilæ as**wān**	متى يقوم القطار... إلى أسوان؟
first/last/next	æl-**æw**wæl/æl-æ**khīr**/ æl-**qā**dim	الأول/ الأخير/ القادم
What time does the train to Alexandria leave?	**mætæ** yæ**qūm** æl-qi**ṭār** ilæ iskændæ**rī**yæ	متى يقوم القطار إلى إسكندرية؟
Please write it down.	min **faḍ**lak ik**tib**ho	من فضلك أكتبه.
What's the fare to Suez?	kæm **tæ**mæn æt-tæz**ka**ra ilæ æs-su**wēs**	كم ثمن التذكرة إلى السويس؟
Is it a through train?	hæl **ho**wæ qi**ṭār** mo**bæ**shir	هل هو قطار مباشر؟
Must I pay a surcharge?	hæl **yæ**gibo æn **æd**fæ' ræsm i**ḍā**fī	هل يجب أن أدفع رسم إضافي؟
Is there a connection to Damascus?	hæl **yū**gæd mo**wā**ṣla ilæ di**mishq**	هل يوجد مواصلة إلى دمشق؟
Do I have to change trains?	hæl **yæ**gib æn a**gay**yar æl-qi**ṭār**	هل يجب أن أغير القطار؟
Is there sufficient time to change?	hæl **yū**gæd waqt **kæ**fiy 'ælæ**shæn** a**gay**yar	هل يوجد وقت كافي علشان أغير؟
Is the train leaving on time?	hæl æl-qi**ṭār** yæ**qūm** fil mī'**æd**	هل القطار يقوم في الميعاد؟
What time does the train arrive in Port Said?	**mætæ** **ya**ṣil æl-qi**ṭār** ilæ bōr sæ'**īd**	متى يصل القطار إلى بور سعيد؟
Is the train arriving on time?	hæl æl-qi**ṭār** **ya**ṣil fil mī'**æd**	هل القطار يصل في الميعاد؟
Does the train stop in Al Minya?	hæl **ya**qif æl-qi**ṭār** fil **min**yæ	هل يقف القطار في المنيا؟

درجة أولى	FIRST CLASS
درجة ثانية	SECOND CLASS

Is there a... on the train?	hæl **tū**gæd... fil qi**ṭār**	هل توجد... في القطار؟
dining car	**'a**rabit ṭa'**ām**	عربة طعام
sleeping car	**'a**rabit nōm	عربة نوم
What platform does the train to... leave from?	min æyy ra**ṣīf** yæ**qūm** æl-qi**ṭār** ilæ	من أي رصيف يقوم القطار إلى...؟
What platform does the train from... arrive at?	**'æ**læ æyy ra**ṣīf ya**ṣil æl-qi**ṭār** min	على أي رصيف يصل القطار من....؟
I'd like to buy a timetable.	o**rīd** æn æsh**tæ**rī **gæd**wæl æl-mæwǣ**'īd**	أريد أن أشتري جدول المواعيد.

هذا قطار مباشر.	It's a through train.
يجب عليك أن تغيّر في...	You have to change at...
غيّر في... واركب قطار الأقاليم.	Change at... and get a local train.
رصيف ٣ يكون...	Platform 3 is...
هناك/ فوق	over there/upstairs
على الشمال/ على اليمين	on the left/on the right
يوجد قطار لـ... الساعة...	There's a train to... at...
قطارك يقوم من رصيف ٤.	Your train will leave from platform 4.
سيوجد تأخير... دقائق.	There will be a delay of...minutes.
الدرجة الأولى في...	First class is...
الأمام	at the front
الوسط	in the middle
النهاية	at the end

Tickets تذاكر

I want a ticket to Cairo.	or**ī**d tæz**ka**ra ilæl q**ā**hira	أريد تذكرة إلى القاهرة.
single (one way)	zih**ǣ**b	ذهاب
return (roundtrip)	zih**ǣ**b wæ iy**ǣ**b	ذهاب وإياب
first class	**da**raga **ū**læ	درجة أولى
second class	**da**raga **tæn**yæ	درجة ثانية
half price	niṣf tæz**ka**ra	نصف تذكرة

Reservation حجز

I want to reserve a...	or**ī**d æn **æḥ**giz	أريد أن أحجز...
seat (by the window)	mæ**kǣn** (bi**gǣ**nib æsh-shib**bǣk**)	مكان (بجانب الشباك)
berth	si**rīr**	سرير
upper	**'ǣ**lī	عالي
middle	fil **wa**saṭ	في الوسط
lower	**wā**ṭi'	واطي
berth in the sleeping car	si**rīr** fī **'a**rabit æn-**nōm**	سرير في عربة النوم

All aboard داخل القطار

Is this the right platform for the train to Alexandria?	hæl **hǣ**zæ ṣa**ḥīḥ** ra**ṣīf** qi**ṭār** iskændæ**rī**yæ	هل هذا صحيح رصيف قطار إسكندرية؟
Is this the train to Port Said?	hæl **hǣ**zæ qi**ṭār** bōr sæ**'īd**	هل هذا قطار بور سعيد؟
Excuse me. May I get by?	es**mæḥ**lī	إسمح لي.
Is this seat taken?	hæl **hǣ**zæl mæ**kǣn** mæḥ**gūz**	هل هذا المكان محجوز؟

I think that's my seat.	æ**zonn ænn**æ **hǣ**zæ mæ**kǣ**nī	أظن أن هذا مكاني.
Would you let me know before we get to Memphis?	**mom**kin tinæ**bih**nī qabl æn-**na**ṣil **il**æ mæm**fīs** min **fad**lak	ممكن تنبهني قبل أن نصل إلى ممفيس من فضلك؟
What station is this?	mǣ hǣ**zi**hil ma**ḥaṭ**ṭa	ما هذه المحطة؟
How long does the train stop here?	kæm min æl-**waqt** ya**gif** **æl**-qi**ṭār** **hon**æ	كم من الوقت يقف القطار هنا؟
When do we get to Aswan?	**mæt**æ **na**ṣil **il**æ as**wān**	متى نصل إلى أسوان؟

تدخين SMOKER	عدم التدخين NONSMOKER

Sleeping في عربة النوم

Are there any free compartments in the sleeping-car?	hæl **tū**gæd maqṣū**rāt** **fāḍ**ya fī **'a**rabit æn-**nōm**	هل توجد مقصورات فاضية في عربة النوم؟
Where's the sleeping-car?	**æy**næ **'a**rabit æn-**nōm**	أين عربة النوم؟
Where's my berth?	**æy**næ si**rī**rī	أين سريري؟
I'd like a lower berth.	o**rīd** si**rīr** **wā**ṭi'	أريد سرير واطي.
Would you make up our berths?	**mom**kin tigæ**h**hiz særæ**yer**næ	ممكن تجهز سرايرنا؟
Would you wake me at 7 o'clock?	æy**qiẓ**nī æs-**sǣ**'æ 7 min **fad**lak	أيقظني الساعة ٧ من فضلك.

Eating في عربة الطعام

Where's the dining-car?	**æy**næ **'a**rabit at-ta**'ām**	أين عربة الطعام؟

Baggage – Porters الحقائب ـ الشيالين

Porter!	shæyy**æl** ['ætt**æl**]	شيال [عتال]!
Can you help me with my luggage?	**mom**kin tisæ'**id**nī fī shēl ḥaqā'ibī	ممكن تساعدني في شيل حقائبي؟
Where are the luggage trolleys (carts)?	æynæ **'a**rabit æl-ḥ**aqā**'ib	أين عربة الحقائب؟
Where's the left-luggage office (baggage check)?	æynæ **mæk**tæb æl-æmæ**næt**	أين مكتب الأمانات؟
I'd like to leave my luggage, please.	or**īd** tark ḥaqā'**i**bī min **fa**ḍlak	أريد ترك حقائبي من فضلك.
I'd like to register (check) my luggage.	or**īd** tæsg**īl** ḥaqā'ibī	أريد تسجيل حقائبي.

تسجيل الحقائب
REGISTERING (CHECKING) BAGGAGE

Bicycle hire تأجير عجلات

I'd like to hire a bicycle.	or**īd** tæ'g**īr** **'æ**gælæ [bisi**klēt**tæ]	أريد تأجير عجلة [بسكلتة].

Or perhaps you prefer:

hitchhiking	ōtō**stop**	أوتوستوب
walking	æs-**sæ**yer	السير

Other means of transport وسائل مواصلات أخرى

camel riding	ro**kūb** æl-**gæ**mæl	ركوب الجمل
donkey riding	ro**kūb** æl-ḥo**mār**	ركوب الحمار
helicopter	hili**kob**tar	هليكوبتر
horse-cab	**'a**rabit khēl	عربة خيل
moped	dar**rā**ga bokhæ**riy**yæ	دراجة بخارية
motorbike	mōtō**sikl**	موتوسيكل
scooter	**skō**ter	سكوتر

Car السيارة

Main roads in Arab countries are generally good. Road signs are sometimes written in English. Roads, however, are not fenced, and night driving at high speed can be dangerous, particularly on desert roads. There are rest areas (isti**rā**ḥa) at frequent intervals where you can refuel, have your car checked or have minor repairs made while having a drink or snack. Driving yourself in town is not recommended, you'll be much more at ease with the services of a chauffeur.

Where's the nearest filling station?	**æy**næ **aq**rab ma**ḥaṭ**ṭit bæn**zīn**	أين أقرب محطة بنزين؟
Full tank, please.	im**læ'** lī min **faḍ**lak	إملأ لي من فضلك.
Give me... litres of petrol (gasoline).	a'ṭīnī...litr bæn**zīn** min **faḍ**lak	أعطني... لتر بنزين من فضلك.
super (premium)/ regular/diesel	sō**bar**/'**ǣ**dī/**dī**zel	سوبر/ عادي/ ديزل
Please check the...	min **faḍ**lak **ik**shif **'æ**læ	من فضلك إكشف على...
battery	æl-baṭṭā**riy**ya	البطارية
brake fluid	zēt æl-fa**rā**mil	زيت الفرامل
oil/water	æz-**zēt**/æl-**mǣ'**	الزيت/ الماء
Would you check the tyre pressure?	min **faḍ**lak **ik**shif **'æ**læ ḍagt æl-**'æ**gæl	من فضلك إكشف على ضغط العجل؟
1.6 front, 1.8 rear.	1,6 lil æ**mǣm** wæ 1,8 lil khælf	١،٦ للأمام و١،٨ للخلف.
Please check the spare tyre, too.	min **faḍ**lak **ik**shif **'æ**læ **'æ**gælæt aṭ-ṭa**wā**ri' **ay**ḍan	من فضلك إكشف على عجلة الطوارىء أيضاً.
Can you mend this puncture (fix this flat)?	min **faḍ**lak **ṣal**laḥ h**ǣ**zihi æl-**'æ**gælæ æl-mo**far**qa'a	من فضلك صلح هذه العجلة المفرقعة.
Would you change the..., please?	min **faḍ**lak **gay**yar	من فضلك غيّر...
bulb	æl-**lam**ba	اللمبة

CAR HIRE, see page 20

fan belt	sīr æl-marwa**ḥ**a	سير المروحة
spark(ing) plugs	æl-bozhī**hǣt**	البوجيهات
tyre	æl-**'æ**gælæ	العجلة
wipers	æl-mæss**ǣḥǣt**	المساحات
Would you clean the windscreen (windshield)?	min **faḍ**lak na**ẓ**if æz-zo**gǣg** æl-æ**mǣ**mī	من فضلك نظف الزجاج الأمامي.

Asking the way—Street directions السؤال عن الطريق ـ الاتجاه

Can you tell me the way to...?	**mom**kin ta**ṣ**if lī aṭ-ṭa**rīq** ilæ	ممكن تصف لي الطريق إلى...؟
How do I get to...?	**kæy**fæ **a**ṣil ilæ	كيف أصل إلى...؟
Are we on the right road for...?	hæl **na**ḥno fī aṭ-ṭa**rīq** aṣ-ṣa**ḥīḥ** ilæ	هل نحن في الطريق الصحيح إلى...؟
How far is the next village?	kæm æl-mæ**sǣ**fæ ilæl **qar**yæ æl-qā**di**mæ	كم المسافة إلى القرية القادمة؟
Is there a road with little traffic?	hæl **yū**gæd ṭa**rīq** gēr moz**dæ**ḥim	هل يوجد طريق غير مزدحم؟
How far is it to... from here?	kæm æl-mæ**sǣ**fæ ilæ... min **ho**næ	كم المسافة إلى... من هنا؟
Is there a motorway (expressway)?	hæl **yū**gæd ōtō**strād**	هل يوجد أوتوستراد؟
How long does it take by car/on foot?	kæm min æl-**waqt** bil sæy**yā**ra/sæy**ran**	كم من الوقت بالسيارة/ سيراً؟
Can I drive to the centre of town?	hæl nasta**ṭī'** æs-su**wǣ**qa fī wasṭ æl-**bæ**læd	هل تستطيع السواقة في وسط البلد؟
Can you tell me, where... is?	**mom**kin tæ**qol**lī **æy**næ	ممكن تقول لي أين...؟
How can I find this place/address?	**æy**næ ægid **hǣ**zæl mæ**kǣn**/'in**wǣn**	أين أجد هذا المكان/ عنوان؟
Where's this?	**æy**næ **hǣ**zæ	أين هذا؟
Can you show me on the map where I am?	min **faḍ**lak wæ**rī**nī mæ**kǣ**nī 'ælæl kha**rī**ṭa	من فضلك وريني مكاني على الخريطة؟

أنت في الطريق الخطأ.	You're on the wrong road.
اتجه إلى الأمام.	Go straight ahead.
هناك على الشمال/ اليمين.	It's down there on the left/right.
أمام/ خلف/ بجانب/ بعد...	opposite/behind/next to/ after...
شمال/ جنوب/ شرق/ غرب	north/south/east/west
اذهب حتى أول/ ثاني تقاطع.	Go to the first/second crossroads (intersection).
إتجه شمالاً بعد إشارة المرور.	Turn left at the traffic lights.
إتجه يميناً حتى الناصية القادمة.	Turn right at the next corner.
خذ طريق الـ...	Take the... road.
هذا شارع اتجاه واحد.	It's a one-way street.
يجب أن ترجع حتى...	You have to go back to...
إتبع اتجاه الجيزة.	Follow signs for Giza.

Parking الركن

Where can I park?	**æy**næ **ær**kin [a**ṣoff**]	أين أركن [أصف]؟
Is there a car park nearby?	hæl **yū**gæd **maw**qif sæyyā**rāt** qa**rīb**	هل يوجد موقف سيارات قريب؟
May I park here?	**mom**kin **ær**kin [a**ṣoff**] **ho**næ	ممكن أركن [أصف] هنا؟
How long can I park here?	kæm min æl-**waqt aq**dar **ær**kin [a**ṣoff**] **ho**næ	كم من الوقت أقدر أركن [أصف] هنا؟
What's the charge per hour?	kæm ḥi**sǣb** æs-**sǣ**'æ	كم حساب الساعة؟
Do you have some change for the parking meter?	hæl '**in**dæk **fæk**kæ lil 'æd**dǣd**	هل عندك فكه للعداد؟

Breakdown—Road assistance الأعطال ـ النجدة

Where's the nearest garage?	•**æy**næ **aq**rab gær**ā**zh	أين أقرب جراج؟
Excuse me. My car has broken down.	'**æf**wæn. sæy**yā**ratī tæ'**ṭa**lat	عفواً، سيارتي تعطلت.
May I use your phone?	**mom**kin isti'**mæl** tili**fō**næk	ممكن استعمال تليفونك؟
I've had a breakdown at...	ænæ '**in**dī 'oṭl fī	أنا عندي عطل في...
Can you send a mechanic?	**mom**kin ir**sæl** mi**kæ**nīkī	ممكن إرسال ميكانيكي؟
My car won't start.	sæy**yā**ratī læ tæ**qūm**	سيارتي لا تقوم.
The battery is dead.	æl-baṭṭa**riy**ya **fa**ḍya	البطارية فاضية.
I've run out of petrol (gasoline).	**læy**sæ '**in**dī bæn**zīn**	ليس عندي بنزين.
I have a flat tyre.	'**in**dī '**æ**gælæ mo**far**qa'a	عندي عجلة مفرقعة.
The engine is overheating.	æl-mō**tōr** **yæs**khæn ki**tīr**	الموتور يسخن كثير.
There is something wrong with the...	fī mosh**ki**læ fī	في مشكلة في...
brakes	æl-fa**rā**mil	الفرامل
carburettor	æl-karbīra**tōr**	الكربيراتور
clutch	æl-dibri**yæzh**	الدبرياج
exhaust pipe	mæ**sū**rit æl-'**æ**dim [æsh-shæk**mæn**]	ماسورة العادم [الشكمان]
radiator	ær-rādy**æ**t**ōr**	الرادياتور
wheel	æl-'**æ**gælæ	العجلة
Can you send a breakdown van (tow truck)?	**mom**kin ir**sæl** sæy**yā**rit **næg**dæ	ممكن إرسال سيارة نجدة؟
How long will you be?	kæm min æl-**waqt** **yæ**khod **hæ**zæl shogl	كم من الوقت يأخذ هذا الشغل؟

Accident—Police حادث ـ بوليس

Please call the police.	min **faḍ**lak **oṭ**lob æl **bōlīs**	من فضلك أطلب البوليس.
There's been an accident. It's about 2 km. from...	**yū**gæd **ḥæ̅**dis **'æ**læ bo'd 2 kīlo**metr** min	يوجد حادث على بعد ٢ كيلومتر من...
Where is there a telephone?	**æy**næ **yu**gæd tili**fōn**	أين يوجد تليفون؟
Call a doctor/an ambulance quickly.	**oṭ**lob dok**tōr**/sæy**yā**rit æl-is'**æ̅f** bi**sor**'æ	أطلب دكتور/سيارة الأسعاف بسرعة.
There are people injured.	**yū**gæd moṣā**būn**	يوجد مصابون.
Here's my driving licence.	hæ̅**zi**hi **rokh**ṣit qiyæ̅**dæ**tī	هذه رخصة قيادتي.
What's your name and address?	mæ̅ **is**mæk wæ 'in**wæ̅**næk	ما اسمك وعنوانك؟
What's your insurance company?	mæ̅ ism shir**kæt** tæ'**mī**næk	ما اسم شركة تأمينك؟

Road signs علامات الطرق

أحترس	Caution
خطر	Danger
إتجاه واحد	One-way street
المشاة	Pedestrians
قف	Stop
مستشفى	Hospital
منحنى خطر	Dangerous bend (curve)
مزلقان	Level (Railroad) crossing
ممنوع الوقوف	No parking
ممنوع الدخول	No entry
موقف	Parking
هدىء السرعة	Slow down

Sightseeing

Where's the tourist office?	æynæ **mæk**tæb æs-siy**ǣ**ḥæ	أين مكتب السياحة؟
What are the main points of interest?	mǣ æl-mæ'**ǣ**lim æs-siyǣ**ḥi**yyæ ar-rai**si**yyæ	ما المعالم السياحية الرئيسية؟
We're here for...	**na**ḥno **ho**næ li	نحن هنا لـ...
only a few hours	ba'ḍ æs-sǣ'**ǣt** fa**q**aṭ	بعض الساعات فقط
a day	yōm	يوم
a week	os**bū'**	أسبوع
Can you recommend a sightseeing tour?	**mom**kin tinṣa**ḥ**nī bi **gæw**læ siyǣ**ḥi**yyæ	ممكن تنصحني بجولة سياحية؟
Where's the point of departure?	min **æy**næ **næb**dæ'	من أين نبدأ؟
Will the bus pick us up at the hotel?	hæl sæyæ**khod**nǣ æl-oto**bīs** min æl-**fon**doq	هل سيأخذنا الأوتوبيس من الفندق؟
How much does the excursion cost?	bi**kæm** æl-**gæw**læ æs-siyǣ**ḥi**yyæ	بكم الجولة السياحية؟
What time does the tour start?	**mæ**tæ **tæb**dæ' æl-**gæw**læ	متى تبدأ الجولة؟
Is lunch included?	hæl æl-gæ**dǣ'** mæḥ**sūb**	هل الغذاء محسوب؟
What time do we get back?	**mæ**tæ **nær**gæ'	متى نرجع؟
Do we have free time in...?	hæl 'indi**næ** **gæw**læ **ḥ**orra fī	هل عندنا جولة حرة في...؟
Is there an English-speaking guide?	hæl **yū**gæd **mor**shid siy**ǣ**ḥī yætæ**kæl**læm ingi**lī**zī	هل يوجد مرشد سياحي يتكلم إنجليزي؟
I'd like to hire a private guide for...	o**rīd** **mor**shid khāṣṣ lī	أريد مرشد خاص لـ...
half a day	nisf yōm	نصف يوم
a full day	yōm **kǣ**mil	يوم كامل

Where is/Where are the...?	**æy**næ	أين...؟
art gallery	**ma'**raḍ æl-fon**ū**n	معرض الفنون
basilica	æl-b**ǣ**zi**lik**	البازيليك
bazaar	æs-**sūq** [æl-baz**ār**]	السوق [البازار]
building	æl-**mæb**nǣ	المبنى
business district	ḥæyy æl-æ'æ**mǣl** æt-togǣ**riy**yæ	حي الأعمال التجارية
castle	æl-**qaṣr**	القصر
catacombs	særǣ**dīb** æl-**mæw**tǣ	سراديب الموتى
cathedral	æl-kǣtidrā'**iy**yæ	الكاتيدرائية
cemetery	æl-mæ**dǣ**fin	المدافن
chapel	æl-kæ**nī**sæ	الكنيسة
church	æl-kæ**nī**sæ	الكنيسة
citadel	æl-**qal'**æ	القلعة
city centre	wasṭ æl-**bæ**læd	وسط البلد
city walls	sūr æl-mæ**dī**næ	سور المدينة
concert hall	**qā**'æt æl-mo**sī**qa	قاعة الموسيقى
convent	æd-**dīr**	الدير
court house	æl-mæḥ**kæ**mæ	المحكمة
dam	æs-**sæd**	السد
downtown area	wasṭ æl-**bæ**læd	وسط البلد
exhibition	æl-**ma'**raḍ	معرض
factory	æl-**maṣ**na'	المصنع
fair	arḍ æl-**ma'**raḍ	أرض المعرض
fortress	æl-**ḥiṣn**	الحصن
fountain	æn-nā**fū**ra	النافورة
gardens	æl-ḥæ**dǣ**'iq	الحدائق
harbour	æl-**mī**nǣ'	الميناء
library	æl-mæk**tæ**bæ æl-'omū**miy**yæ	المكتبة العمومية
market	æs-**sūq**	السوق
monastery	æd-**dīr**	الدير
monument	æn-**naṣb** æt-tiz**kǣ**rī	النصب التذكاري
mosque	æl-**mæs**gid	المسجد

museum	æl-**mæt**ḥæf	المتحف
obelisk	æl-**mi**sælæ	المسلة
old town	æl-mæ**dī**næ æl-qa**dī**mæ	المدينة القديمة
palace	æl-**qaṣr**	القصر
park	æl-ḥæ**dī**qa	الحديقة
parliament building	**mæbnæ** æl-barlæ**mān**	مبنى البرلمان
pyramids	æl-ah**rām**	الأهرام
royal palace	æl-**qaṣr** æl-**mæ**lækī	القصر الملكي
ruins	æl-aṭ**lāl**	الأطلال
shopping area	æl-**ḥæyy** æt-to**gæ**rī	الحي التجاري
Sphinx	**æ**būl hōl	أبو الهول
square	æl-mī**dæn**	الميدان
stadium	æl-is**tæd**	الأستاد
statue	æt-tim**sæl**	التمثال
temple	æl-mæ'**bæd**	المعبد
theatre	æl-**mæs**raḥ	المسرح
tomb	æl-**qabr**	القبر
tower	æl-**borg**	البرج
town hall	**mæbnæ** æl-mo**ḥā**faẓa	مبنى المحافظة
university	æl-**gæ**mi'æ	الجامعة
Valley of the Kings	**wæ**dī æl-mi**lūk**	وادي الملوك
Valley of the Queens	**wæ**dī æl-**mæ**li**kæt**	وادي الملكات
zoo	ḥæ**dī**qat æl-ḥæyæ**wæn**	حديقة الحيوان

Admission الدخول

Is... open on Fridays/Sundays?	hæl æl-... mæf**tūḥ** yōm æl-**gom**'æ/æl-**æ**ḥæd	هل الـ... مفتوح يوم الجمعة/الأحد؟
When does... open?	**mæ**tæ **yæf**tæḥ	متى يفتح...؟
When does it close?	**mæ**tæ **yaq**fil	متى يقفل؟
How much is the entrance fee?	**bi**kæm æd-do**khūl**	بكم الدخول؟
I'd like tickets for...	o**rīd** tæ**zæ**kir li	أريد تذاكر لـ...
...adults	...ki**bār**	...كبار
...children	...aṭ**fāl**	...أطفال

Is there any reduction for (the)...?	hæl **yū**gæd takh**fīḍ** lil	هل يوجد تخْفيض للـ...؟
disabled	**'æ**gæzæ	عجزة
groups	mægmū'**ǣt**	مجموعات
pensioners	mæ'ǣ**shǣt**	معاشات
students	**ṭ**alaba	طلبة
Have you a guidebook (in English)?	hæl **'in**dæk dæ**līl** siy**ǣ**ḥī (bil ingi**līz**ī)	هل عندك دليل سياحي (بالإنجليزي)؟
Can I buy a catalogue?	**mom**kin æsht**æ**rī kætæ**lōg**	ممكن أشتري كتالوج؟
Is it all right to take pictures?	mæs**mūḥ** **æ**khod **ṣu**war	مسموح أخذ صور؟

الدخول مجاناً	ADMISSION FREE
ممنوع التصوير	NO CAMERAS ALLOWED

Who—What—When? من ـ ماذا ـ متى؟

What's that building?	mǣ **hǣ**zæl **mæb**nǣ	ما هذا المبنى؟
Who was the...?	mæn kǣn	من كان...؟
architect	æl-mo**hæn**dis	المهندس
artist	æl-fæ**nǣn**	الفنان
painter	ær-ræs**sǣm**	الرسام
sculptor	æn-næḥ**ḥǣt**	النحات
Who built it?	mæn bæ**nǣh**	من بناه؟
When did he live?	**mæ**tæ 'ǣsh	متى عاش؟
When was it built/painted?	**mæ**tæ **bu**niyæ/ **ru**simæ	متى بنى/رسم؟
Where's the house where... lived?	**æy**næ æl-**bēt** æl**læ**zī **'ǣ**shæ fīh	أين البيت الذي عاش فيه...؟
Who painted that picture?	mæn **ræ**sæmæ hǣ**zi**hi aṣ-**ṣū**ra	من رسم هذه الصورة؟

We're interested in...	næ**ḥ**no mohtæm**mīn** bi	نحن مهتمين بـ...
antiques	æl-æntī**kæt**	الأنتيكات
archaeology	æl-**asār**	الآثار
art	æl-**fænn**	الفن
ceramics	æl-fokh**khār**	الفخار
coins	æl-'om**læt**	العملات
Coptic art	æl-**fænn** æl-**qop**ṭī	الفن القبطي
fine arts	æl-fo**nūn** æl-gæ**mī**læ	الفنون الجميلة
folk art	æl-**fænn** æsh-**shæ**'bī	الفن الشعبي
geology	æl-zhiyo**lozh**yæ	الجيولوجيا
handicrafts	æl-sinā**'āt** æl-yædæ**wiy**yæ	الصناعات اليدوية
hieroglyphics	æl-hiroglifiyyæ	الهيروغليفية
history	æt-tæ**rīkh**	التاريخ
Islamic art	æl-**fænn** æl-is**læ**mī	الفن الإسلامي
medicine	aṭ-**ṭibb**	الطب
music	æl-mo**sī**qa	الموسيقى
natural history	æt-tæ**rīkh** aṭ-ṭa**bī**'ī	التاريخ الطبيعي
painting	ær-**ræsm**	الرسم
pottery	æl-**khæ**zæf	الخزف
prehistory	mæ̅ qabl æt-tæ**rīkh**	ما قبل التاريخ
religion	æd-**dīn**	الدين
sculpture	æn-**næḥt**	النحت
zoology	'ilm æl-ḥæyæ**wæn**	علم الحيوان
Where's the... department?	**æy**næ qism	أين قسم...؟
It's...	**hæ**zæ	هذا
amazing	**mod**hish	مدهش
beautiful	gæ**mīl**	جميل
impressive	**rā**'i'	رائع
interesting	mo**himm**	مهم
pretty	**ḥil**wæ	حلوة
strange	gæ**rīb**	غريب
superb	bæ**dī'**	بديع

Religious services الخدمات الدينية

The Middle East is predominantly Muslim. However, other religions are represented as well. Largest and most significant of the Christian denominations is the Coptic Church, one of the most ancient forms of Christianity, whose main following is in Egypt. Most mosques are open to visitors, except during hours of worship—Muslims pray five times a day. When visiting a mosque, you are expected to take off your shoes before entering (at larger mosques, over-slippers are provided).

Is there a... near here?	hæl **yū**gæd... qa**rīb** min **ho**næ	هل يوجد... قريب من هنا؟
Catholic church	kæ**nī**sæ kæsoli**kiy**yæ	كنيسة كاثوليكية
Protestant church	kæ**nī**sæ brotis**tant**	كنيسة بروتستانت
Orthodox church	kæ**nī**sæ orto**doks**	كنيسة أرثوذكس
mosque	**mæs**gid	مسجد
synagogue	mæ'**bæd** yæ**hū**dī	معبد يهودي
At what time is...?	mæ̃ **hi**yæ mæ**wæ̃qīt**	ما هي مواقيت...؟
mass/the service	aṣ-ṣa**lāh**	الصلاة
Where can I find a... who speaks English?	**æy**næ **æ**gid... yætæ**kæl**læm ingi**lī**zī	أين أجد... يتكلم إنجليزي؟
priest/minister/rabbi	qis**sīs**/qis**sīs**/ḥæ̃**khæ̃m**	قسيس/قسيس/حاخام
I'd like to visit the mosque/church.	o**rīd** æn æ**zūr** æl-**mæs**gid/ æl-kæ**nī**sæ	أريد أن أزور المسجد/الكنيسة.

In the countryside في الريف

Is there a scenic route to...?	hæl **yū**gæd ṭa**rīq** si**yæ̃**ḥī ilæ	هل يوجد طريق سياحي إلى...؟
How far is it to...?	kæm æl-mæ**sæ̃**fæ ilæ	كم المسافة إلى...؟
Can we walk?	**mom**kin **nim**shi	ممكن نمشي؟
How high is that mountain?	mæ̃ irti**fæ̃' hæ̃**zæl **gæ**bæl	ما ارتفاع هذا الجبل؟

What's the name of...	mæ ism	ما اسم...؟
that animal/bird	**hæ**zæl ḥæyæ**wæn**/ṭīr	هذا الحيوان / الطير
that flower/tree	hæ**zi**hil **wær**dæ/**sha**gara	هذه الوردة / الشجرة

Landmarks أماكن التقاء

bridge	**ko**brī [zhisr]	كوبري [جسر]
canal	qa**næl**	قنال
desert	**ṣa**ḥarā'	صحراء
excavations	tan**qīb** 'æn æl-a**sār**	تنقيب عن الآثار
farm	**'iz**bæ	عزبة
field	ḥaql	حقل
hill	tæll	تل
house	bēt	بيت
inn	isti**rā**ḥa	استراحة
island	gæ**zī**ræ	جزيرة
lake	bo**ḥæy**ra	بحيرة
minaret	**mi**'zænæ	مئذنة
oasis	**wæ**ḥæ	واحة
path	**sik**kæ	سكة
plain	sæhl	سهل
plantation	mæz**ræ**'æ	مزرعة
pond	**bir**kæ	بركة
river	nahr	نهر
road	ṭa**rīq**	طريق
sand dunes	ti**læl** ram**liy**yæ	تلال رملية
sea	baḥr	بحر
track	**sik**kæ	سكة
valley	**wæ**dī	وادي
village	**qar**yæ	قرية
vineyard	mæ**zæ**ri' æl-ko**rūm**	مزارع الكروم
wadi	**wæ**dī	وادي
well	bi'r	بئر
wood	gāba	غابة

ASKING THE WAY, see page 76

Relaxing

Cinema (movies) – Theatre السينما ـ المسرح

Besides the conventional indoor cinema, many open-air cinemas operate from June to September. In Egypt, films in English are shown regularly, as well as Arabic films, of which Egypt is a prolific producer. Seats are numbered, and cinemas almost always crowded, so arrive in good time.

At the theatre, the curtain rises usually at 9.30 p.m. Advance booking is essential.

What's showing at the cinema tonight?	**mǣ**zæ **yū**gæd fil **sī**nimæ æl-**læy**læ	ماذا يوجد في السينما الليلة؟
What's playing at the... Theatre?	**mǣ**zæ **yū**gæd fī **mæs**ræḥ	ماذا يوجد في مسرح...؟
What sort of play is it?	mǣ nū' æl-mæsræ**ḥiy**yæ	ما نوع المسرحية؟
Can you recommend a...?	**mom**kin tin**ṣaḥ**nī bi	ممكن تنصحني بـ...؟
good film	film **kwæy**yis	فيلم كويس
comedy	ko**med**yǣ	كوميديا
drama	**drā**mā	دراما
musical	ōbe**rēt**	أوبريت
revue	'arḍ **fæn**nī [skētsh]	عرض فني [سكتش]
At which theatre is the play by... being performed?	fī æyy **mæs**ræḥ **to**'raḍ mæsræ**ḥiy**yæt	في أي مسرح تعرض مسرحية...؟
I'd like to see a...	orīd mo**shǣ**hædæt	أريد مشاهدة...
puppet show	'arḍ lil 'æ**rā**'is	عرض للعرائس
sound-and-light show	'arḍ aṣ-**ṣōt** wæl ḍō'	عرض الصوت والضوء

What time does it begin/finish?	**mæ**tæ **yæb**dæ'/**yæn**tæhī	متى يبدأ/ينتهي؟
Are there any seats for tonight?	hæl **tū**gæd æ**mǣ**kin æl-**læy**læ	هل توجد أماكن الليلة؟
How much are the seats?	bi**kæm** æt-tæ**zǣ**kir	بكم التذاكر؟
I'd like to reserve 2 seats for the show on... evening.	o**rīd** æn **æ**ḥgiz tæzkar**tēn** li 'arḍ... mæ**sǣ**'æn	أريد أن أحجز تذكرتين لعرض... مساءاً.
Can I have a ticket for the matinée on...?	o**rīd** tæz**ka**ra li 'arḍ æl-mǣtī**nē**	أريد تذكرة لعرض الماتينيه...
I'd like a seat in the...	o**rīd** mæ**kǣn** fī	أريد مكان في...
stalls (orchestra)	aṣ-**ṣā**la	الصالة
circle (mezzanine)	æl-bæl**kōn**	البلكون
Not too far back.	**læy**sæ lil wa**rā**' ki**tīr**	ليس للوراء كثير.
How much are the seats in the circle (mezzanine)?	bi**kæm** æt-tæ**zǣ**kir fil bæl**kōn**	بكم التذاكر في البلكون؟
May I have a programme, please?	**mom**kin bir**nǣ**mig min **fa**ḍlak	ممكن برنامج من فضلك؟
Where can I leave my coat?	**æy**næ **æ**trok **hǣ**zæl **bal**ṭō	أين أترك هذا البالطو؟

متأسف. العدد كامل.	I'm sorry, we're sold out.
يوجد بعض الأماكن في البلكون.	There are only a few seats left in the circle (mezzanine).
تذكرتك من فضلك.	May I see your ticket?
هذا مكانك.	This is your seat.

* It's customary to tip theatre usherettes (**blā**zar) in Egypt.

DAYS OF THE WEEK, see page 152

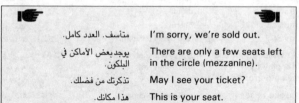

Opera—Ballet—Concert أوبرا ـ باليه ـ حفلة موسيقية

Can you recommend a ballet?	**mom**kin tinṣ**aḥ**nī bi **bǣ**lēh	ممكن تنصحني بباليه؟
concert/opera	**ḥæ**flæ mosī**qiy**yæ/**ō**brā	حفلة موسيقية / أوبرا
Where's the opera house/concert hall?	**æy**næ dār æl-**ō**brā/ **qā**'æt æl-mosīqa	أين دار الأوبرا / قاعة الموسيقى؟
What's on at the opera tonight?	**mǣ**zæ fil **ō**brā **hǣ**zæl mæ**sǣ'**	ماذا في الأوبرا هذا المساء؟
Who's singing/ dancing?	mæn yog**æn**nī/**yær**qoṣ	من يغني / يرقص؟
Which orchestra is playing?	mǣ æl-**fir**qa æl**læ**tī **tæ**'æzif	ما الفرقة التي تعزف؟
What are they playing?	**mǣ**zæ yæ'æzi**fūn**	ماذا يعزفون؟
Who's the . . .?	mæn	من...؟
conductor/soloist	ra'**īs** æl-**fir**qa/æl-'**ǣ**zif	رئيس الفرقة / العازف

Nightclubs—Discos ملهى ليلي ـ مرقص

Can you recommend a good nightclub?	**mom**kin tinṣ**aḥ**nī bi **mæl**hæ **læy**lī **kwæy**yis	ممكن تنصحني بملهى ليلي كويس؟
Is there a floor show?	hæl **yū**gæd 'arḍ **fæn**nī	هل يوجد عرض فني؟
Are there belly-dancers?	hæl **tū**gæd raqqa**ṣāt** shar**qiy**yæ	هل توجد رقصات شرقية؟
What time does the show start?	**mæ**tæ **yæb**dæ' æl-'**arḍ**	متى يبدأ العرض؟
Is evening dress required?	hæl libs æs-**sæh**ra ḍa**rū**rī	هل لبس السهرة ضروري؟
Where can we go dancing?	**æy**næ **yom**kin æz-zi**hǣb** lil raqṣ	أين يمكن الذهاب للرقص؟
Is there a discotheque in town?	hæl **yū**gæd **mar**qaṣ [**dis**kō] fil **bæ**læd	هل يوجد مرقص [ديسكو] في البلد؟
Would you like to dance?	hæl to**ḥibb** æn **tar**qoṣ (hæl to**ḥib**bi æn tar**qoṣ**ṣi)	هل تحب أن ترقص (هل تحب أن ترقصي)؟

Sports الرياضة

I'd like to see a football (soccer) match.	o**rīd** mo**shæ**hædæt mobā**rāt** ko**rat** qa**dæm**	أريد مشاهدة مباراة كرة قدم.
Is there a match on...?	hæl **tū**gæd mo**bā**rā	هل توجد مباراة...؟
Which teams are playing?	mæ æl-**firaq** æl**læ**tī **tæl**'æb	ما الفرق التي تلعب؟
Can you get me a ticket?	**mom**kin æn tæḥ**ṣol**lī '**æ**læ tæz**ka**ra	ممكن أن تحصل لي على تذاكر؟

basketball	**bas**kēt [**sæl**læ]	باسكيت [سلة]
boxing	bōx	بوكس
football (soccer)	**korat** qa**dæm**	كرة قدم
horse racing	si**bæq** æl-**khēl**	سباق الخيل
(horseback) riding	ro**kūb** æl-**khēl**	ركوب الخيل
rowing	tæg**dīf**	تجديف
swimming	si**bæ**ḥæ	سباحة
tennis	**tē**nis	تنس
volleyball	**vō**lī [æl-**kora** aṭ-ṭā'**ira**]	ڤولي [الكرة الطائرة]

I'd like to see a boxing match.	o**rīd** mo**shæ**hædæt mobā**rāt** bōx	أريد مشاهدة مباراة بوكس.
What's the admission charge?	bi**kæm** æd-do**khūl**	بكم الدخول؟
Where is/are the...?	**æy**næ	أين...؟
golf course	arḍ gōlf	أرض جولف
race course (track)	arḍ si**bæq** æl-**khēl**	ارض سباق الخيل
squash club	**næ**dī skwāsh	نادي اسكواش
tennis courts	mæ**læ**'ib æt-**tē**nis	ملاعب التنس
What's the charge per...?	kæm æl-ḥi**sæb** li**mod**dæt	كم الحساب لمدة...؟
day/round/hour	yōm/**daw**ra/**sæ**'æ	يوم/دورة/ساعة
Can I hire (rent) clubs/rackets?	**mom**kin tæ'**gīr** ma**ḍā**rib	ممكن تأجير مضارب؟

DAYS OF THE WEEK, see page 152

Is there any good hunting/fishing here?	hæl æṣ-**ṣēd**/ṣēd æs-sæmæk **kwæy**yis **ho**næ	هل الصيد/صيد السمك كويس هنا؟
Do I need a permit?	hæl **æ**næ miḥ**tǣg** tar**khīṣ**	هل أنا محتاج ترخيص؟
Is there... here?	hæl **yū**gæd... **ho**næ	هل يوجد... هنا؟
a good sandy beach	**shā**ṭi' **ram**lī **kwæy**yis	شاطىء رملي كويس
a swimming pool	ḥæm**mǣm** si**bǣ**ḥæ	حمام سباحة
What's the temperature of the water?	mǣ dara**git** ḥa**rā**rit æl-**mǣ'**	ما درجة حرارة الماء؟

On the beach على الشاطىء

Is it safe to swim?	hæl æs-si**bǣ**ḥæ æ**mǣn**	هل السباحة أمان؟
Is there a lifeguard?	hæl **yū**gæd **ḥǣ**ris	هل يوجد حارس؟
The waves are big.	æl-am**wǣg 'ǣl**yæ	الأمواج عالية.
Is there a good place for...?	hæl **yū**gæd mæ**kǣn** **kwæy**yis lil...	هل يوجد مكان كويس لـ...؟
snorkeling/wind-surfing	gaṭs/tæ**zæḥ**loq shi**rā**'ī	غطس / تزحلق شراعي
Are there any dangerous currents?	hæl **tū**gæd tayyā**rāt** **kha**ṭera	هل توجد تيارات خطرة؟
I want to hire a/an/some...	o**rīd** tæ'**gīr**	أريد تأجير...
bathing hut (cabana)	kæ**bī**næ li khæl' æl-mæ**lǣ**bis	كابينه لخلع الملابس
deck chair	**kor**sī blǣzh qo**mǣsh**	كرسي بلاج قماش
sailboard	loḥ shi**rā**'ī	لوح شراعي
sailing boat	**mær**kib shirā'**iy**yæ	مركب شراعية
sunshade (umbrella)	shæm**siy**yæ	شمسية
water-skis	ædæ**wǣt** inzi**lǣq** **'æ**læl mǣ'	أدوات انزلاق على الماء

PRIVATE BEACH	شاطىء خاص
NO SWIMMING	ممنوع الاستحمام

Making friends

Introductions التعرف

May I introduce...?	oqaddim læk (lik)*	أقدم لك (لكِ)...
John, this is...	John hǣzæ (hǣzihi)	جون هذا (هذه)...
My name is...	ismī	اسمي...
Pleased to meet you.	tæshærrafna	تشرفنا.
What's your name?	mǣ ismæk (ismik)	ما اسمَك (اسمِك)؟
How are you?	kæyfæ ḥǣlæk (ḥǣlik)	كيف حالك (حالِك)؟
Fine, thanks.	kwæyyis (kwæyyisæ) æl-ḥæmdu lillǣh	كويس (كويسة) الحمد للّه.
And you?	wæ intæ (intī)	وأنتَ (أنتِ)؟

Follow up المحادثة

How long have you been here?	monzo mætæ intæ (intī) honæ	منذ متى أنتَ (أنتِ) هنا؟
Is this your first visit?	hæl hǣzihi æwwæl ziyāra læk (lik)	هل هذه أول زيارة لَك (لكِ)؟
Are you enjoying your stay?	hæl intæ mæsrūr (intī mæsrūræ) min æl-iqāmæ	هل أنتَ مسرور (أنتِ مسرورة) من الإقامةَ؟
I like the landscape a lot.	yo'gibonī æl-manẓar giddæn	يعجبني المنظر جداً.
What do you think of the country/people?	mǣ ræ'yæk (ræ'yik) fil bælæd/æn-nǣs	ما رأيَك (رأيِك) في البلد / الناس؟
Where do you come from?	min æynæ tæ'tī	من أين تأتي؟
I'm from...	ænæ min	أنا من...
What nationality are you?	mǣ hiyæ ginseyyætæk (ginseyyætik)	ما هي جنسيتَك (جنسيتِك)؟

* The feminine form is given in parentheses.

COUNTRIES, see page 154

I'm American.	**æ**næ æmr**ī**kī (æmrī**kiy**yæ)	أنا أمريكي (أمريكية).
British/Canadian	brit**a**nī (briṭ**ā**n**iy**yæ)/ **kæ**nædī (kænæ**diy**yæ)	بريطاني (بريطانية)/ كندي (كندية)
English/Irish	ingil**ī**zī (ingil**īziy**yæ)/ irl**æ**ndī (irlæn**diy**yæ)	إنجليزي (إنجليزية) / ايرلندي (ايرلندية)
Where are you staying?	**æy**næ **tæs**kon **ho**næ	أين تسكن هنا؟
Are you on your own?	hæl **in**tæ **wæḥ**dæk (**in**tī **wæḥ**dik)	هل أنت وحدك (أنتِ وحدِك)؟
I'm with my...	**æ**næ **mæ**'æ	أنا مع...
family/wife/husband	osr**a**tī/zæw**gæ**tī/**zæw**gī	أسرتي/زوجتي/زوجي
children/parents	aṭ**fā**lī/w**ǣ**li**dæy**	أطفالي/والديْ
boyfriend/girlfriend	ṣa**dī**qī/ṣadī**qa**tī	صديقي/صديقتي

father/mother	**wǣ**lid/wǣ**li**dæ	والد/والدة
son/daughter	ibn/bint	ابن/بنت
brother/sister	ækh/okht	أخ/أخت
uncle/aunt	'æmm/'**æm**mæ	عم/عمه
nephew/niece	ibn ækh/bint ækh	ابن أخ/بنت أخ
cousin	ibn 'æmm/bint 'æmm	ابن عم/بنت عم

Are you...?	hæl **in**tæ (**in**tī)	هل أنتَ (أنتِ)...؟
married/single	motæ**zaw**wig (motæzaw**wi**gæ)/'**ǣ**zib ('**æz**bæ)	متزوج (متزوجة)/عازب (عازبة)
What do you do?	m**ǣ** **hi**yæ mih**næ**tæk (mih**næ**tik)	ما هي مهنتكَ (مهنتكِ)؟
I'm a student.	**æ**næ **ṭā**lib (ṭā**li**bæ)	أنا طالب (طالبة).
What are you studying?	**mǣ**zæ **tæd**ross (tæd**ros**sī)	ماذا تدرسْ (تدرسي)؟
I'm here on a business trip.	**æ**næ **ho**næ fī **riḥ**læt shogl	أنا هنا في رحلة شغل.
Do you travel a lot?	hæl to**sǣ**fir (tosǣ**fi**ri) ki**tīr**	هل تسافر (تسافرِ) كثير؟
Do you play cards/chess?	hæl **tæl**'æb (tæl'**æ**bī) kot**shī**næ/shata**rang**?	هل تلعب (تلعبِ) كوتشينه/ شطرنج؟

The weather الجو

What a lovely day!	innæho yōm gæ**mīl**	إنه يوم جميل!
What awful weather!	æl-**gæww sæ**yyi' [**wi**ḥish]	الجو سيء [وحش]!
Isn't it cold/ hot today?	æ**læy**sæ æl-**gæww** bærd/ ḥārr æl-**yōm**	أليس الجو برد / حار اليوم؟
Is it usually as warm as this?	hæl æl-**gæww dæy**mæn ḥārr kæl yōm	هل الجو دايماً حار كاليوم؟
Do you think it's going to... tomorrow?	hæl tæ**ẓonn æn**næ gædæn	هل تظن أن غداً...؟
be a nice day	sæyæ**kūn** yōm gæ**mīl**	سيكون يوم جميل
rain	sæto**maṭ**er	ستمطر
What is the weather forecast?	mǣ **hi**yæ æt-tænæbbo'**ǣt** æl-gæw**wiy**yæ	ما هي التنبؤات الجوية؟

cloud	sa**ḥǣ**bæ	سحابة
moon	**qa**mar	قمر
rain	**ma**ṭar	مطر
sky	sæ**mǣ'**	سماء
star	nigm	نجم
sun	shæms	شمس
thunderstorm	**'ā**ṣifa	عاصفة
wind	rīḥ	ريح

Invitations الدعوات

Would you like to have dinner with us on...?	hæl to**ḥib**bo (to**ḥib**bi) æn tæ**tæ'**shæ (tæ**tæ'**shi) **mæ'**ænǣ yōm	هل تحبُ (تحب) أن تتعشى (تتعشي) معنا يوم ....؟
May I invite you for lunch?	**mom**kin æ'æ**zi**mæk (æ'æ**zi**mik) **'æ**læl gæ**dǣ'**	ممكن أعزمك (أعزمِك) على الغذاء؟
Can you come round for a drink this evening?	**mom**kin **tæ'**tī li mæsh**rūb hǣ**zæl mæ**sǣ'**	ممكن تأتي لمشروب هذا المساء؟

DAYS OF THE WEEK, see page 152

There's a party. Are you coming?	yūgæd **ḥæ**flæ. hæl **tæ'**tī	يوجد حفلة. هل تأتي؟
That's very kind of you.	**hǣ**zæ la**ṭīf gid**dæn minæk (**mi**nik)	هذا لطيف جداً منكَ (منكِ).
Great. I'd love to come.	'a**ẓīm.** æ**ḥib**bo æn **æ**tī	عظيم. أحب أن أتي.
What time shall we come?	**mæ**tæ **næ'**tī	متى نأتي؟
May I bring a friend (girlfriend)?	**mom**kin **yæ'**ti ṣa**dīq** (**tæ'**ti ṣa**dīqa**) **mæ'**ī	ممكن يأتي صديق (تأتي صديقة) معي؟
I'm afraid we've got to leave now.	næs**tæ'**zin lil ra**ḥīl** æl'**æn**	نستأذن للرحيل الآن.
Next time you must come to visit us.	æl-**mar**ra æl-**qā**dimæ **yæ**gib æn **tæ'**tī li ziyā**ra**tinæ	المرة القادمة يجب أن تأتي لزيارتنا.
Thanks for the evening. It was great.	**shok**ran 'ælæl **sæh**ra. **kǣ**næt 'a**ẓī**ma	شكراً على السهرة. كانت عظيمة.

Dating موعد

Do you mind if I...?	hæl '**in**dæk ('**in**dik) **mǣ**ni' læw	هل عَندك (عِندِك) مانع لو...؟
sit down here	gæ**læst hon**æ	جلست هنا
smoke	dækh**khænt**	دخنت
Do you have a light, please?	hæl **mæ'**æk (mæ'**æ**ki) wæl**lǣ**'æ min **faḍ**lak (**faḍ**lik)	هل معَك (معك) ولاعة من فضلَك (فضلِك)؟
Would you like a cigarette?	si**gā**ra	سيجارة؟
Why are you laughing?	li**mǣ**zæ **taḍ**ḥak (taḍ**ḥa**ki)	لماذا تضحك (تضحكِ)؟
Is my pronunciation that bad?	hæl **noṭ**qī **sæy**yi'	هل نطقي سيء؟
Are you waiting for someone?	hæl tan**ta**ẓir (tan**ta**ẓiri) æ**ḥ**æd	هل تنتظر (تنتظر) أحد؟

Are you free this evening?	hæl **intæ fāḍī** (**inti** faḍyæ) **hǣ**zæl mæ**sǣ'**	هل أنت فاضي (انتِ فاضية) هذا المساء؟
Would you like to...?	hæl to**ḥibb** (to**ḥibbi**)	هل تحب (تحبِ)...؟
go out with me tonight	æl-khor**ūg** **mæ'**ī æl-**læy**læ	الخروج معي الليلة
go dancing	æz-zi**hǣb** lil raqṣ	الذهاب للرقص
go for a drive	æn **næ**lif bil sæy**yā**ra	أن نلف بالسيارة
Shall we go to the cinema (movies)?	hæl **næz**hæb ilæl **sī**nimæ	هل نذهب إلى السينما؟
Where shall we meet?	**æy**næ nætæ**qā**bæl	أين نتقابل؟
I'll pick you up at your hotel.	sæ'æ**khod**æk (sæ'æ-**khod**ik) min æl-**fon**doq	سأخذَك (سأخذِك) من الفندق.
I'll call for you at 8.	sæ'**aḥ**dar æs-**sǣ**'æ 8	سأحضر الساعة ٨.
May I take you home?	hæl awaṣ**ṣa**lak (awaṣ-**ṣa**lik) **i**læ mæn**zi**læk (mæn**zi**lik)	هل أوصلك (أوصلِك) إلى منزلك (منزلِك)؟
Can I see you tomorrow?	hæl nætæ**qā**bæl **gæ**dæn	هل نتقابل غداً؟
I hope we'll meet again.	ætæ**mæn**næ æn nætæ**qā**bæl **mar**ra **tæn**yæ	أتمنى أن نتقابل مرة ثانية.

... and you might answer:

I'd love to, thank you.	bi koll so**rūr**	بكل سرور.
Thank you, but I'm busy.	**shok**ran. læ**kin**nī mæsh**gūl** (mæsh**gū**læ)	شكراً لكني مشغول (مشغولة).
No, I'm not interested, thank you.	**shok**ran. lǣ o**rīd**	شكراً. لا أريد.
Leave me alone, please!	**itrok**nī fī **ḥǣ**lī min **faḍ**lak	أتركني في حالي من فضلك!
Thank you, it's been a wonderful evening.	**shok**ran. **kǣ**næt **sæh**ra momt**ǣ**zæ	شكراً كانت سهرة ممتازة.
I've enjoyed myself.	ænæ inba**saṭṭ**	أنا أنبسطت.

Shopping Guide

This shopping guide is designed to help you find what you want with ease, accuracy and speed. It features:

1. A list of all major shops, stores and services (p. 99).
2. Some general expressions required when shopping, to allow you to be specific and selective (p. 101).
3. Full details of the shops and services most likely to concern you. Here you'll find advice, alphabetical lists of items and conversion charts listed under the headings below.

LAUNDRY, see page 29/HAIRDRESSER'S, see page 30

Advice مقدمة

Opening hours of shops, offices and banks differ from country to country. Many shops close in the middle of the day and reopen in the afternoon. There may also be seasonal variations, with businesses starting and ending early in summer.

In some countries, Friday, the Muslim holy day, is the weekly closing day for most businesses. In others, in keeping with Western custom, Sunday is the official holiday.

Souk means "market" in Arabic. It's composed of a maze of narrow winding alleys where tradesmen and artisans of all kinds are grouped together.

In the souk you'll see jewellers and artisans at work inlaying wood with enamel and ivory, engraving or hammering copper or making pottery. Antique dealers abound, and merchants sell fine rugs and brocades—all this in an atmosphere scented with sandalwood, cinnamon and musk.

If you are interested in antiques, with a little luck you might come across an ancient coin, a piece of Coptic cloth or a statuette dating back to the pharaohs. Be sure to ask for a museum certificate guaranteeing the authenticity of any very old objects you buy.

Remember that bargaining is an Eastern custom not without a certain charm. As you browse through the souk, take your time, and don't hesitate to accept a cup of coffee or mint tea offered you by a merchant.

Is the... open on Friday?	hæl... mæf**tūḥ** yōm æl-**gom**'æ	هل... مفتوح يوم الجمعة؟
Is the... closed on Sunday?	hæl... mæq**fūl** yōm æl-**æ**ḥæd	هل... مقفول يوم الأحد؟
When does... open/close?	**mæ**tæ **yæf**tæḥ/**yaq**fil	متى يفتح/يقفل...؟

Shops, stores and services محلات وخدمات

Where's the nearest...?	**æy**næ **aq**rab	أين أقرب...؟
antique shop	mæ**ḥæll** æntī**kǣt**	محل انتيكات
baker's	**mækh**bæz	مخبز
bank	bænk	بنك
barber's	**ṣalōn** ḥi**lǣ**qa	صالون حلاقة
bazaar	sūq [ba**zār**]	سوق [بازار]
beauty salon	**ṣalōn** tæg**mīl**	صالون تجميل
bookshop	mæk**tæ**bæ	مكتبة
butcher's	gaz**zār** [læḥ**ḥǣm**]	جزار [لحام]
cake shop	mæ**ḥæll** ḥælæwiy**yǣt**	محل حلويات
camera shop	mæ**ḥæll** kæmi**rāt**	محل كاميرات
chemist's	ægzæ**khǣ**næ [færmæ**siy**yæ]	أجزخانة [فرماسية]
clothing store	mæ**ḥæll** mæ**lǣ**bis	محل ملابس
dairy	mæ**ḥæll** æl**bǣn**	محل ألبان
dentist	**ṭabīb** æs**nǣn**	طبيب أسنان
department store	mæ**ḥæll** to**gǣ**rī	محل تجاري
dressmaker	khay**yāṭ**	خياط
drugstore	ægzæ**khǣ**næ [færmæ**siy**yæ]	أجزخانة [فرماسية]
dry cleaner's	mæ**ḥæll** tan**ẓīf** mæ**lǣ**bis	محل تنظيف ملابس
electrician	kahra**bā**'ī	كهربائي
fishmonger's	mæ**ḥæll** **sæ**mæk	محل سمك
florist's	mæ**ḥæll** zo**hūr**	محل زهور
furrier's	mæ**ḥæll** farw	محل فرو
greengrocer's	mæ**ḥæll** æl-kho**ḍār**	محل الخضار
grocer's	mæ**ḥæll** æl-bi**qā**læ	محل البقالة
hairdresser's	**ṣalōn** ḥi**lǣ**qa	صالون حلاقة
hardware store	mæ**ḥæll** ædæ**wǣt** mænzi**liy**yæ	محل أدوات منزلية
hospital	mos**tæsh**fæ	مستشفى
ironmonger's	mæ**ḥæll** ædæ**wǣt** mænzi**liy**yæ	محل أدوات منزلية

jeweller's	mæḥæll æl-mogæwharāt	محل المجوهرات
laundry	mæḥæll gæsīl wæ mækwæ	محل غسيل ومكوة
leather-goods store	mæḥæll maṣnū'āt gildiyyæ	محل مصنوعات جلدية
market	sūq	سوق
newsstand	koshk æl-garā'id	كشك الجرائد
optician	æn-naẓārātī	النظاراتي
pastry shop	mæḥæll ḥælæwiyyǣt	محل حلويات
photographer	moṣawwir	مصور
police station	qism æl-bōlīs [shorṭa]	قسم البوليس [شرطة]
post office	mæktæb bærīd [bōstæ]	مكتب بريد [بوستة]
second-hand shop	mæḥæll ædæwǣt mostæ'mælæ	محل أدوات مستعملة
shoemaker's (repairs)	gæzmægī	جزمجي
shoe shop	mæḥæll gizæm [æḥziyyæ]	محل جزم [أحذية]
shopping centre	mærkæz togǣrī	مركز تجاري
souvenir shop	mæḥæll hædǣyæ tizkǣriyyæ	محل هدايا تذكارية
sporting goods shop	mæḥæll ædæwǣt riyaḍiyya	محل أدوات رياضية
stationer's	mæḥæll ædæwǣt kitǣbiyyæ	محل أدوات كتابية
supermarket	sōbar markit	سوبر ماركت
tailor's	tærzī [khayyāṭ]	ترزي [خياط]
telegraph office	mæktæb tiligrāf	مكتب تلغراف
tobacconist's	mæḥæll sægǣyir [mæḥæll dokhǣn]	محل سجاير [محل دخان]
toy shop	mæḥæll li'æb	محل لعب
travel agency	mæktæb siyǣḥæ	مكتب سياحة
vegetable store	khoḍarī	خضري
veterinarian	ṭabīb bīṭarī	طبيب بيطري
watchmaker's	mæḥæll sǣ'ǣt	محل ساعات

دخول	خروج	مخرج الطوارئ
ENTRANCE	EXIT	EMERGENCY EXIT

General expressions تعبيرات عامة

Where? أين

Where's a good...?	æynæ yūgæd... kwæyyis	أين يوجد... كويس؟
Where can I find a...?	æynæ ægid	أين أجد...؟
Where do they sell...?	æynæ yobæ'	أين يباع...؟
Where can I buy...?	æynæ æshtærī	أين أشتري...؟
Where's the main shopping area?	æynæ æl-ḥæyy æt-togærī ar-ra'īsī	أين الحي التجاري الرئيسي؟
Is it far from here?	hæl æl-mæsæfæ bæ'īdæ	هل المسافة بعيدة؟
How do I get there?	kæyfæ aṣil ilæyhæ	كيف أصل إليها؟

Service الخدمة

Can you help me?	momkin tisæ'idnī	ممكن تساعدني؟
I'm just looking.	ænæ ætfarrag faqaṭ	أنا أتفرج فقط.
I'd like...	orīd	أريد...
Can you show me some...?	momkin torīnī ba'ḍ	ممكن تريني بعض...؟
Do you have any...?	hæl 'indæk	هل عندك...؟
Can you show me...?	momkin torīnī	ممكن تريني...؟
this/that	hæzæ	هذا
the one in the window	hæzæ illī fil vitrīnæ	هذا إللي في الفترينة
Where's the... department?	æynæ qism æl-	أين قسم الـ...؟
Where is the lift (elevator)/escalator?	æynæ æl-maṣ'ad/ æs-sellem æl-kahrabā'ī	أين المصعد/السلم الكهربائي؟

SALE أوكازيون

Defining the article—Preference وصف السلعة ـ التفضيل

It must be...	**hǣ**zæ **yæ**gib æn yæ**kūn**	هذا يجب أن يكون...
big	kæ**bīr**	كبير
cheap	ra**khīṣ**	رخيص
dark	**gǣ**miq	غامق
good	**kwæ**yyis	كويس
heavy	tæ**qīl**	تقيل
large	kæ**bīr**	كبير
light (weight)	khæ**fīf**	خفيف
light (colour)	**fǣ**tiḥ	فاتح
oval	bay**ḍā**wī	بيضاوي
rectangular	mosta**ṭīl**	مستطيل
round	mostæ**dīr**	مستدير
small	ṣa**gīr**	صغير
square	mo**rab**ba'	مربع
sturdy	mæ**tīn**	متين
Can you show me some others?	**mom**kin to**rī**nī she' **a**khar	ممكن تريني شيء آخر؟
Haven't you anything...?	hæl '**in**dæk she'	هل عندك شيء...؟
cheaper/better	**ar**khaṣ/**æḥ**sæn	أرخص / أحسن
larger/smaller	**ak**bar/**aṣ**gar	أكبر / أصغر

How much بكم

How much is this?	bi**kæm hǣ**zæ	بكم هذا؟
I don't understand.	**æ**næ **lǣ æf**hæm	أنا لا أفهم.
Please write it down.	min **faḍ**lak iktibho	من فضلك أكتبه.
I don't want...	**lǣ** o**rīd**	لا أريد...
anything too expensive	she' **gǣ**lī ki**tīr**	شيء غالي كتير
to spend more than...	æn **aṣ**rof **ak**tar min	أن أصرف اكثر من...

COLOURS, see page 111

Decision القرار

It's not quite what I want.	**hæ̅**zæ **læy**sæ bil ḍabṭ æ**llæ**zī orīdoh	هذا ليس بالضبط الذي أريده.
No. I don't like it.	læ. læ̅ to'**gi**bonī	لا. لا تعجبني.
I'll take it.	sæ'æ**khod**hæ̅	سأخذها.

Ordering—Delivery الطلبيات ـ التسليم

Can you order it for me?	**mom**kin **toṭ**lob **hæ̅**zæ lī	ممكن تطلب هذا لي؟
When will it be ready?	**mæ**tæ yæ**kūn gæ̅**hiz	متى يكون جاهز؟
I'll take it with me.	sæ'æ**khod hæ̅**zæ **mæ'**ī	سأخذ هذا معي.
Deliver it to the ... Hotel.	waṣ**ṣil**ho ilæ **fon**doq	وصله إلى فندق...
Please send it to this address.	min **faḍ**lak æ**rsil**ho **ilæ hæ̅**zæl 'in**wæ̅n**	من فضلك أرسله إلى هذا العنوان.
Will I have any difficulty with the customs?	hæl sæ'**æ**gid ṣo'**ū**ba fil **gom**rok	هل سأجد صعوبة في الجمرك؟

Paying الدفع

How much is it?	bi**kæm**	بكم؟
Can I pay by traveller's cheque?	**mom**kin **æd**fæ' bi shī**kæt** siyæ̅**ḥiy**yæ	ممكن أدفع بشيكات سياحية؟
Do you accept ...?	hæl **taq**bal	هل تقبل...؟
credit cards	kært maṣ**ra**fī	كارت مصرفي
dollars	æd-dōlā**rāt**	الدولارات
pounds	æl-gonē**hæ̅t**	الجنيهات
May I have a receipt?	**mom**kin **æ**khod æl-ī**ṣāl**	ممكن أخذ الإيصال؟
I think there's a mistake in the bill.	æ**ẓonn** yū**gæd** kha**ṭa'** fil ḥi**sæ̅b**	أظن يوجد خطأ في الحساب.

Anything else? شيء آخر؟

No thanks, that's all.	lǣ **shokran hǣzæ** koll she'	لا، شكراً، هذا كل شيء.
Yes, I want...	**næ'æm orīd**	نعم، أريد...
Show me...	**wærīnī**	وريني...
May I have a bag, please?	**momkin æ**khod kīs min **faḍlak**	ممكن أخذ كيس من فضلك؟
Could you wrap it up for me, please?	**momkin togallif hǣzæ** lī	ممكن تغلف هذا لي؟

Dissatisfied? عدم الرضا

Can you please exchange this?	**momkin tagyīr hǣzæ min faḍlak**	ممكن تغيير هذا من فضلك؟
I want to return this.	**orīd irgǣ' hǣzæ**	أريد إرجاع هذا.
I'd like a refund. Here's the receipt.	**orīd istirdǣd** æt-tæmæn. **hǣzæ howæl īṣāl**	أريد استرداد الثمن. هذا هو الايصال.

ممكن أساعدك؟	Can I help you?
ماذا تريد؟	What would you like?
أي... تريد؟	What... would you like?
لون/شكل/نوع/كمية	colour/shape/quality/quantity
أسف، ليس عندنا.	I'm sorry, we don't have any.
البضاعة نفذت.	We're out of stock.
ممكن نطلبها لك؟	Shall we order it for you?
ستأخذها معك أو نرسلها لك؟	Will you take it with you or shall we send it?
شيء آخر؟	Anything else?
...جنيه/دينار، من فضلك.	... pounds/dinars, please.
الخزينة هناك.	The cash desk is over there.

Bookshop—Stationer's مكتبة ـ محل أدوات كتابية

Bookshops and stationer's may be combined or separate.

Where's the nearest...?	æynæ aqrab	أين أقرب...؟
bookshop	mæktæbæ	مكتبة
stationer's	mæḥæll ædæwǣt kitǣbiyyæ	محل أدوات كتابية
newsstand	koshk æl-garā'id	كشك الجرائد
Where can I buy an English-language newspaper?	æynæ æshtærī gærīdæ ingilīziyyæ	أين اشتري جريدة إنجليزية؟
Where's the guide-book section?	æynæ qism kotob æd-dælīl æs-siyǣḥī	أين قسم كتب الدليل السياحي؟
Where do you keep the English books?	æynæ qism æl-kotob æl-ingilīziyyæ	أين قسم الكتب الأنجليزية؟
Have you any of...'s books in English?	hæl 'indæk kotob li... bil ingilīzī	هل عندك كتب لـ... بالإنجليزية؟
I'd like a/an/some...	orīd	أريد...
address book	daftar 'ænǣwīn	دفتر عناوين
adhesive tape	waraq læzq	ورق لصق
ball-point pen	qalæm ḥibr gǣf	قلم حبر جاف
book	kitǣb	كتاب
calendar	nætīgæ	نتيجة
carbon paper	waraq karbōn	ورق كربون
crayons	aqlǣm ælwǣn	أقلام ألوان
dictionary	qāmūs	قاموس
English-Arabic	ingilīzī-'arabī	إنجليزي ـ عربي
pocket	lil gēb	للجيب
drawing paper	waraq ræsm	ورق رسم
drawing pins	dæbǣbīs ræsm	دبابيس رسم
envelopes	ẓorūf	ظروف
eraser	æstīkæ [mimḥǣh]	استيكة [ممحاة]
exercise book	daftar	دفتر

English	Transliteration	Arabic
felt-tip pen	qalæm fotr	قلم فوتر
fountain pen	qalæm ḥibr	قلم حبر
glue	ṣamg	صمغ
grammar book	kitǣb næḥw	كتاب نحو
guidebook	dælīl siyǣḥī	دليل سياحي
ink	ḥibr	حبر
labels	tikitǣt	تكتات
magazine	mægællæ	مجلة
map	kharīṭa	خريطة
map of the town	kharīṭa lil bælæd	خريطة للبلد
road map	kharīṭa lil ṭoroq	خريطة للطرق
newspaper	gærīdæ	جريدة
American/English	æmrikiyyæ/ingiliziyyæ	أمريكية / أنجليزية
notebook	mofækkira	مفكرة
notepaper	waraq lil kitǣbæ	ورق للكتابة
paintbox	'ilbit ælwǣn	علبة ألوان
paper	waraq	ورق
paperback	kitǣb gēb	كتاب جيب
paperclips	mæshǣbik klibs	مشابك كلبس
paper napkins	fowaṭ waraq	فوط ورق
paste	ṣamg	صمغ
pencil	qalæm roṣāṣ	قلم رصاص
pencil sharpener	bærrǣyæ	براية
playing cards	kotshīnæ	كوتشينه
pocket calculator	ælæ ḥāsbæ lil gēb	آلة حاسبة للجيب
postcard	kært bostǣl	كارت بوستال
refill (for a pen)	anbūbit ḥibr gāf	أنبوبة حبر جاف
rubber	æstīkæ [mimḥǣh]	استيكة [ممحاة]
ruler	masṭara	مسطرة
string	dōbār	دوبار
thumbtacks	dæbǣbīs ræsm	دبابيس رسم
travel guide	dælīl siyǣḥī	دليل سياحي
typewriter ribbon	shirīṭ lil ælæl kætbæ	شريط للآلة الكاتبة
typing paper	waraq lil ælæl kætbæ	ورق للآلة الكاتبة
writing pad	blōk nōt	بلوك نوت

Chemist's (drugstore) أجزخانة [فرماسية]

In the Middle East, chemist's don't normally stock the great range of goods that you'll find in Britain or the U.S. The address of the nearest all-night chemist's is displayed in the window.

For reading ease, this section has been divided into two parts:

1. Pharmaceutical—medicine, first-aid, etc.
2. Toiletry—toilet articles, cosmetics.

General كلمات عامة

Where's the nearest (all-night) chemist's?	**æy**næ **aq**rab ægzæ**khǣ**næ [færmæ**siy**yæ] (læy**ley**yæ]	أين أقرب أجزخانة [فرماسية] (ليلية)؟
What time does the chemist's...?	**mæ**tæ... æl-ægzæ**khǣ**næ [æl-færmæ**siy**yæ]	متى... الأجزخانة [الفرماسية]؟
open	**tæf**tæḥ	تفتح
close	**taq**fil	تقفل

1—Pharmaceutical أدوية وإسعافات أولية

I want something for...	o**rīd** she' li	أريد شيء لـ...
a cold	zo**kǣm**	زكام
a cough	so'**ǣl**	سعال
insect bites	qarṣ æl-ḥasha**rāt**	قرص الحشرات
sunburn	**ḍar**bit shæms	ضربة شمس
travel sickness	do**wār** æs-**sa**far	دوار السفر
an upset stomach	'osr haḍm	عسر هضم
Can you prepare this prescription for me?	**mom**kin to**gæh**hiz lī **hǣ**zihil ro**shet**tæ	ممكن تجهّز لي هذه الروشته؟
Can I get it without a prescription?	**mom**kin **aḥ**ṣol æ**leh** bi**dūn** ro**shet**tæ	ممكن أحصل عليه بدون روشته؟
Shall I wait?	hæl an**ta**ẓir	هل أنتظر؟

DOCTOR, see page 136

I'd like a/an/some...	orīd	أريد...
analgesic	mosækkin	مسكن
antiseptic cream	krem moṭahhir	كريم مطهر
aspirin	aspirīn	أسبرين
(elastic) bandage	robāṭ (maṭṭāṭ)	رباط (مطاط)
Band-Aids	blāstar	بلاستر
condom	kæbbūt ingilīzī	كبوت إنجليزي
contraceptives	'ǣzil	عازل
corn plasters	blāstar lil kallō	بلاستر للكالو
cotton wool (absorbent cotton)	qoṭn ṭibbī	قطن طبي
cough drops	aqrāṣ lil so'āl	أقراص للسعال
disinfectant	moṭahhir	مطهر
ear drops	qaṭra lil ozon	قطرة للأذن
Elastoplast	blāstar	بلاستر
eye drops	qaṭra lil 'oyūn	قطرة للعيون
first-aid kit	'ilbit is'ǣfǣt æwwæliyyæ	علبة إسعافات أولية
gauze	shǣsh	شاش
insect repellent	dæhǣn ḍidd æl-hasharāt	دهان ضد الحشرات
insecticide	qātil lil hasharāt	قاتل للحشرات
iodine	ṣabgit yūd	صبغة يود
laxative	molæyyin	ملين
mouthwash	gæsīl lil fæmm	غسيل للفم
sanitary towels (napkins)	fowaṭ waraq ṭibbī	فوط ورق طبي
suppositories	libūṣ	لبوس
(quinine) tablets	aqrāṣ (kīnǣ)	أقراص (كينا)
tampons	tǣmbōn ṭibbī	تامبون طبي
thermometer	tirmometr	ترمومتر
throat lozenges	aqrāṣ lil zōr	أقراص للزور
vitamin pills	aqrāṣ vītæmīn	أقراص فيتامين

سم	POISON
للاستعمال الخارجي فقط	FOR EXTERNAL USE ONLY

2—Toiletry أدوات التجميل

I'd like a/an/ some...	orīd	أريد...
after-shave lotion	losyōn bæ'd æl-ḥilǣqa	لوسيون بعد الحلاقة
astringent	mozīl lil wægh	مزيل للوجه
blusher	bodra lil tægmīl	بودرة للتجميل
bubble bath	ḥæmmǣm rægǣwī	حمام رغاوي
cosmetics	ædæwǣt tægmīl	أدوات تجميل
cream	krem	كريم
cleansing cream	krem lil tanẓīf	كريم للتنظيف
foundation cream	krem æsǣsī	كريم أساسي
moisturizing cream	krem moraṭṭib	كريم مرطب
night cream	krem lil nōm	كريم للنوم
cuticle remover	mozīl li gild æl-aẓāfir	مزيل لجلد الأظافر
deodorant	mozīl li rā'iḥæt æl-'æraq	مزيل لرائحة العرق
eyebrow pencil	qalæm koḥl	قلم كحل
eyeliner	qalæm lil 'oyūn	قلم للعيون
eye shadow	ẓill lil 'oyūn	ظل للعيون
face powder	bodra lil wægh	بودرة للوجه
foot cream	krem lil qadæm	كريم للقدم
hand cream	krem lil yæd	كريم لليد
hair remover	mozīl lil sha'r	مزيل للشعر
lipsalve	krem shæfǣyif	كريم شفايف
lipstick	aḥmar lil shæfǣyif	أحمر للشفايف
nail brush	forshæ lil aẓāfir	فرشة للأظافر
nail clippers	qaṣṣāfa lil aẓāfir	قصافة للأظافر
nail file	mabrad aẓāfir	مبرد أظافر
nail polish	monokīr	مونوكير
nail polish remover	mozīl lil monokīr	مزيل للمونوكير
nail scissors	maqaṣṣ lil aẓāfir	مقص للأظافر
perfume	pærfan ['iṭr]	برفان [عطر]
powder	bodra	بودرة
razor	mækænit ḥilǣqa	ماكينة حلاقة
razor blades	æmwǣs ḥilǣqa	أمواس حلاقة

safety pins	dæbæbīs mæshbæk	دبابيس مشبك
shaving cream	krem lil ḥilæqa	كريم للحلاقة
soap	ṣābūn	صابون
sponge	sæfingæ	سفنجة
sun-tan cream/oil	krem/zēt lil shæms	كريم/زيت للشمس
talcum powder	bodrat tælk	بودرة تلك
tissues	mænædīl waraq	مناديل ورق
toilet paper	waraq tæwælīt	ورق تواليت
toilet water	kolonyæ	كولونيا
toothbrush	forshæt æsnæn	فورشة أسنان
toothpaste	mæ'gūn æsnæn	معجون أسنان
tweezers	molqāṭ	ملقاط

For your hair لشعرك

colour shampoo	shambo lil tælwīn	شامبو للتلوين
comb	mishṭ	مشط
dye	ṣabga lil sha'r	صبغة للشعر
hairbrush	forshæ lil sha'r	فرشة للشعر
hair gel	sæ'il li formet æsh-sha'r	سائل لفورمة الشعر
hairgrips	binæs	بنس
hair lotion	moqawwī lil sha'r	مقوي للشعر
hair slide	dæbbūs sha'r	دبوس شعر
hair spray	sbray lil sha'r	سبراي للشعر
shampoo for ... hair	shambo li sha'r	شامبو لشعر...
dry/greasy (oily)	gæf/dohnī	جاف/دهني
tint	tælwīn	تلوين
wig	barūka	باروكة

For the baby للطفل

baby food	gizæ' aṭ-ṭifl	غذاء الطفل
dummy (pacifier)	bæzzæzæ	بزازة
feeding bottle	zogægit æl-ækl	زجاجة الأكل
nappies (diapers)	tægyīrāt aṭ-ṭifl	تغييرات الطفل

Clothing الملبس

If you want to buy something specific, prepare yourself in advance. Look at the list of clothing on page 115. Get some idea of the colour, material and size you want. They're all listed on the next few pages.

I'd like...	or**ī**d	أريد ...
I'd like something for an...	or**ī**d she' li	أريد شيء لـ...
11-year-old boy	**wæ**læd '**om**ro 11 sænæ	ولد عمره ١١ سنة
11-year-old girl	bint 'omr**a**hǣ 11 sænæ	بنت عمرها ١١ سنة
Where's the... department?	**æy**næ qism	أين قسم...؟
children's/men's women's	æl-aṭ**fāl**/ær-ri**gǣl**/ æs-sæyyi**dǣt**	الأطفال / الرجال / السيدات
I want something like this.	or**ī**d she' misl **hǣ**zæ	أريد شيء مثل هذا.
I like the one in the window.	yo'**gi**bonī mǣ fil vitrīnæ	يعجبني ما في الڤترينة.

Colour اللون

I want something in...	or**ī**d lōn	أريد لون...
I want a darker/ lighter shade.	or**ī**d **æg**maq/**æf**tæḥ **da**raga	أريد أغمق / أفتح درجة.
I want something to match this.	or**ī**d she' yon**ǣ**sib **hǣ**zæ	أريد شيء يناسب هذا.
I don't like the...	lǣ yo'**gi**bonī	لا يعجبني ...
colour/pattern	æl-**lōn**/æsh-**shækl**	اللون / الشكل

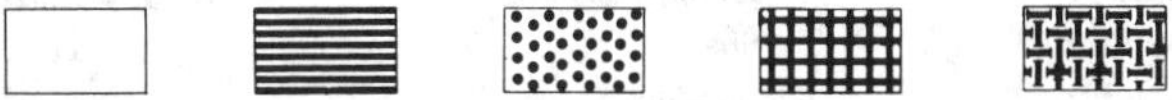

سادة	مخطط	منقط	مربعات	مزركش
(s**ǣ**dæ)	(mo**kha**ṭṭaṭ)	(mo**naq**qaṭ)	(morabba'**āt**)	(mo**zar**kæsh)

beige	bēzh	بيج
black	æswæd	أسود
blue	æzraq	أزرق
brown	bonnī	بني
golden	zæhæbī	ذهبي
green	akhḍar	أخضر
grey	ramādī	رمادي
mauve	mōv	موف
orange	bortoqālī	برتقالي
pink	wærdī	وردي
purple	bænæfsigī	بنفسجي
red	aḥmar	أحمر
silver	faḍḍī	فضي
turquoise	terkwæz	تركواز
white	abyaḍ	أبيض
yellow	aṣfar	أصفر
light...	... fætiḥ	...فاتح
dark...	... gæmiq	...غامق

Fabric قماش

Do you have anything in...?	hæl 'indæk she' min	هل عندك شيء من...؟
Is that...?	hæl hæzæ	هل هذا...؟
handmade	shogl yæd	شغل يد
imported	mostæwrad	مستورد
made here	mæḥællī	محلي
pure cotton	qoṭn mīyæ fil mīyæ	قطن مية في المية
pure wool	ṣūf mīyæ fil mīyæ	صوف مية في المية
synthetic	ṣinā'ī	صناعي
colourfast	lōn sæbit	لون ثابت
crease (wrinkle) resistant	gēr miḥtæg li mækwæ	غير محتاج لمكوة

Is it… washable?	hæl **hǣzæ** lil gæ**sīl**	هل هذا للغسيل...؟
hand	bil yæd	باليد
machine	bil mæ**kæ**næ	بالماكينة
Will it shrink?	hæl **hǣzæ** yæ**kish**	هل هذا يكش؟
I want something thinner.	o**rīd** she' khæ**fīf**	أريد شيء خفيف.
Do you have anything of better quality?	hæl **'in**dæk no' æ**ḥ**sæn	هل عندك نوع أحسن؟
What's it made of?	maṣ**nū'** min **mǣ**zæ	مصنوع من ماذا؟

cambric	tīl khæ**fīf**	تيل خفيف
camel-hair	**wa**bar æl-**gæ**mæl	وبر الجمل
chiffon	shi**fōn**	شيفون
corduroy	qa**ṭī**fa mo**ḍal**la'a	قطيفة مضلعة
cotton	qoṭn	قطن
cotton voile	**lī**nō	لينو
crepe	kreb	كريب
denim	zhinz	جينز
felt	gūkh	جوخ
flannel	fæ**nil**læ	فانله
gabardine	gæbær**dīn**	جبردين
lace	dæn**til**læ	دانتيلا
linen	kit**tǣn** [tīl]	كتان [تيل]
leather	gild	جلد
poplin	bob**līn**	بوبلين
satin	sæ**tǣn**	ساتان
silk	ḥæ**rīr**	حرير
suede	**shæm**wa	شاموا
towelling	qo**mǣsh** fūṭa	قماش فوطة
velvet	qa**ṭī**fa	قطيفة
velveteen	qa**ṭī**fa qoṭn	قطيفة قطن
wool	ṣūf	صوف
worsted	ṣūf ingi**lī**zī	صوف إنجليزي

How much is that per metre?	bi**kæm** æl-**mitr** min **hǣ**zæ	بكم المتر من هذا؟

1 centimetre (cm.) =	0.39 in.	1 inch =	2.54 cm.
1 metre (m.)	= 39.37 in.	1 foot =	30.5 cm.
10 metres	= 32.81 ft.	1 yard =	0.91 m.

Size المقاس

Sizes can vary from one manufacturer to another, so be sure to try on shoes and clothing before you buy.

I don't know my size.	lǣ æ'ærif maqāsī	لا أعرف مقاسي.
In England I take size 38.	fī ingiltēra maqāsī 38	في إنجلترا مقاسي ٣٨.
small/medium	ṣagīr/mutæ**wæs**siṭ	صغير/متوسط
large/extra large	kæbīr/kæbīr giddæn	كبير/كبير جداً
Could you measure me?	momkin taqīs lī	ممكن تقيس لي؟

A good fit? القياس

Can I try it on?	momkin aqīs hǣzæ	ممكن أقيس هذا؟
Where's the fitting room?	æynæ kæbīnæt æl-qiyǣs	أين كابينة القياس؟
Is there a mirror?	hæl tūgæd mirǣyæ	هل توجد مرايا؟
It fits very well.	æl-mæqās mazbūṭ giddæn	المقاس مضبوط جداً.
It doesn't fit.	æl-mæqās læysæ mazbūṭ	المقاس ليس مضبوط.
It's too...	innæho... kitīr	إنه... كثير
short/long	qasīr/tawīl	قصير/طويل
tight/loose	dæyyæq/wǣsi'	ضيق/واسع
How long will it take to alter?	kæm min æl-waqt li 'æmæl æt-taṣlīḥ	كم من الوقت لعمل التصليح؟

NUMBERS, see page 146

Clothes and accessories الملابس ولوازمها

I'd like a/an/ some...	orīd	أريد...
bathrobe	**bor**nos	برنس
blouse	**blō**sæ [qamīṣ ḥærīmī]	بلوزة [قميص حريمي]
bow tie	kara**vatta** baby**ōn**	كرافتة بابيون
bra	suty**ǣ**næ	سوتيانة
braces	hæmmæ**læt**	حمالات
briefs	slib	سليب
cap	kæs**kitt**æ	كاسكيتة
cardigan	zhæ**kēt** trīkō [**kæn**zæ]	جاكيت تريكو [كنزة]
coat	**bal**ṭō	بالطو
dress	fos**tǣn**	فستان
with long sleeves	bi æk**mǣm** ṭawīla	بأكمام طويلة
with short sleeves	bi æk**mǣm** qaṣīra	بأكمام قصيرة
sleeveless	bi**dūn** æk**mǣm**	بدون أكمام
dressing gown	rōb	روب
evening dress (woman's)	fos**tǣn** lil **sæh**ra	فستان للسهرة
garter belt	ḥi**zǣm mæsh**bæk	حزام مشبك
gloves	go**wǣn**tī [ko**fūf**]	جوانتي [كفوف]
handbag	**shan**ṭit yæd	شنطة يد
hat	bar**nī**ṭa	برنيطة
jacket	zhæ**kēt**	جاكيت
jeans	banṭa**lōn** zhinz	بنطلون جينز
nightdress	qa**mīṣ** nōm	قميص نوم
panties	slib	سليب
pants (Am.)	banṭa**lōn**	بنطلون
panty girdle	kor**sey**	كورسيه
panty hose	shor**rāb** ḥærīmī ṭa**wīl**	شراب حريمي طويل
pullover	bo**lō**var	بلوفر
roll-neck (turtle-neck)	bi **yǣ**qa **'ǣl**yæ	بياقة عالية
round-neck	bi **yǣ**qa modaw**wara**	بياقة مدورة
V-neck	bi **sæ**bæ'æ	بسبعة

SPORTSWEAR, see page 127

pyjamas	bizhǣmǣ	بيجاما
raincoat	balṭō maṭar	بالطو مطر
scarf	isharb	ايشارب
shirt	qamīṣ	قميص
shorts	short	شورت
skirt	zhūb	جوب
slip	kombinēson	كومبينيزون
socks	shorrāb [kælsæt]	شراب [كلسات]
stockings	shorrāb ḥærīmī	شراب حريمي
suit (man's)	bædlæ	بدلة
suit (woman's)	bædlæ ḥærīmī	بدلة حريمي
suspender belt	ḥizǣm mæshbæk	حزام مشبك
suspenders (Am.)	ḥæmmǣlǣt	حمالات
sweater	bolōvar	بلوفر
sweatshirt	swīt shert	سويت شيرت
tie	karavatta	كرافتة
tights	shorrāb ḥærīmī ṭawīl	شراب حريمي طويل
trousers	banṭalōn	بنطلون
T-shirt	tī shert	تي شيرت
umbrella	shæmsiyyæ	شمسية
underpants	slib	سليب
undershirt	fǣnillæ	فانيلا
vest (Am.)	ṣidērī	صديري
vest (Br.)	fǣnillæ	فانيلا
waistcoat	ṣidērī	صديري

belt	ḥizǣm	حزام
buckle	tōkæ	توكة
button	zorār	زرار
collar	yǣqa	ياقة
pocket	gēb	جيب
press stud (snap fastener)	kæbsūn	كبسون
zip (zipper)	sōstæ	سوستة

Shoes جَزْمٌ [احذية]

I'd like some...	orīd	أريد...
boots	būt	بوت
moccasins	mækǣsǣn	ماكاسان
sandals	ṣandal	صندل
shoes	gæzma [ḥizǣ']	جزمة [حذاء]
flat/with a heel	wāṭya/bi kæ'b	واطية/بكعب
with leather soles	bi næ'l gild	بنعل جلد
with rubber soles	bi næ'l kǣwitsh	بنعل كاوتش
slippers	shibshib	شبشب
These are too...	innæhǣ... kitīr	إنها... كثير
narrow/wide	ḍæyyaq/wāsi'	ضيق/واسع
large/small	kæbīr/ṣagīr	كبير/صغير
Do you have a larger/smaller size?	hæl 'indæk maqās akbar/aṣgar	هل عندك مقاس أكبر/أصغر؟
Do you have the same in black?	hæl 'indæk næfs æsh-she' æswæd	هل عندك نفس الشيء أسود؟
cloth/rubber	qomǣsh/kǣwitsh	قماش/كاوتش
leather/suede	gild/shæmwa	جلد/شاموا
Is it genuine leather?	hæl hǣzæ gild ṭabī'ī	هل هذا جلد طبيعي؟
I need some shoe polish/shoelaces.	æhtǣg ilæ wærnīsh/robāṭ æḥziyyæ	احتاج إلى ورنيش/رباط أحذية.

Shoes worn out? Here's the key to getting them fixed again:

Can you repair these shoes?	momkin iṣlāḥ hǣzihil gæzmæ [ḥizǣ']	ممكن إصلاح هذه الجزمة [الحذاء]؟
Can you stitch this?	momkin khiyāṭit hǣzæ	ممكن خياطة هذا؟
I want new heels.	orīd kæ'b gædīd	أريد كعب جديد.
I want new soles.	orīd næ'l gædīd	أريد نعل جديد.
When will they be ready?	mætæ tækūn gæhzæ	متى تكون جاهزة؟

COLOURS, see page 111

Electrical appliances أدوات كهربائية

There is no standard voltage within any single Middle-Eastern country. Most places have 220 volts AC, 50 cycles, some 110 volts.

What's the voltage?	kæm vōlt æl-kahr**a**ba'	كم ڤولت الكهرباء؟
Do you have an adaptor/a battery for this?	hæl **'in**dæk mo**ḥæw**wil/ baṭṭ**āriy**ya li **hǣ**zæ	هل عندك محول/بطارية لهذا؟
This is broken. Can you repair it?	**hǣ**zæ mak**sūr**. **mom**kin iṣ**lā**ḥo	هذا مكسور. ممكن إصلاحه؟
Can you show me how it works?	**mom**kin to**rī**nī **kæy**fæ **yæ'**mæl	ممكن تريني كيف يعمل؟
I'd like a/an/ some...	o**rīd**...	أريد...
amplifier	mo**kæb**bir ṣawt	مكبر صوت
bulb	**lam**ba	لمبة
clock-radio	**rad**yō bi **sǣ**'æ	راديو بساعة
electric toothbrush	**for**shæt æs**nǣn** kahraba**'iy**yæ	فرشة أسنان كهربائية
flashlight	baṭṭ**āriy**yit gēb	بطارية جيب
hair dryer	sish**wār**	سيشوار
headphones	sæmm**ǣ'ǣt** lil ra's	سماعات للرأس
(travelling) iron	**mæk**wæ (lil **sa**far)	مكوة (للسفر)
lamp	miṣ**bāḥ**	مصباح
plug	kobs	كوبس
portable radio	**rad**yō ṣa**gīr**	راديو صغير
recorder player	bīk ab	بيك أب
shaver	mæki**nat** ḥi**lǣ**qa	ماكينة حلاقة
speakers	sæmm**ǣ'ǣt**	سماعات
cassette recorder	kæs**set** ri**kōr**dar	كاسيت ريكوردر
(colour) television	tilivis**yōn** (mi**læw**win)	تليفزيون (ملون)
torch	baṭṭ**āriy**yit gēb	بطارية جيب
transformer	mo**ḥæw**wil [trāns]	محول [ترانس]
video-recorder	gi**hǣz** **vīd**yō	جهاز ڤيديو

Grocery محل البقالة

I'd like some bread, please.	orīd khobz min fadlak	أريد خبز من فضلك.
What sort of cheese do you have?	mææ aṣnāf æl-gibæn 'indæk	ما أصناف الجبن عندك؟
A piece of that one.	qiṭ'a min hǣzæ	قطعة من هذا.
a bit more	shwæyæ kæmǣn	شوية كمان
a bit less	shwæyæ aqall	شوية أقل
That's enough.	yækfī	يكفي.
I'll have one of those, please.	orīd wāḥid min hǣzæ min fadlak	أريد واحد من هذا من فضلك
May I help myself?	momkin ækhod bi nafsī	ممكن أخذ بنفسي؟
I'd like...	orīd	أريد...
a kilo of apples	kīlō toffǣḥ	كيلو تفاح
half a kilo of tomatoes	niṣf kīlō ṭamāṭim [banadūra]	نصف كيلو طماطم [بندورة]
100 grams of butter	100 grām zibdæ	١٠٠ جرام زبدة
a litre of milk	litr læbæn [ḥælīb]	لتر لبن [حليب]
half a dozen eggs	niṣf dæstæ bēḍ	نصف دستة بيض
4 slices of ham	4 qiṭ'a zhambon	٤ قطعة جامبون
a packet of tea	bǣkō shæy	باكو شاي
a jar of jam	barṭamān mirabba	برطمان مربى
a tin (can) of olives	'ilbit zætūn	علبة زيتون
a tube of mustard	anbūbit mosṭarda	أنبوبة مسطردة
a box of chocolates	'ilbit shokolāta	علبة شوكولاتة

---

1 kilogram or kilo (kg.) = 1000 grams (g.)

100 g. = 3.5 oz.	½ kg. = 1.1 lb.	1 oz. = 28.35 g.
200 g. = 7.0 oz.	1 kg. = 2.2 lb.	1 lb. = 453.60 g.

1 litre (l.) = 0.88 imp. qt. or 1.06 U.S. qt.

1 imp. qt. = 1.14 l.	1 U.S. qt. = 0.95 l.
1 imp. gal. = 4.55 l.	1 U.S. gal. = 3.8 l.

FOOD, see also page 64

دليل التسوق

Jeweller's—Watchmaker's محل مجوهرات وساعات

In the markets and jewellery shops of the Middle East, you'll find excellent copies of ancient jewellery. Gold and silver is rarely available in the same shop.

Could I see that, please.	momkin ara hǣzihi	ممكن أرى هذه؟
Do you have anything in white gold?	hæl 'indæk she' min zæhæb abyaḍ	هل عندك شيء من ذهب أبيض؟
How many carats is this?	kæm qīrāṭ	كم قيراط؟
Is this real silver?	hæl hǣzæ faḍḍa ḥaqīqiyyæ	هل هذا فضة حقيقية؟
Can you repair this watch?	momkin iṣlāḥ hǣzihi æs-sǣ æ	ممكن إصلاح هذه الساعة؟
I'd like a/an/some ...	orīd	أريد...
alarm clock	minæbbih	منبه
bangle	gwēshæ	غويشة
battery	baṭṭāriyya	بطارية
bracelet	gwēshæ	غويشة
(chain) bracelet	gwēshæ (silsilæ)	غويشة (سلسلة)
brooch	brōsh	بروش
chain	silsilæ	سلسلة
charm	ḥilyæ	حلية
cigarette case	'ilbit sægāyir	علبة سجاير
cigarette lighter	wællā'æ	ولاعة
(wall) clock	sǣ'it (ḥā'iṭ)	ساعة (حائط)
cuff links	zarāyir qomṣān	زراير قمصان
cutlery	faḍḍiyya lil ækl	فضية للأكل
earrings	ḥælæq	حلق
gem	ḥagar kærīm	حجر كريم
jewellery box	'ilbit gæwāhir	علبة جواهر
mechanical pencil	qalæm roṣāṣ mæ'dænī	قلم رصاص معدني
necklace	'oqd	عقد
pendant	qilǣdæ	قلادة

pin	dæb**būs**	دبوس
propelling pencil	**qa**læm ro**ṣāṣ** mæ'**dæ**nī	قلم رصاص معدني
ring	**khæ**tim	خاتم
engagement ring	**khæ**tim khoṭūba	خاتم خطوبة
signet ring	**khæ**tim ri**gæ**lī	خاتم رجالي
wedding ring	**dib**lit zæ**wæg**	دبلة زواج
tie pin	dæb**būs** kara**vat**ta	دبوس كرافتة
watch	**sæ**'æ	ساعة
digital	raqa**miy**yæ	رقمية
with a second hand	bi **'æq**ræb sæ**wæ**nī	بعقرب ثواني
waterproof	ḍidd æl-**mæ**'	ضد الماء
watchstrap	**gil**dit **sæ**'æ	جلدة ساعة

alabaster	ala**bās**tar	الباستر
amethyst	ræg**mæst**	رجمست
coral	mor**gæn**	مرجان
crystal	krīs**tæl**	كريستال
diamond	al**māẓ**	ألماظ
emerald	**zo**morrod	زمرد
enamel	**ṣa**daf	صدف
(cut) glass	**zo**gæg (mæsh**gūl**)	زجاج (مشغول)
gold	**zæ**hæb	ذهب
gold-plated	mo**zæh**hæb	مذهب
ivory	**'æg**	عاج
onyx	'æ**qīq**	عقيق
pearl	**lū**lī	لولي
pewter	**mæ**'dæn	معدن
platinum	blæ**tīn**	بلاتين
ruby	**yæ**qūt	ياقوت
sapphire	**yæ**qūt æzraq	ياقوت أزرق
silver	**faḍ**ḍa	فضة
silver-plated	mo**faḍ**ḍaḍ	مفضض
topaz	**zæ**bærgæd	زبرجد
turquoise	fæy**rūz**	فيروز

Optician النظاراتي

I've broken my glasses.	**kasart** nazzāratī ['owæy**nætī**]	كسرت نظاراتي [عويناتي].
Can you repair them?	**mom**kin iṣlāḥæhæ	ممكن إصلاحها؟
When will they be ready?	mætæ tæ**kūn gæh**zæ	متى تكون جاهزة؟
Can you change the lenses?	**mom**kin tæg**yīr** æl-'ædæ**sæt**	ممكن تغيير العدسات؟
I want tinted lenses.	**orīd** 'ædæ**sæt** mo**læw**wænæ	أريد عدسات ملونة.
The frame is broken.	æsh-**sham**bar mak**sūr**	الشمبر مكسور.
I'd like a spectacle case.	**orīd girææb** lil naz**zāra**	أريد جراب للنظارة.
I'd like to have my eyesight checked.	**orīd** æn **æk**shif **'æ**læ **na**ẓarī	أريد أن أكشف على نظري.
I'm short-sighted/ long-sighted.	**æ**næ **'indī qi**ṣar **na**ẓar/ ṭūl **na**ẓar	أنا عندي قصر نظر/طول نظر.
I'd like some contact lenses.	**orīd** 'ædæ**sæt lā**ṣiqa	أريد عدسات لاصقة.
I've lost one of my contact lenses.	fæ**qadt iḥ**dæ 'ædæ**sætī** æl-**lā**ṣiqa	فقدت إحدى عدساتي اللاصقة.
Could you give me another one?	**mom**kin to'**ṭī**nī **'æ**dæsæ **tæn**yæ	ممكن تعطيني عدسة ثانية؟
I have hard/soft lenses.	**'indī** æl-'ædæ**sæt næsh**fæ/ læ**yyi**næ	عندي العدسات ناشفة/لينة.
Do you have any contact-lens fluid?	hæl **'in**dæk **sæ**'il lil 'ædæ**sæt** æl-**lā**ṣiqa	هل عندك سائل للعدسات اللاصقة؟
I'd like to buy...	**orīd** shi**rā'**	أريد شراء...
a pair of binoculars	naz**zā**ra mo'**az**zama	نظارة معظمة
a pair of sunglasses	naz**zā**rit shæms	نظارة شمس
May I look in a mirror?	**mom**kin æt**far**rag fil mi**ræ**yæ	ممكن أتفرج في المرايا؟

Photography التصوير

I want a(n)... camera.	orīd **kǣ**mira	أريد كاميرا...
automatic	oto**mǣ**tik	أوتوماتيك
inexpensive	ra**khī**ṣa	رخيصة
simple	**sæh**læ	سهلة
Show me some cine (movie)/video cameras, please.	o**rī**nī ba'ḍ kǣmi**rāt** æs-**sī**nimæ/æl-**vī**dyō min **faḍ**lak	أريني بعض كاميرات السينما / الڤيديو من فضلك.
I'd like some passport photos taken.	o**rīd** æn æ**khod** **ṣo**war li gæ**wǣz** æs-**sa**far	أريد أن أخذ صور لجواز السفر.

Film—Developing فيلم ـ تحميض

I'd like a film for this camera.	o**rīd** film li hǣ**zi**hil **kǣ**mira	أريد فيلم لهذه الكاميرا.
black and white	**æs**wæd wæ **ab**yaḍ	أسود وأبيض
colour	æl**wǣn**	ألوان
colour negative	nigæ**tīf** bil æl**wǣn**	نيجاتيف بالألوان
colour slide	slæyd bil æl**wǣn**	سلايد بالألوان
cartridge	**kar**tridzh	كارتريدج
disc film	film disk	فيلم دسك
roll film	æl-bo**bī**næ	البوبينة
video cassette	kæs**set** **vī**dyō	كاسيت ڤيديو
24 exposures	ar**bā**'a wæ 'ish**rīn** **ṣū**ra	أربعة وعشرين صورة
36 exposures	**sit**tæ wæ tælæ**tīn** **ṣū**ra	ستة وثلاثين صورة
this size	**hǣ**zæl ma**qās**	هذا المقاس
this ASA/DIN number	**da**ragit æl-ḥæsǣ**siy**yæ aza/dīn	درجة الحساسية أذا / دين
artificial light type	li ḍo' ṣi**nā**'ī	لضوء صناعي
daylight type	li ḍo' æn-na**hār**	لضوء النهار
fast (high-speed)	sæ**rī**'	سريع
fine grain	qa**līl** æl-ḥæsǣ**siy**yæ	قليل الحساسية
How much is the proccessing?	bi**kæm** æt-taḥ**mīd**	بكم التحميض؟

I'd like... prints of each negative.	orīd... ṣūra min koll nigætīf	أريد... صورة من كل نيجاتيف.
with a mat finish	bi waraq 'ǣdī	بورق عادي
with a glossy finish	bi waraq læmmī'	بورق لميع
Will you enlarge this, please?	momkin tækbīr hǣzihi min faḍlak	ممكن تكبير هذه من فضلك؟
When will the photos be ready?	mætæ tækūn aṣ-ṣowar gæhzæ	متى تكون الصور جاهزة؟

Accessories and repairs قطع غيار وتصليح

I'd like a/an/some...	orīd	أريد...
battery	baṭṭāriyya	بطارية
cable release	moftǣḥ æt-taṣwīr æl-'ǣlī	مفتاح التصوير العالي
camera case	shanṭa lil kǣmira	شنطة للكاميرا
(electronic) flash	flǣsh (electrōnī)	فلاش (إليكتروني)
filter	filtar	فلتر
for black and white	li æswæd wæ abyaḍ	لأسود وأبيض
for colour	li ælwǣn	لألوان
telephoto lens	'ædæsæ mokæbbira	عدسة مكبرة
wide-angle lens	'ædæsæ mo'aẓẓama	عدسة معظمة
Can you repair this camera?	momkin iṣlāḥ hæzihil kǣmira	ممكن إصلاح هذه الكاميرا؟
The film is jammed.	æl-film mæznūq	الفيلم مزنوق.
There's something wrong with the...	yūgæd 'oṭl fī	يوجد عطل في...
exposure counter	'addǣd aṣ-ṣowar	عداد الصور
film winder	moftǣḥ læff æl-film	مفتاح لف الفيلم
flash attachment	tasbīt æl-flǣsh	تثبيت الفلاش
lens	æl-'ædæsæ	العدسة
light meter	miqyǣs aḍ-ḍo'	مقياس الضوء
rangefinder	ḍābiṭ æl-mæsǣfæ	ضابط المسافة
shutter	monaẓẓim fæthit æl-'ædæsæ	منظم فتحة العدسة

NUMBERS, see page 146

Tobacconist's محل الدخان

As well as at tobacconist's, you can buy cigarettes at news-stands. Cigars and accessories are often available only in specialized shops.

A packet of cigarettes, please.	**'il**bit sæg**ǣ**yir min fa**ḍ**lak	علبة سجاير من فضلك.
Do you have any American/English cigarettes?	**'in**dæk sæg**ǣ**yir amri**kǣ**nī/ingi**lī**zī	عندك سجاير أمريكاني / إنجليزي؟
I'd like a carton.	o**rīd** khar**ṭū**sha	أريد خرطوشة.
Give me a/some..., please.	o**rīd**... min **faḍ**lak	أريد... من فضلك.
candy	bon**bō**nī	بونبوني
chewing gum	mæs**tī**kæ [li**bǣ**næ]	مستيكة [لبانة]
chocolate	shoko**lā**ta	شوكولاتة
cigarette holder	fomm sæg**ǣ**yir [**mæb**sæm]	فم سجاير [مبسم]
cigarettes	sæg**ǣ**yir	سجاير
filter-tipped	bi **fil**tar	بفلتر
without filter	bi**dūn fil**tar	بدون فلتر
mild/strong	khæ**fī**fæ/qa**wiy**yæ	خفيفة / قوية
menthol	bil næ'**nǣ**'	بالنعناع
king-size	ṭa**wī**la	طويلة
cigars	si**gār**	سيجار
lighter	wæl**lǣ**'æ	ولاعة
lighter fluid/gas	bæn**zīn**/**gǣ**z wæl**lǣ**'æ	بنزين / جاز ولاعة
matches	kæb**rīt**	كبريت
pipe	payp	بايب
pipe cleaners	mon**naẓ**ẓif payp	منظف بايب
pipe tobacco	do**khǣn** payp	دخان بايب
pipe tool	**'id**dit payp	عدة بايب
stamps	ṭa**wā**bi'	طوابع
sweets	bon**bō**nī	بونبوني
(light/dark) tobacco	do**khǣn** (**fǣ**tiḥ/**gǣ**miq)	دخان (فاتح / غامق)
wick	shi**rīṭ** wæl**lǣ**'æ	شريط ولاعة

Miscellaneous منوعات

Souvenirs هدايا تذكارية

Browsing through the bustling markets will turn up countless treasured souvenirs of your visit to the Middle East. Here are some suggestions for articles which you might like to bring back.

I'd like a souvenir from here.	orīd tiz**kār** min **ho**næ	أريد تذكار من هنا.
antiques	æntī**kæt**	انتيكات
brassware	maṣnū**'āt** ni**ḥæs** a**ṣ**far	مصنوعات نحاس أصفر
carpets	sægæ**gīd**	سجاجيد
ceramics	fokh**khār**	فخار
copperware	maṣnū**'āt** ni**ḥæs**	مصنوعات نحاس
dagger	**khan**gar	خنجر
gallabiya (full length robe)	gællæ**biy**yæ	جلابية
(hand-blown) glass	zo**gæg** (**yæ**dæwī)	زجاج (يدوي)
gold filigree	mæshgū**læt** zæhæ**biy**yæ	مشغولات ذهبية
hand-embroidered garments	mæ**læ**bis taṭ**rīz yæ**dæwī	ملابس تطريز يدوي
handicrafts	ṣinā**'āt** yædæ**wiy**yæ	صناعات يدوية
handkerchief	mæn**dīl**	منديل
jewellery	mogawha**rāt**	مجوهرات
kaftan	qof**ṭān**	قفطان
leather goods	maṣnū**'āt** gil**diy**yæ	مصنوعات جلدية
nargile (water pipe)	**shī**shæ [nær**gī**læ]	شيشة [نرجيله]
oriental lamp	miṣ**bāḥ shar**qī	مصباح شرقي
sandals	**ṣan**dal	صندل
stones	aḥ**gār**	أحجار
precious	kærīmæ	كريمة
semi-precious	shibh kærīmæ	شبه كريمة
Turkish coffee service	ṭaqm **qah**wa **tor**kī	طقم قهوة تركي
woodwork	maṣnū**'āt** khæshæ**biy**yæ	مصنوعات خشبية

Records—Cassettes إسطوانات ـ كاسيتات

Do you have any records by...?	hæl **'indæk** is**ṭiwā**nāt li	هل عندك إسطوانات لـ...؟
I'd like a ...	o**rīd**	أريد...
cassette	kæs**set**	كاسيت
compact disc	isṭ**iwā**na kom**pakt**	إسطوانة كومباكت

L.P. (33 rpm)	tæ**læ**tæ wæ tælæ**tīn** **læf**fæ	ثلاثة وثلاثين لفة
E.P. (45 rpm)	**khæm**sæ wæ arba**'īn** **læf**fæ	خمسة وأربعين لفة
single	**khæm**sæ wæ arba**'īn** **læf**fæ ṣa**gī**ra	خمسة وأربعين لفة صغيرة

Can I listen to this record?	**mom**kin **æs**mæ' hæ**zi**hil isṭi**wā**na	ممكن أسمع هذه الإسطوانة؟
Arabic music	mo**sī**qa 'ara**biy**ya	موسيقى عربية
classical music	mo**sī**qa **klæ**sik	موسيقى كلاسيك
folk music	mo**sī**qa shæ**'biy**yæ	موسيقى شعبية
instrumental music	mo**sī**qa	موسيقى
light music	mo**sī**qa khæ**fī**fæ	موسيقى خفيفة
orchestral music	mo**sī**qa gæ**mæ'iy**yæ	موسيقى جماعية
pop music	mo**sī**qa gar**biy**yæ	موسيقى غربية
song	og**nī**yæ	أغنية

Sports articles أدوات رياضية

I'd like (to hire) ... equipment	o**rīd** (tæ'**gīr**) ædæ**wæt**	أريد (تأجير) أدوات...
snorkelling	æl-**gaṭs**	الغطس
scuba-diving	æl-**gaṭs** æl-'æ**mīq**	الغطس العميق
I'd like a/an/some...	o**rīd**	أريد...
bathing cap	**bo**neh lil **baḥr**	بونية للبحر
plimsolls (sneakers)	**gæz**mæ **kæ**witsh	جزمة كاوتش

swimming trunks/ swimsuit	**mǣyō**	مايوة
tracksuit	**trēning**	ترنج

Toys اللعب

I'd like a toy/game.	o**rīd li'bæ**	أريد لعبة .
backgammon set	**ṭawla**	طاولة
(beach) ball	**kora** (lil baḥr)	كرة (للبحر)
building blocks (bricks)	mokæ'æ**bǣt**	مكعبات
card game	kot**shī**næ	كوتشينة
chess set	shaṭa**rang**	شطرنج
doll	'**arū**sa	عروسة
electronic game	**li'**bæ elek**trō**nī	لعبة اليكتروني
racket game	ræk**ket**	راكت
roller skates	'**æ**gæl tæ**zæ**ḥloq	عجل تزحلق

Useful Items أشياء مهمة

bottle-opener	fæt**tǣ**ḥit zogǣ**gǣt**	فتاحة زجاجات
can opener	fæt**tǣ**ḥit 'ilæb	فتاحة علب
compass	**bær**gæl	برجل
corkscrew	bær**rī**mæ li fæth æz-zogǣ**gǣt**	بريمة لفتح الزجاجات
frying pan	**ṭā**sa	طاسة
hammer	shǣ**kūsh**	شاكوش
penknife	**maṭ**wa	مطواة
rope	**ḥæ**bl	حبل
saucepan	**ḥæl**læ	حلة
scissors	ma**qaṣṣ**	مقص
screwdriver	mi**fækk**	مفك
tin-opener	fæt**tǣ**ḥit 'ilæb	فتاحة علب
tool	'**id**dæ	عدة

Your money: banks-currency

In the Middle East, there's generally no limit on the import of foreign currency. In Egypt, however, it must be declared upon arrival. Foreign currency may be exchanged only at a bank or other authorized establishment. Traveller's cheques are readily cashed at banks. Be sure to take your passport with you for identification when changing money, and don't forget to ask for a receipt or have the transaction noted on your declaration form; you'll need it to reconvert Egyptian money to foreign currency when leaving. Credit cards are accepted by an increasing number of establishments.

Monetary units: The basic unit of currency in Egypt is the *pound* (gi**nēh**), which is divided into 100 *piastre* ('irsh).

In other Arab countries one of the following basic units of currency is used: the *dinar* (**dī**nar) divided into 1000 *fils* (fils) in Jordan; the *riyal* (ri**yāl**), the *lira* (**li**ræ) and the *dirham* (**dir**hæm).

Banking hours: Opening hours vary from country to country, but generally banks are open from 8.30 a.m. to noon or 1 p.m. and close on Friday, the Muslim holy day. Some places have shorter opening hours on Sunday. In others, in keeping with Western custom, Sunday is the official holiday.

Where's the nearest bank?	æynæ **aq**rab bænk	أين أقرب بنك؟
Where's the currency exchange office?	æynæ **mæk**tæb æt-tæḥ**wīl**	أين مكتب التحويل؟

At the bank في البنك

I want to change some dollars/pounds sterling.	o**rīd** tæḥ**wīl** dōlā**rāt**/ gonē**hæt** istir**līnī**	أريد تحويل دولارات/ جنيهات أسترليني.

I want to cash a traveller's cheque.	**orīd** ṣarf shīk siy**æ**ḥī	أريد صرف شيك سياحي.
What's the exchange rate?	mæ si'r æt-tæḥ**wīl**	ما سعر التحويل؟
Would you..., please?	**mom**kin... min **fa**ḍlak	ممكن... من فضلك.
fill in this form	**tæm**læ' hæ**zi**hi æl-isti**mā**ra	تملأ هذه الاستمارة
give me a receipt	a'**ṭī**nī ī**ṣāl**	أعطني إيصال
How much commission do you charge?	kæm **tæ**ḥsib æl-'o**mū**læ	كم تحسب العمولة؟
I have a/an/some...	**'in**dī	عندي...
credit card	kært **maṣ**rafī	كارت مصرفي
introduction from...	khi**ṭāb** taw**ṣi**ya min	خطاب توصية من...
letter of credit	khi**ṭāb** ḍa**mān**	خطاب ضمان
I'm expecting some money from New York. Has it arrived?	**æ**næ mon**ta**ẓir no**qūd** min nyū york. hæl **wa**ṣalat	أنا منتظر نقود من نيويورك. هل وصلت؟
Can you telex my bank in...?	**mom**kin **tor**sil **te**lex ilæ **bæn**kī fī	ممكن ترسل تلكس إلى بنكي في...؟
Please give me...	min **fa**ḍlak a'**ṭī**nī	من فضلك أعطني...
10... notes (bills)	10 wara**qāt** bi	١٠ ورقات بـ...
some small change	ba'ḍ æl-**fæk**kæ	بعض الفكة

Deposits—Withdrawals إيداع ـ سحب

I want to...	**orīd**	أريد...
open an account	**æf**tæḥ ḥi**sæb**	افتح حساب
withdraw... pounds	**æs**ḥæb... gonē**hæt**	أسحب... جنيهات
Where should I sign?	**æy**næ a**waq**qa'	أين أوقع؟
I'd like to pay this into my account.	**mom**kin ūdi' **hæ**zæ fī ḥi**sæ**bī	ممكن أودع هذا في حسابي.

NUMBERS, see page 146

Business terms تعبيرات تجارية

My name is...	**ismī...**	اسمي...
Here's my card.	**hǣzæ kærtī**	هذا كارتي.
I have an appointment with...	**'indī mæw'id mæ'æ**	عندي موعد مع...
Can you give me an estimate of the cost?	**momkin ta'ṭīnī si'r taqrībī**	ممكن تعطيني سعر تقريبي؟
What's the rate of inflation?	**mǣ nisbæt æt-taḍakhkhom**	ما نسبة التضخم؟
Can you provide me with an interpreter/a secretary?	**momkin īgǣd motærgim/sekertēræ**	ممكن إيجاد مترجم/سكرتيرة؟
Where can I make photocopies?	**æynæ æ'æmil fotokōpī**	أين أعمل فوتوكوبي؟

amount	**mæblæg**	مبلغ
balance	**raṣīd**	رصيد
capital	**ræ's æl-mǣl**	رأس المال
contract	**'aqd**	عقد
discount	**takhfīḍ**	تخفيض
expenses	**maṣārīf**	مصاريف
interest	**fæydæ**	فائدة
investment	**istismār**	استثمار
invoice	**fātūra**	فاتورة
loss	**khosāra**	خسارة
payment	**dæf'**	دفع
percentage	**nisbæ**	نسبة
profit	**mæksæb [ribḥ]**	مكسب [ربح]
purchase	**shirā'**	شراء
sale	**bē'**	بيع
share	**sæhm**	سهم
transfer	**tæḥwīl**	تحويل
value	**qīmæ**	قيمة

At the post office

Post office opening hours vary from country to country. On the whole, you can count on them being open from 8.30 a.m. to 1 p.m.; some reopen later in the afternoon. Friday is the official closing day, with some post offices closing earlier on Thursday. The postal service is usually slow, so for urgent messages it is safer to resort to telephone, telegraph or telex services.

There are different letter boxes (mailboxes) depending on the destination and type of letter: for ordinary mail, express (special delivery) and airmail. In big towns, boxes may be marked in English.

Where's the nearest post office?	æynæ **aqrab mæk**tæb bæ**rīd** [**bōs**tæ]	أين أقرب مكتب بريد [بوستة]؟
What time does the post office...?	**mæ**tæ... **mæk**tæb æl-bæ**rīd** [**bōs**tæ]	متى... مكتب البريد [بوستة]؟
open/close	**yæf**tæḥ/**yaq**fil	يفتح/يقفل
Which counter do I go to for stamps?	**æy**næ shib**bæk** aṭ-ṭa**wā**bi'	أين شباك الطوابع؟
A stamp for this..., please.	**ṭā**bi' li **hæ**zæl... min **faḍ**lak	طابع لهذا الـ... من فضلك.
letter/postcard	khi**ṭāb**/kært bos**tæl**	خطاب/كارت بوستال
What's the postage for a letter to...?	bi**kæm** aṭ-**ṭā**bi' li khi**ṭāb** ilæ	بكم الطابع لخطاب إلى...؟
What's the postage for a postcard to...?	bi**kæm** aṭ-**ṭā**bi' li kært bos**tæl** ilæ	بكم الطابع لكارت بوستال إلى...؟
Where's the letter box (mailbox)?	**æy**næ ṣon**dūq** æl-khiṭā**bāt**	أين صندوق الخطابات؟
I want to send this parcel.	o**rīd** ir**sæl hæ**zæl ṭard	اريد إرسال هذا الطرد.
Do I need to fill in a customs declaration?	hæl **yæ**gib æn **æm**læ' isti**mā**rit æl-**gom**rok	هل يجب أن أملأ استمارة الجمرك؟

COUNTRIES, see page 154

I want to send this by...	orīd irsæl hæzæ bi	أريد إرسال هذا بـ...
air mail	æl-bærīd æl-gæwwī	البريد الجوي
express (special delivery)	æl-bærīd æl-mostæ'gil	البريد المستعجل
registered mail	æl-bærīd æl-mosæggæl	البريد المسجل
At which counter can I cash an international money order?	min æyy shibbæk yomkinonī ṣarf ḥiwælæ bærīdiyyæ ægnæbiyyæ	من أي شباك يمكنني صرف حوالة بريدية أجنبية؟
Where's the poste restante (general delivery)?	æynæ mæktæb tæslīm æl-khiṭābāt	أين مكتب تسليم الخطابات؟
Is there any post (mail) for me? My name is...	hæl tūgæd khiṭābāt lī. ismī	هل توجد خطابات لي؟ اسمي...

طوابع STAMPS	طرود PARCELS	حوالات MONEY ORDERS

Telegrams تلغراف

In the Middle East, telegrams are sent through post offices, which also have telex service. Major hotels may offer the same services.

I want to send a...	orīd irsæl	أريد ارسال...
telegram/telex	tiligrāf/telex	تلغراف/ تلكس
May I have a form, please?	min faḍlak a'ṭīnī istimāra	من فضلك اعطني استمارة
How much is it per word?	bikæm æl-kelmæ	بكم الكلمة؟
How long will a cable to Boston take?	mætæ yaṣil æt-tiligrāf ilæ bosṭon	متى يصل التلغراف الى بوسطن؟
How much will this telex cost?	bikæm hæzæl telex	بكم هذا التلكس؟

Telephoning تليفون

Phone calls are handled by post offices and (at a surcharge) by big hotels. For a local call, you can also go into a store.

Where's the telephone/telephone booth?	**æ**ynæ æt-tili**fōn**/ **kæ**binet æt-tili**fōn**	أين التليفون/كابينة التليفون؟
I need some coins for the telephone.	æh**tæg** **fæk**kæ lil tili**fōn**	احتاج فكة للتليفون.
May I use your phone for a/an...?	**mom**kin isti'**māl** tili**fō**næk li	ممكن استعمال تليفونك لـ...؟
local call	mo**kæl**mæ mæh**æl**liyyæ	مكالمة محلية
international call	mo**kæl**mæ khæ**ri**gi**yy**æ	مكالمة خارجية
Do you have a telephone directory?	hæl **'in**dæk dæ**līl** tili**fōn**	هل عندك دليل تليفون؟
I want to telephone to England.	o**rīd** æl-iti**ṣāl** bi ingil**tē**ra	أريد الاتصال بانجلترا.
Can I dial direct?	**mom**kin at**ta**ṣil mo**bæ**sharatæn	ممكن اتصل مباشرة؟
Can you help me get this number?	min **faḍ**lak **sæ'id**nī fil itti**ṣāl** bi **hæ**zæl **ra**qam	من فضلك ساعدني في الاتصال بهذا الرقم.
The dialling (area) code for London is...	**ra**qam mof**tæḥ** **lan**dan **ho**wæ	رقم مفتاح لندن هو...
Where's the (international) operator's office?	**æ**ynæ **mæk**tæb æl-itti**ṣā**lāt (æl-khæ**ri**gi**yy**æ)	أين مكتب الاتصالات (الخارجية)؟

Operator عامل التليفون

Good morning, I want Cairo 23 45 67.	ṣa**bāḥ** æl-**khēr**. o**rīd** æl-**qā**hira 23 45 67	صباح الخير. أريد القاهرة ٢٣ ٤٥ ٦٧
I want to place a personal (person-to-person) call.	o**rīd** mo**kæl**mæ shakh**ṣi**yyæ	أريد مكالمة شخصية.

يمكنك الاتصال في كابينه ٤	You can take your call in booth 4.
لا يوجد رد.	There's no reply.

Would you try again later, please?	min **faḍ**lak **ḥǣ**wil **marra tæ**nyæ bæ**'dēn**	من فضلك حاول مرة ثانية بعدين.
Operator, you gave me the wrong number.	yæ **sæ**yyid a'**aṭ**ay**tæ**nī raqam **ga**laṭ	يا سيد أعطيتني رقم غلط.
Operator, we were cut off.	yæ **sæ**yyid inqaṭa'at æl-mo**kǣ**lmæ	يا سيد انقطعت المكالمة.

Speaking—Not there التحدث ـ ليس هنا

Hello this is... speaking.	ælo ænæ	ألو أنا...
I want to speak to...	o**rīd** æn ætæ**kæl**læm mæ'æ	أريد أن أتكلم مع...
I want extension...	o**rīd** ær-**ra**qam æd-**dǣ**khilī	أريد الرقم الداخلي...
Is that...?	hæl **hǣ**zæ	هل هذا...؟
Speak..., please.	tæ**kæl**læm... min **faḍ**lak	تكلم... من فضلك.
louder/more slowly	bi ṣawt **'ālī**/bi**boṭ'**	بصوت عالي/ببطىء
Will you tell him/her I called? My name is...	min **faḍ**lak qūl **læ**ho/**læ**hæ **in**nī itta**ṣalt. ism**ī	من فضلك قول له/لها إنني اتصلت. اسمي...
Would you ask him/her to call me?	min **faḍ**lak o**ṭ**lob **min**ho/**min**hæ æl-itti**ṣāl** bī	من فضلك أطلب منه/منها الاتصال بي.
Would you take a message, please?	min **faḍ**lak khod hǣ**zi**hil ri**sǣ**læ	من فضلك خذ هذه الرسالة.

Charges السعر

What was the cost of that call?	**bi**kæm hǣ**zi**hil mo**kǣ**lmæ	بكم هذه المكالمة؟

Doctor

Many doctors speak good English, others will have some knowledge of medical terms. In certain cases or in an emergency, however, you may find yourself needing to explain your problem in Arabic.

General كلمات عامة

Can you get me a doctor?	momkin toṭlob lī doktōr	ممكن تطلب لي دكتور.
Is there a doctor here?	hæl yūgæd doktōr honæ	هل يوجد دكتور هنا؟
I need a doctor, quickly.	æḥtæg ilæ doktōr bisor'æ	احتاج إلى دكتور بسرعة.
Where can I find a doctor who speaks English?	æynæ ægid doktōr yætækællæm ingilīzī bi ṭalāqa	أين أجد دكتور يتكلم إنجليزي بطلاقة؟
Where's the surgery (doctor's office)?	æynæ 'iyædæt æd-doktōr	أين عيادة الدكتور؟
What are the surgery (office) hours?	mæ hiyæ mæwæ'īd æl-'iyædæ	ما هي مواعيد العيادة؟
Could the doctor come to see me here?	momkin yæ'tī æd-doktōr lil kæshf 'ællæyyæ honæ	ممكن يأتي الدكتور للكشف عليَّ هنا؟
What time can the doctor come?	mætæ yomkin lil doktōr æn yæ'tī	متى يمكن للدكتور أن يأتي؟
Can you recommend a/an...?	momkin tinṣaḥnī bi	ممكن تنصحني بـ...؟
general practitioner	doktōr 'æm	دكتور عام
children's doctor	doktōr aṭfāl	دكتور أطفال
eye specialist	doktōr 'oyūn	دكتور عيون
gynaecologist	doktōr amrāḍ nisæ'	دكتور أمراض نساء
Can I have an appointment...?	momkin ækhod mæw'id	ممكن أخذ موعد؟
tomorrow	gædæn	غداً
as soon as possible	fī aqrab waqt	في أقرب وقت

CHEMIST'S, see page 107

Parts of the body أعضاء الجسم

ankle	kæ'b æl-qa**dæm**	كعب القدم
appendix	æz-**zæy**dæ	الزايدة
arm	zi**rā'**	ذراع
artery	shir**yæn**	شريان
back	ẓahr	ظهر
bladder	mæ**sǣ**næ	مثانة
bone	'aẓm	عظم
bowels	æḥ**shǣ'**	أحشاء
breast	**sæ**dy	ثدي
chest	ṣadr	صدر
ear	**o**zon	أذن
eye/eyes	'æyn/o**yūn**	عين/عيون
face	wægh	وجه
finger	**a**ṣbā'	إصبع
foot	qa**dæm**	قدم
genitals	a'**ḍā'** æt-tæ**nǣ**sol	أعضاء التناسل
gland	**god**dæ	غدة
hand	yæd	يد
head	ra's	رأس
heart	qalb	قلب
jaw	fækk	فك
joint	**maf**ṣal	مفصل
kidney	**kil**yæ	كلية
knee	**rok**bæ	ركبة
leg	sǣq	ساق
ligament	ri**bāṭ**	رباط
lip	**shif**fæ	شفة
liver	kibd	كبد
lung	**ri**'æ	رئة
mouth	fæmm	فم
muscle	**'a**ḍal	عضل
neck	**ra**qabæ	رقبة
nerve	**'a**ṣab	عصب
nervous system	æl-gi**hǣz** æl-'**a**ṣabī	الجهاز العصبي

nose	ænf	أنف
rib	ḍil'	ضلع
shoulder	kitf	كتف
skin	gild	جلد
spine	æl-'æ**mūd** æl-**faq**rī	العمود الفقري
stomach	**mi**'dæ	معدة
tendon	**wa**tar	وتر
thigh	fækhd	فخذ
throat	zōr	ذور
thumb	**aṣ**ba' æl-ib**hǣm**	أصبع الأبهام
toe	**aṣ**ba' æl-**qa**dæm	أصبع القدم
tongue	**li**sǣn	لسان
tonsils	**li**wæz	لوز
vein	'irq	عرق

Accident—Injury حادث - إصابة

There's been an accident.	kǣn **yū**gæd **ḥǣ**dis	كان يوجد حادث.
My son has had a fall.	ib**nī** **sa**qaṭ	ابني سقط.
My daughter has had a fall.	bin**tī** **sa**qaṭit	بنتي سقطت.
He/She is...	**ho**wæ/**hi**yæ	هو/هي...
unconscious	**mog**mæ 'æ**lēh**/**mog**mæ 'æ**lē**hæ	مغمى عليه/مغمى عليها
bleeding	**yæn**ẓif/**tæn**ẓif	ينزف/تنزف
injured	mo**ṣāb**/mo**ṣā**ba	مصاب/مصابة
His/Her leg is ...	**sǣ**qoh/**sǣ**qhæ	ساقه/ساقها
hurt	mag**rū**ḥæ	مجروحة
broken	mak**sū**ra	مكسورة
swollen	**wǣr**mæ	وارمة
I've been stung.	**æ**næ maq**rūṣ**	أنا مقروص.
I've got something in my eye.	**yū**gæd she' fī **'æy**nī	يوجد شيء في عيني.

I've got a/an...	**'ind**ī	عندي...
blister	kīs mǣ'	كيس ماء
boil	kho**rāg**	خراج
bruise	ri**ḍūḍ**	رضوض
burn	ḥarq	حرق
cut	qaṭ'	قطع
graze	sælkh	سلخ
insect bite	qarṣ **ḥ**ashara	قرص حشرة
lump	**wa**ram	ورم
rash	ṭafḥ **gil**dī	طفح جلدي
sting	**qar**ṣa	قرصة
swelling	**wa**ram	ورم
wound	gærḥ	جرح
Could you have a look at it?	**mom**kin **taf**ḥaṣ **hǣ**zæ	ممكن تفحص هذا؟
I can't move...	lǣ **yom**kin æ**ḥ**arrak	لا يمكن أحرك...
It hurts.	**hǣ**zæ yo'**li**monī	هذا يؤلمني.

أين الألم؟	Where does it hurt?
من أي ألم تعاني؟	What kind of pain is it?
دائم/ متردد/ ضعيف/حاد	dull/sharp/constant/on and off
هذا...	It's...
مكسور/مملوخ/مخلوع/ممزق	broken/sprained/dislocated/torn
يجب عمل أشعة.	I want you to have an X-ray.
يجب أن تضع جبس.	You'll have to have a plaster.
هذا ملوث.	It's infected.
هل تطعمت ضد التيتانوس من قبل؟	Have you been vaccinated against tetanus?
سأعطيك مطهر/مهدىء.	I'll give you an antiseptic/ a painkiller.

Symptoms أعراض

I'm not feeling well.	**ash**'or bi tæ'b	أشعر بتعب.
I feel...	**ash**'or bi	أشعر بـ...
dizzy/nauseous/ shivery	**dō**khæ/qi'/**ræ**'shæ	دوخة/قيء/رعشة
I've been vomiting.	tæqa**yæ't**	تقيأت.
I'm constipated.	**'indī** ims**ǣk**	عندي إمساك.
I've got diarrhoea.	**'indī** ish**ǣl**	عندي إسهال.
My... hurt(s).	**'indī** ælæm fī	عندي ألم في...
I have difficulties breathing.	**'indī** ṣo'ūba fil tænæffos	عندي صعوبة في التنفس.
I have a pain in my chest.	**'indī** ælæm fī **ṣadrī**	عندي ألم في صدري.
I had a heart attack ... years ago.	kǣn **'indī** **næw**bæ qal**biy**yæ min... sænæ**wǣt**	كان عندي نوبة قلبية من... سنوات.
My blood pressure is too high/too low.	dagṭ **dæm**mī **'ǣlī**/**wāṭi'**	ضغط دمي عالي/واطي.

Illness أمراض

I'm diabetic.	**'indī** æs-**sok**kar	عندي السكر.
I'm ill.	ænæ ma**rīḍ**	أنا مريض.
I've got a fever.	**'indī** ḥarāra	عندي حرارة.
My temperature is ... degrees.	ḥa**rār**tī... **daraga**	حرارتي... درجة.
I've got (a/an)...	**'indī**	عندي...
Have I got (a/an)...?	hæl **'indī**	هل عندي...؟
appendicitis	ilti**hǣb** æz-**zæy**dæ	التهاب الزايدة
asthma	**rabw**	ربو
backache	ælæm fil ẓahr	ألم في الظهر

cough	so'**ǣl**	سعال
cramps	taqallo**ṣāt**	تقلصات
cystitis	iltih**ǣb** æl-mæs**ǣ**næ	التهاب المثانة
dysentery	dusint**ǣ**riǣ	دوسنتاريا
earache	**æ**læm fil **o**zon	ألم في الأذن
flu	infil**wæ**nzæ	انفلونزا
food poisoning	tæ**sæm**mom giz**ǣ**'ī	تسمم غذائي
gastritis	ḥomūḍa fil **mi**'dæ	حموضة في المعدة
headache	ṣo**dā'**	صداع
indigestion	'osr haḍm	عسر هضم
inflammation of...	iltih**ǣb** fī	التهاب في ...
jaundice	iltih**ǣb** æl-**kæ**bid	التهاب الكبد
measles	**ḥaṣ**ba	حصبة
nosebleed	næ**zīf æn**fī	نزيف أنفي
palpitations	khafa**qān** æl-**qalb**	خفقان القلب
pneumonia	iltih**ǣb ri**'æwī	التهاب رئوي
rheumatism	rom**ǣtīsm**	روماتيزم
sore throat	**æ**læm fil zōr	ألم في الزور
stiff neck	**æ**læm fil **'o**noq	ألم في العنق
stomach ache	**æ**læm fil **mi**'dæ	ألم في المعدة
sunstroke	**ḍar**bit shæms	ضربة شمس
venereal disease	**ma**raḍ tæn**ǣ**solī	مرض تناسلي

Women's section خاص بالنساء

I have period pains.	**'in**dī **æ**læm æl-**'ǣ**dæ æsh-shæh**rī**yyæ	عندي ألم العادة الشهرية.
I have a vaginal infection.	**'in**dī tæ**læw**wos fil **mih**bal	عندي تلوث في المهبل.
I'm on the pill.	**æ**khod ḥo**būb** man' æl-**ḥæml**	أخذ حبوب منع الحمل.
I haven't had my period for...	in**qaṭ**'at æl-**'ǣ**dæ æsh-shæh**riy**yæ limod**dat**	انقطعت العادة الشهرية لمدة...
I'm (... months) pregnant.	**æ**næ **ḥǣ**mil (fī... ash**hōr**)	أنا حامل (في... أشهر).

منذ متى تعاني من هذا؟	How long have you been feeling like this?
هل هذه أول مرة تعاني من هذا؟	Is this the first time you've had this?
هل تتبرز بانتظام؟	Are you having regular bowel movements?
هل عندك غازات؟	Do you have wind?
سأقيس لك الحرارة/ ضغط الدم.	I'll take your temperature/ blood pressure.
إرفع كمك من فضلك.	Roll up your sleeve, please.
إخلع ملابسك (العليا).	Please undress (down to the waist).
تمدد هنا.	Please lie down over here.
أفتح فمك.	Open your mouth.
خذ نفس عميق.	Breathe deeply.
كح، من فضلك.	Cough, please.
أين مكان الألم؟	Where does it hurt?
عندك...	You've got (a/an)...
ليس هناك خطر.	It's nothing serious.
هذا (ليس) معدي.	It's (not) contagious.
سأعطيك حقنة.	I'll give you an injection.
أريد عينة من دمك/ براز/ بول.	I want a specimen of your blood/stools/urine.
يجب أن تلزم السرير لـ... يوم.	You must stay in bed for ... days.
أريد أن تعرض نفسك على أخصائي.	I want you to see a specialist.
أريد أن تذهب إلى المستشفى لعمل كشف عام.	I want you to go to the hospital for a general check-up.

Prescription—Treatment روشتة ـ علاج

This is my usual medicine.	**hǣ**zæ **ho**wæ dæ**wǣ**'ī æl-mo'**tǣd**	هذا هو دوائي المعتاد.
Can you give me a prescription for this?	o**rīd** ro**shet**tæ li **hǣ**zæ	أريد روشتة لهذا.
Can you prescribe a/an/some...?	min **faḍ**lak iktib**lī** dæ**wǣ'**	من فضلك اكتب لي دواء...
antidepressant	ḍidd æl-'ikti'**ǣb**	ضد الاكتئاب
sleeping pills	mo**næw**wim	منوم
tranquillizer	mo**hæd**di'	مهدىء
I'm allergic to antibiotics/penicillin.	'**in**dī ḥæsǣ**siy**yæ ḍidd æl-moḍad**dǣt** æl-ḥæyæ**wiy**yæ/æl-bensi**līn**	عندي حساسية ضد المضادات الحيوية/ البنسلين.
How many times a day should I take it?	kæm **mar**ra fil yōm **yæ**gib æn **a**khod **hǣ**zæ	كم مرة في اليوم يجب أن أخذ هذا؟
Must I swallow them whole?	hæl **æb**læ' **hǣ**zæ bil **kǣ**mil	هل أبلع هذا بالكامل؟

ما هو العلاج الذي تتبعه؟	What treatment are you having?
ما هي الأدوية التي تأخذها؟	What medicine are you taking?
عن طريق الحقن أم الفم؟	By injection or orally?
خذ... ملعقة صغيرة من هذا الدواء...	Take... teaspoons of this medicine...
خذ حبة مع كوب من الماء...	Take one pill with a glass of water...
كل... ساعات/ ... مرة في اليوم	every... hours/... times a day
قبل/بعد كل وجبة	before/after each meal
في الصباح/ في المساء	in the morning/at night
في حالة وجود ألم	if there is any pain
خلال... أيام	for... days

CHEMIST'S, see page 107

Fee الأتعاب

How much do I owe you?	kæm **yæ**gib æn **æd**fæ' læk	كم يجب أن أدفع لك؟
May I have a receipt for my health insurance?	o**rīd** īṣ**āl** li tæ'**mī**nī aṣ-**ṣih**ḥī	أريد ايصال لتأميني الصحي.
Can I have a medical certificate?	**mom**kin **æh**ṣol '**æ**læ shi**hǣ**dæ ṭib**biy**yæ	ممكن أحصل على شهادة طبية؟
Would you fill in this health insurance form, please?	min **faḍ**lak **im**læ' isti**mā**rat æt-tæ'**mīn** aṣ-**ṣih**ḥī	من فضلك إملا استمارة التأمين الصحي.

Hospital المستشفى

Please notify my family.	min **faḍ**lak **bæl**læg os**ra**tī	من فضلك بلغ أسرتي.
What are the visiting hours?	mǣ **hi**yæ mæwǣ'**īd** æz-zi**yā**ra	ما هي مواعيد الزيارة؟
When can I get up?	**mæ**tæ astati' æn **an**haḍ	متى استطيع أن أنهض؟
When will the doctor come?	**mæ**tæ sæyæ**morr** æd-dok**tōr**	متى سيمر الدكتور؟
I'm in pain.	**æ**næ '**in**dī **æ**læm	أنا عندي ألم.
I can't eat/sleep.	**æ**næ lǣ **aq**dar æ**kol**/æ**nǣm**	أنا لا أقدر أكل/أنام.
Where is the bell?	**æy**næ æl-**ga**ras	أين الجرس؟

nurse	moma**ri**ḍa	ممرضة
patient	ma**rīḍ**	مريض
anaesthesia	mo**khæd**dir	مخدر
blood transfusion	naql dæmm	نقل دم
injection	æl-**ḥaqn**	الحقن
operation	'æmæ**liy**yæ	عملية
bed/bedpan	si**rīr**/qaṣ**riy**yæ	سرير/قصرية
thermometer	tirmo**metr**	ترمومتر

Dentist طبيب أسنان

English	Transliteration	Arabic
Can you recommend a good dentist?	momkin tinṣaḥnī bi ṭabīb æsnæn kwæyyis	ممكن تنصحني بطبيب أسنان كويس.
Can I make an (urgent) appointment to see Dr....?	orīd mæw'id ('āgil) mæ'æ doktōr	أريد موعد (عاجل) مع دكتور...
Couldn't you make it earlier?	hæl yomkin æn yækūn æl-mæw'id qabl zǣlik	هل يمكن أن يكون الموعد قبل ذلك؟
I have a broken tooth.	'indī sinnæ maksūra	عندي سنة مكسورة.
I have a toothache.	'indī ælæm fī sinnitī	عندي ألم في سنتي.
I have an abscess.	'indī khorāg	عندي خراج.
This tooth hurts.	hǣzihi æs-sinnæ to'limonī	هذه السنة تؤلمني.
at the top	foq	فوق
at the bottom	tæḥt	تحت
at the front	fil æmǣm	في الأمام
at the back	fil khælf	في الخلف
Can you fix it temporarily?	momkin ti'ǣlighæ mowaqqatæn	ممكن تعالجها مؤقتاً؟
I don't want it taken out.	lǣ orīd khælæ'hæ	لا أريد خلعها.
Could you give me an anaesthetic?	momkin ta'ṭīnī mokhæddir	ممكن تعطيني مخدر؟
I've lost a filling.	fæqadt ḥæshw æs-sinnæ	فقدت حشو السنة.
The gum...	æl-lisæ	اللثة...
is very sore	mo'limæ	مؤلمة
is bleeding (heavily)	tænẓif (bi kæsra)	تنزف (بكثرة)
I've broken this denture.	kasart hǣzæl ṭaqm	كسرت هذا الطقم.
Can you repair this denture?	momkin iṣlāḥ hǣzæl ṭaqm	ممكن إصلاح هذا الطقم؟
When will it be ready?	mætæ yækūn gǣhiz	متى يكون جاهز؟

Reference section

Numbers الأرقام

Unlike the script, numbers are written from left to right. When referring to two of anything, the dual plural form is used, and the number two dispensed with (see p. 159).

0	٠	ṣifr	صفر
1	١	wǣḥid/wǣḥdæ	واحد/واحدة
2	٢	itnēn	اثنين
3	٣	tælǣtæ	ثلاثة
4	٤	arba'a	أربعة
5	٥	khæmsæ	خمسة
6	٦	sittæ	ستة
7	٧	sæbæ'	سبعة
8	٨	tæmǣnyæ	ثمانية
9	٩	tis'æ	تسعة
10	١٠	'ashara	عشرة
11	١١	ḥidāshar	حداشر
12	١٢	itnāshar	اثناشر
13	١٣	tælættāshar	تلتاشر
14	١٤	arba'atāshar	أربعتاشر
15	١٥	khæmæstāshar	خمستاشر
16	١٦	sittāshar	ستاشر
17	١٧	sæbæ'tāshar	سبعتاشر
18	١٨	tæmæntāshar	ثمنتاشر
19	١٩	tis'ætāshar	تسعتاشر
20	٢٠	'ishrīn	عشرين
21	٢١	wǣḥid wæ 'ishrīn	واحد وعشرين
22	٢٢	itnēn wæ 'ishrīn	اثنين وعشرين
23	٢٣	tælǣtæ wæ 'ishrīn	ثلاثة وعشرين
24	٢٤	arba'a wæ 'ishrīn	أربعة وعشرين
25	٢٥	khæmsæ wæ 'ishrīn	خمسة وعشرين
26	٢٦	sittæ wæ 'ishrīn	ستة وعشرين
27	٢٧	sæbæ'æ wæ 'ishrīn	سبعة وعشرين

28	٢٨	**tæmænyæ wæ 'ishrīn**	ثمانية وعشرين
29	٢٩	**tis'æ wæ 'ishrīn**	تسعة وعشرين
30	٣٠	**tælætīn**	ثلاثين
31	٣١	**wæḥid wæ tælætīn**	واحد وثلاثين
32	٣٢	**itnēn wæ tælætīn**	اثنين وثلاثين
40	٤٠	**arba'īn**	أربعين
50	٥٠	**khæmsīn**	خمسين
60	٦٠	**sittīn**	ستين
70	٧٠	**sæb'īn**	سبعين
80	٨٠	**tæmænīn**	ثمانين
90	٩٠	**tis'īn**	تسعين
100	١٠٠	**mīyæ**	مية
101	١٠١	**mīyæ wæ wæḥid**	مية وواحد
102	١٠٢	**mīyæ wæ itnēn**	مية واثنين
110	١١٠	**mīyæ wæ 'ashara**	مية وعشرة
120	١٢٠	**mīyæ wæ 'ishrīn**	مية وعشرين
150	١٥٠	**mīyæ wæ khæmsīn**	مية وخمسين
160	١٦٠	**mīyæ wæ sittīn**	مية وستين
170	١٧٠	**mīyæ wæ sæb'īn**	مية وسبعين
180	١٨٠	**mīyæ wæ tæmænīn**	مية وثمانين
190	١٩٠	**mīyæ wæ tis'īn**	مية وتسعين
200	٢٠٠	**mītēn**	متين
300	٣٠٠	**toltomīyæ**	تلتمية
400	٤٠٠	**rob'omīyæ**	ربعمية
500	٥٠٠	**khomsomīyæ**	خمسمية
600	٦٠٠	**sittomīyæ**	ستمية
700	٧٠٠	**sob'omīyæ**	سبعمية
800	٨٠٠	**tomnomīyæ**	تمنمية
900	٩٠٠	**tos'omīyæ**	تسعمية
1000	١٠٠٠	**ælf**	ألف
2000	٢٠٠٠	**ælfēn**	ألفين
5000	٥٠٠٠	**khæmsæt ælæf**	خمسة آلاف
10,000	١٠ ٠٠٠	**'asharat ælæf**	عشرة آلاف
100,000	١٠٠ ٠٠٠	**mīt ælf**	ميت ألف
1,000,000	١ ٠٠٠ ٠٠٠	**milyōn**	مليون

first	æwwæl/ūlæ	أول/أولى
second	tǣnī	ثاني
third	tǣlit	ثالث
fourth	rābi'	رابع
fifth	khǣmis	خامس
sixth	sǣdis	سادس
seventh	sǣbi'	سابع
eighth	tǣmin	ثامن
ninth	tǣsi'	تاسع
tenth	'ǣshir	عاشر
once/twice	marra/marratēn	مرة/مرتين
three times	tælǣt marrāt	ثلاث مرات
a half/half (adj.)	niṣf	نصف
half a.../half of...	niṣf	نصف...
a quarter/one third	rob'/tilt	ربع/تلت
a pair of	zōg min	زوج من
a dozen	dæstæ	دستة
one per cent	wǣḥid fil mīyæ	واحد في المية
3%	tælǣtæ fil mīyæ	٣٪
1981	ælf tos'omīyæ wǣḥid wæ tæmænīn	ألف تسعمية واحد وثمانين
1992	ælf tos'omīyæ itnēn wæ tis'īn	ألف تسعمية اثنين وتسعين
2003	ælfēn wæ tælǣtæ	ألفين وثلاثة

Seasons فصول السنة

spring/summer	rabī'/ṣēf	ربيع/صيف
autumn/winter	khærīf/shitǣ'	خريف/شتاء
in spring	fil rabī'	في الربيع
during the summer	æsnæ' aṣ-ṣēf	أثناء الصيف
high season/in season	fil mūsim	في الموسم
low season/off season	khǣrig æl-mūsim	خارج الموسم

Year and age السنة والعمر

year	**sæ**næ	سنة
leap year	**sæ**næ kæ**bī**sæ	سنة كبيسة
decade	'aqd	عقد
century	qarn	قرن
this year	hǣ**zi**hil **sæ**næ	هذه السنة
each year	koll **sæ**næ	كل سنة
last year	æs-**sæ**næ æl-mā**ḍi**yya	السنة الماضية
next year	æs-**sæ**næ æl-qā**di**mæ	السنة القادمة
2 years ago	min sænæ**tēn**	من سنتين
in one year	bæ'd **sæ**næ	بعد سنة
How old are you?	kæm **'om**rak	كم عمرك؟
I'm... years old.	**'om**rī... **sæ**næ	عمري... سنة.
He was born in...	**how**æ **wu**lidæ **sæ**næt	هو ولد سنة...
She was born in...	**hi**yæ **wu**lidæt **sæ**næt	هي ولدت سنة...
What's his/her age?	mæ 'omroho/'om**ro**hæ	ما عمره/عمرها؟

Months الشهور

January	yæ**nǣ**yir [kǣ**nūn** æt-**tǣ**nī]	يناير [كانون الثاني]
February	fib**rā**yir [sha**bāṭ**]	فبراير [شباط]
March	**mǣ**ris [a**zār**]	مارس [أذار]
April	æb**rīl** [ni**sǣn**]	ابريل [نيسان]
May	**mæ**yo [ay**yār**]	مايو [أيار]
June	**yon**yo [hozæy**rān**]	يونيو [حزيران]
July	**yol**yo [tæm**mūz**]	يوليو [تموز]
August	a**gos**ṭos [æb]	أغسطس [أب]
September	sib**tæm**bir [æy**lūl**]	سبتمبر [أيلول]
October	ok**tō**bar [tish**rīn** æl-**æ**wwæl]	أكتوبر [تشرين الأول]
November	no**væm**bir [tish**rīn** æt-**tǣ**nī]	نوفمبر [تشرين الثاني]
December	di**sæm**bir [kǣ**nūn** æl-**æ**wwæl]	ديسمبر [كانون الأول]

in September	fī sibt**æ**mbir [æy**lūl**]	في سبتمبر [أيلول]
since...	**mon**zo	منذ...
the beginning of...	**æw**wæl	أول...
the middle of...	**wa**saṭ	وسط...
the end of...	**æ**khir	أخر...

Public holidays الإجازات الرسمية

Two kinds of calendar are in use in the Middle East. The Gregorian calendar—used in the West—is current in normal daily activities. Official documents and certain public holidays follow the Islamic lunar calendar, while newspapers cite both. The lunar calendar begins with the Hegira, or emigration of the Prophet Muhammad from Mecca to Medina in A.D. 622. The lunar year has twelve months of 29 or 30 days, and thus is approximately 10 days shorter than the Gregorian or solar year.

The names of the hegira months are:

rægæb	رجب	mo**ḥar**ram	محرم
shæ'**bæn**	شعبان	**ṣa**far	صفر
rama**ḍān**	رمضان	ra**bī**' æl-**æw**wæl	ربيع الأول
shæw**wæl**	شوال	ra**bī**' æt-**tæ**nī	ربيع الثاني
zūl **qi**'dæ	ذو القعدة	gæ**mæ**dæ æl-**æw**wæl	جمادي الأول
zūl **ḥig**gæ	ذو الحجة	gæ**mæ**dæ æt-tæny	جمادي الثاني

Given below are the most important Muslim holidays.

1st mo**ḥar**ram	Hegira or Muslim New Year's Day ('īd ra's æs-**sæ**næ æl-ḥig**riy**yæ)
12th ra**bī**' æl-**æw**wæl	Birth of the Prophet Muhammad (**mū**lid æn-**na**bī)
1st to 3rd shæw**wæl**	Ramadan Baïram ('īd æl-**fiṭr**) celebrating the end of the holy month of Ramadan (see page 35).
9th to 13th zūl **ḥig**gæ	Kurban Baïram ('īd æl-aḍ**ḥā**) celebrating God's mercy towards Abraham in sparing his son; this is the period during which Muslims make a pilgrimage to Mecca.

Secular holidays follow the Gregorian calendar and vary from country to country. A few important ones are:

1st January	New Year's Day (ra's æs-**sæ**næ), celebrated in places where there is Western influence. It is not an official holiday everywhere.
1st May	Labour Day ('īd æl-'**omǣl**), a holiday in many Middle Eastern countries.
movable dates	Spring Festival (shæmm æn-ni**sīm**), celebrated in Egypt on Coptic Easter Monday.

Christian holidays are observed officially in countries where there are large Christian communities. The Coptic Christmas and Easter are celebrated regionally in Egypt, but like the Eastern Orthodox holidays, they fall about two weeks later than their Western equivalents.

7th January	Coptic Christmas ('īd æl-mi**lǣd**—literally the Feast of the Birth)
movable dates	Coptic Easter ('īd æl-qi**yǣ**ma—Feast of the Resurrection).

Greetings and wishes التحيات والتمنيات

There is no direct equivalent to certain Western greetings like Merry Christmas and Happy Easter. However, there is a general greeting "koll **sæ**næ wæ **in**tæ ṭayyib" that can be used on the above occasions as well as on birthdays and during Ramadan and other festivals.

Happy birthday!	'īd mī**lǣd** sæ'**īd**	عيد ميلاد سعيد!
Best wishes!	**a**ṭyab æt-tæmæni**yǣt**	أطيب التمنيات!
Congratulations!	tæ**hǣ**nī	تهاني!
Good luck/ All the best!	ḥaẓẓ sæ'**īd**	حظ سعيد!
Have a good trip!	**ri**ḥlæ sæ'īdæ	رحلة سعيدة!
Have a good holiday!	æ**gǣ**zæ sæ'īdæ	إجازة سعيدة!
Best regards from...	æl-**mokh**liṣ	المخلص...
My regards to...	tæḥi**yǣ**tī ilæ	تحياتي إلى...

Days and Date أيام وتاريخ

What date is it today?	**mǣ tærīkh** æl-**yōm**	ما تاريخ اليوم؟
July 1	**æw**wæl **yol**yo [tæm**mūz**]	أول يوليو [تموز]
May 4th	**arba'**a min **mæ**yo [ay**yār**]	أربعة من مايو [أيار]
What day is it today?	æyy yōm æl-**yōm**	أي يوم اليوم؟
Sunday	(yōm) æl-**æ**ḥæd	(يوم) الأحد
Monday	(yōm) æl-it**nēn**	(يوم) الإثنين
Tuesday	(yōm) æl-tæ**lǣt**	(يوم) الثلاث
Wednesday	(yōm) æl-**arba**'a	(يوم) الأربع
Thursday	(yōm) æl-khæ**mīs**	(يوم) الخميس
Friday	(yōm) æl-**gom**'æ	(يوم) الجمعة
Saturday	(yōm) æs-**sæbt**	(يوم) السبت
in the morning	fil ṣa**bāḥ**	في الصباح
in the afternoon	bæ'd aẓ-**ẓohr**	بعد الظهر
in the evening	fil mæ**sǣ'**	في المساء
at night	fil **lēl**	في الليل
yesterday	æms	أمس
today	æl-**yōm**	اليوم
tonight	æl-**læy**læ	الليلة
tomorrow	**gæ**dæn	غداً
the day before	æl-**yōm** æs-**sǣ**biq	اليوم السابق
two days ago	min yo**mēn**	من يومين
in three days' time	bæ'd **tæ**læt æy**yǣm**	بعد ثلاثة أيام
last week	æl-os**bū'** æl-**mā**ḍī	الأسبوع الماضي
next week	æl-os**bū'** æl-**qā**dim	الأسبوع القادم
a fortnight (two weeks)	osbū'**ēn**	أسبوعين
birthday	'īd mī**lǣd**	عيد ميلاد
day off	yōm æ**gǣ**zæ	يوم إجازة
holiday	æl-æ**gǣ**zæ	الإجازة
holidays/vacation	æ**gǣ**zæ	إجازة
week	os**bū'**	أسبوع
weekend	ni**hǣ**yæt æl-os**bū'**	نهاية الأسبوع
working day	yōm **'æ**mæl	يوم عمل

What time is it? الساعة كم؟

Excuse me. Can you tell me the time?	**'æf**wæn. æs-**sǣ**'æ kæm	عفواً. الساعة كم؟
It's one o'clock	æs-**sǣ**'æ **wæḥ**dæ	الساعة واحدة.
It's...	æs-**sǣ**'æ	الساعة...
five past...	... wæ **khæm**sæ *	... وخمسة
ten past...	... wæ **'a**shara	... وعشرة
a quarter past...	... wæ rob'	... وربع
twenty past...	... wæ tilt	... وتلت
twenty-five past...	... wæ niṣf **il**læ **khæm**sæ	... ونصف إلا خمسة
half past...	... wæ niṣf	... ونصف
twenty-five to...	... wæ niṣf wæ **khæm**sæ	... ونصف وخمسة
twenty to...	... **il**læ tilt	... إلا تلت
a quarter to...	... **il**læ rob'	... إلا ربع
ten to...	... **il**læ **'a**shara	... إلا عشرة
five to...	... **il**læ **khæm**sæ	... إلا خمسة
12 o'clock (noon/ midnight)	it**nā**shar (**ẓoh**ran/monta**ṣ**af æl-lēl)	اثناشر (ظهراً / منتصف الليل)
in the morning	fil ṣa**bāḥ**	في الصباح
in the afternoon	bæ'd aẓ-**ẓohr**	بعد الظهر
in the evening	fil mæ**sæ'**	في المساء
The train leaves at...	æl-qi**ṭār** yæ**qum** æl-	القطار يقوم الـ...
13.04 (1.04 p.m.)	**wæḥ**dæ wæ ar**ba'** da**qā**'iq bæ'd aẓ-**ẓohr**	واحدة وأربع دقائق بعد الظهر
0.40 (0.40 a.m.)	**wæḥ**dæ **il**læ tilt ṣa**bā**ḥan	واحدة إلا تلت صباحاً
hour/minute/second	**sǣ**'æ/da**qī**qa/**sæn**yæ	ساعة/دقيقة/ثانية
quarter of an hour	rob' **sǣ**'æ	ربع ساعة
half an hour	niṣf **sǣ**'æ	نصف ساعة
The clock is fast/ slow.	æs-**sǣ**'æ mo**qad**dimæ/ mo'**ækh**khira	الساعة مقدمة/ مؤخرة.

* in ordinary conversation, time is expressed as shown here. However, official time uses a 24-hour clock which means that afternoon hours are counted from 13 to 24.

Countries البلاد

Africa	æ**frī**qyæ	أفريقيا
Asia	**æ**syǣ	أسيا
Australia	ost**rā**lyǣ	أستراليا
Europe	o**rob**ba	أوروبا
North America	æm**rī**kæ æsh-shæ**mǣ**liyyæ	أمريكا الشمالية
South America	æm**rī**kæ æl-gænū**biy**yæ	أمريكا الجنوبية
Algeria	æl-gæ**zǣ**'ir	الجزائر
Canada	**kæ**nædæ	كندا
Egypt	miṣr	مصر
England	ingil**tē**ra	إنجلترا
France	fa**ran**sa	فرنسا
Great Britain	brī**ṭān**yā	بريطانيا
Greece	æl-yo**nǣn**	اليونان
India	æl-**hind**	الهند
Iraq	æl-'i**rāq**	العراق
Ireland	ir**læn**dæ	ايرلندة
Italy	i**ṭā**lyā	إيطاليا
Jordan	æl-**or**don	الأردن
Lebanon	lib**nǣn**	لبنان
Libya	**lī**byǣ	ليبيا
Middle East	æsh-**sharq** æl-**aw**saṭ	الشرق الأوسط
Morocco	æl-**mæg**rib	المغرب
New Zealand	nyu zī**læn**dæ	نيوزيلندة
Saudi Arabia	æs-sa'**udiy**yæ	السعودية
Scotland	skot**læn**dæ	سكوتلندة
South Africa	gæ**nūb** æf**rī**qyæ	جنوب أفريقيا
Soviet Union	**rō**syǣ	روسيا
Soudan	æs-sū**dǣn**	السودان
Syria	**so**ryæ	سوريا
Tunisia	**tū**nis	تونس
Turkey	tor**ki**yæ	تركيا
United States	æl-wilǣ**yǣt** æl-mot**tæ**ḥidæ	الولايات المتحدة
Wales	wīlz	ويلز

Emergency الطوارىء

DANGER	**kha**ṭar	خطر
FIRE	ḥæ**rīq**	حريق
Gas	gǣz	غاز
Get a doctor	**o**ṭlob dok**tōr**	أطلب دكتور
Go away	**im**shi	إمشي
HELP	æn-**næg**dæ	النجدة
Get help quickly	**o**ṭlob æn-**næg**dæ bi**sor**'æ	أطلب النجدة بسرعة
I'm ill	ænæ ma**rīḍ**	أنا مريض
I'm lost	ænæ toht	أنا تهت
Leave me alone	it**rok**nī fī **ḥǣ**lī	اتركني في حالي
LOOK OUT	iḥ**tæ**ris	إحترس
Poison	simm	سم
POLICE	bō**līs**	بوليس
STOP THIEF	**im**sik ḥa**rā**mī	إمسك حرامي
Call the...	**o**ṭlob æl-	أطلب الـ...
(American) consulate	qonṣo**ley**yæ (æmrī**kiy**yæ)	قنصلية (أمريكية)
(Canadian) embassy	si**fā**ra (kænæ**diy**yæ)	سفارة (كندية)
police	bō**līs**	بوليس

Lost! المفقودات

Where's the...?	**æy**næ	أين...؟
lost property (lost and found) office?	**mæk**tæb æl-mæfqū**dǣt**	مكتب المفقودات
police station	qism æl-bō**līs**	قسم البوليس
I want to report a theft.	o**rīd** tæ**b**lig 'æn **sir**qa	أريد تبليغ عن سرقة.
My... has been stolen.	... **so**riqat	... سرقت.
I've lost my...	fæ**qadt**	فقدت...
handbag	**shan**ṭit **yæ**dī	شنطة يدي
passport	gæ**wǣz sa**farī	جواز سفري
wallet	maḥ**faẓ**tī	محفظتي

CAR ACCIDENTS, see page 78

Conversion tables جدول التحويل

Kilometres into miles

1 kilometre (km.) = 0.62 miles

km.	10	20	30	40	50	60	70	80	90	100	110	120	130
miles	6	12	19	25	31	37	44	50	56	62	68	75	81

Miles into kilometres

1 mile = 1.609 kilometres (km.)

miles	10	20	30	40	50	60	70	80	90	100
km.	16	32	48	64	80	97	113	129	145	161

Fluid measures

1 litre (l.) = 0.88 imp. quart or 1.06 U.S. quart

1 imp. quart = 1.14 l. 1 U.S. quart = 0.95 l.
1 imp. gallon = 4.55 l. 1 U.S. gallon = 3.8 l.

litres	5	10	15	20	25	30	35	40	45	50
imp. gal.	1.1	2.2	3.3	4.4	5.5	6.6	7.7	8.8	9.9	11.0
U.S. gal.	1.3	2.6	3.9	5.2	6.5	7.8	9.1	10.4	11.7	13.0

Weights and measures

1 kilogram or kilo (kg.) = 1000 grams (g.)

100 g. = 3.5 oz. ½ kg. = 1.1 lb.
200 g. = 7.0 oz. 1 kg. = 2.2 lb.

1 oz. = 28.35 g.
1 lb. = 453.60 g.

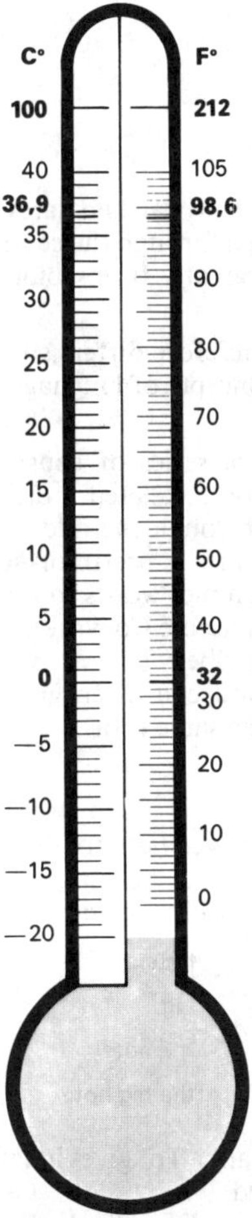

Centimetres and inches

To change centimetres into inches, multiply by .39.

To change inches into centimetres, multiply by 2.54.

	in.	feet	yards
1 mm.	0.039	0.003	0.001
1 cm.	0.39	0.03	0.01
1 dm.	3.94	0.32	0.10
1 m.	39.40	3.28	1.09

	mm.	cm.	m.
1 in.	25.4	2.54	0.025
1 ft.	304.8	30.48	0.305
1 yd.	914.4	91.44	0.914

(32 metres = 35 yards)

Temperature

To convert centigrade into degrees Fahrenheit, multiply centigrade by 1.8 and add 32.

To convert degrees Fahrenheit into centigrade, subtract 32 from Fahrenheit and divide by 1.8.

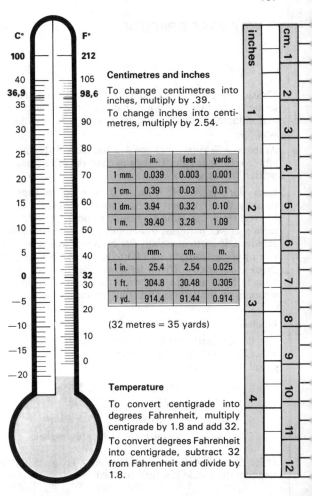

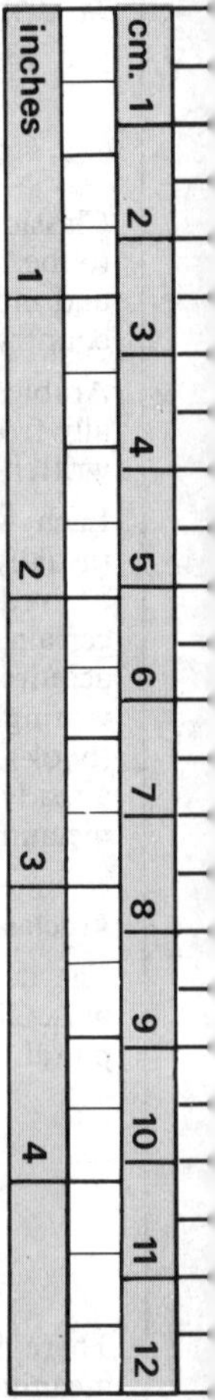

A very basic grammar

Classical Arabic is the language of the Koran and dates back to the 7th century. But it has changed through the centuries, and modern spoken Arabic varies greatly from country to country.

Arabic is a Semitic language and therefore differs structurally from English and European concepts of language. It is written from right to left.

Each word in Arabic is based on a series of consonants (usually three) known as the "root". Related words are derived from the same root and, through the addition of certain vowel patterns, and sometimes a prefix or suffix, acquire a specific meaning. For example, words to do with writing come from the root **k t b**: **kæ**tæbæ (to write), ki**tǣb** (book), **mæk**tæb (office), **kǣ**tib (scribe). Thus, if you are already familiar with one word, you can often guess the meaning of another derived from the same root.

Articles

The definite article (the) in Arabic is الـ **(æl)** for both the masculine and feminine genders, and the singular and plural. It precedes the noun and generally the adjective.

فندق	**fondoq**	hotel
كبير	kæ**bīr**	big
الفندق	æl-**fondoq**	the hotel
الفندق الكبير	æl-**fondoq** æl-kæ**bīr**	the big hotel

There is no indefinite article (a/an). To give indefinite meaning the article is simply omitted.

Nouns

There are two genders, masculine and feminine. In general words ending in **æ** or **a** are feminine. The names of towns and countries are nearly always feminine.

	Masculine			Feminine	
طالب	ṭālib	student (m.)	طالبة	ṭālibæ	student (f.)
شارع	shæri'	street	وردة	wærdæ	flower
مطعم	maṭ'am	restaurant	فرنسا	faransa	France

There are two sorts of plurals in Arabic: one for two things (dual), and another for three or more. Basically, to form the dual add the ending ين **(ēn)** to a singular masculine noun, or تين **(tēn)** to a feminine noun. To make the plural for three or more, add the ending ين **(īn)** to singular masculine nouns and ات **(æt** or **āt)** to feminine nouns. There are, however, numerous exceptions and irregular plurals where the word changes, like the English "child" to "children". Here are a few examples:

Regular

فنان	fænn**æn**	an artist	شجرة	**sha**gara	a tree
فنانين	fænnæ**nēn**	two artists	شجرتين	shagar**tēn**	two trees
فنانين	fænnæ**nīn**	artists	شجرات	shaga**rāt**	trees

Irregular

ولد	**wæ**læd	a boy	تذكرة	taz**ka**ra	ticket
ولدين	wælæ**dēn**	two boys	تذكرتين	tazkar**tēn**	two tickets
أولاد	æw**læd**	boys	تذاكر	ta**zæ**kir	tickets

Adjectives

Adjectives do not come before the noun as in English, but afterwards. They agree with the noun in gender and number. Don't forget that when there is a definite article in front of the noun, the adjective must also be preceded by the definite article. However, the verb "to be" doesn't exist in the present tense in Arabic. In order to describe something, just put the noun with the definite article, and then the adjective without the article.

البيت الكبير	æl-**bēt** æl-kæ**bīr**	the big house
البيت كبير.	æl-**bēt** æl-kæ**bīr**	The house is big.

When an adjective qualifies a plural noun that is not human, the adjective is put in the feminine singular.

شجرة كبيرة	**sha**gara kæ**bī**ræ	a big tree
شجرات كبيرة	shaga**rāt** kæ**bī**ræ	big trees

There are no possessive adjectives; instead a suffix is added to the noun. Here are the suffixes for masculine nouns (for feminine nouns insert the letter **t** shown in parentheses):

my	...ي	...(t)ī	our	...نا	...(t)næ
your (m.)	...ك	...(t)æk			
your (f.)	...ك	...(t)ik	your (pl.)	...كم	...(t)kom
his/its	...ـه	...(t)oh			
her/its	...ـها	...(t)hæ	their	...ـهم	...(t)hom

Adding a possessive pronoun suffix to a noun makes it definite, and therefore if an adjective follows, the adjective must have the definite article.

كتاب كبير	ki**tǣb** kæ**bīr**	a big book
كتابي الكبير	ki**tǣ**bī æl-kæ**bīr**	my big book

Verbs

One particularity of Arabic verbs is that they change not only according to the subject (I, you, he, etc.), but also according to whether a man or a woman is spoken to. You'll find examples of this in the sections "Some basic expressions" (pages 11–16) and "Making friends" (pages 92–96). In Arabic the verb "to be" does not exist in the present tense (see above); "to have" is rendered by the preposition **to** عند ('ind) plus a personal pronoun suffix, e.g. عنده(**inda**-ho—literally "to him") means "he has".

The following is the past and present conjugation of the verb "to write". Note that the subject pronoun is normally omitted.

	Present tense	Past tense
I	أكتب **æk**tob	كتبت kæ**tæb**to
you (m.)	تكتب **tæk**tob	كتبت kæ**tæb**tæ
you (f.)	تكتبي tæk**to**bi	كتبتي kæ**tæb**tī
he/it	يكتب **yæk**tob	كتب **kæ**tæbæ
she/it	تكتب **tæk**tob	كتبت **kæ**tæbæt
we	نكتب **næk**tob	كتبنا kæ**tæb**næ
you	تكتبوا tæk**to**bū	كتبتوا kæ**tæb**tū
they	يكتبوا yæk**to**bū	كتبوا **kæ**tæbū

To form the future tense, add the prefix سـ (**sæ**) to the present tense.

When you want to make a negative sentence, put لا (**læ**) in front of the verb.

أنا أكتب.	ænæ **æk**tob	I write.
أنا لا أكتب.	ænæ læ **æk**tob	I don't write.

To ask a question, simply put هل (**hæl**) at the beginning of the sentence:

البيت كبير.	æl-**bēt** kæ**bīr**	The house is big.
هل البيت كبير؟	hæl æl-**bēt** kæ**bīr**	Is the house big?

Personal pronouns

I	انا **æ**næ	we	نحن **næḥ**no
you (m.)	انت **in**tæ		
you (f.)	انت **in**tī	you	انتم **in**tom
he/it	هو **ho**wæ		
she/it	هي **hi**yæ	they	هم hom

DICTIONARY

Dictionary
and alphabetical index

English—Arabic

f feminine *m* masculine *pl* plural *dl* du

able, to be ممكن **mom**kin 14
about *(approximately)* حوالي ḥæ**wæ**lī 31
above فوق foq 16, 63
abscess خراج kho**rāg** *m* 145
absorbent cotton قطن طبي qoṭn **ṭib**bī *m* 108
accept, to قبل **qa**bala 61,103
accident حادث **hæ**dis *m* 79, 138
account حساب ḥi**sæb** *m* 130
ache ألم ælæm *m* 141
adaptor محول mo**ḥæw**wil *m* 118
additional زيادة zi**yæ**da 24, 27
address عنوان 'in**wæn** *m* 21, 31, 76, 79, 103
address book دفتر عناوين **daf**tar 'ænæ**wīn** *m* 105
adhesive tape ورق لزق **wa**raq læzq *m* 105
admission دخول do**khūl** *m* 82, 90
adult كبير kæ**bīr** *m* 82
after بعد bæ'd 16, 77
afternoon بعد الظهر bæ'd aẓ-**ẓohr** 152, 153
after-shave lotion لوسيون بعد الحلاقة los**yōn** bæ'd æl-ḥi**læ**qa *m* 109
again مرة ثانية **mar**ra **tæn**yæ 96, 135
age عمر 'omr *m* 149
air conditioning تكييف هواء tæk**yīf** **hæ**wæ' *m* 23, 28
air mail بريد جوي bæ**rīd** **gæw**wī *m* 133
airplane طائرة **ṭā**'ira *f* 65
airport مطار ma**ṭār** *m* 21, 65
alarm clock منبه mi**næb**bih *m* 120
alcohol كحول ko**ḥol** *m* 38
alcoholic كحولية koḥo**liy**yæ 58
Alexandria أسكندرية iskændæ**rī**yæ *f* 70, 72
all كل koll 104
allergic (to) حساسية (ضد) ḥæsæ**siy**yæ (ḍidd) 143
almond لوزة **lō**zæ *f* 63
alphabet حروف ḥo**rūf** *m/pl* 10
also أيضاً **ay**ḍan 16
ambulance سيارة إسعاف sæy**yā**rit is'**æf** *f* 79
American أمريكي æm**rī**kī 93, 106, 125, 155
amount مبلغ **mæb**læg *m* 61, 131
amplifier مكبر صوت mo**kæb**bir ṣawt *m* 118
anaesthetic مخدر mo**khæd**dir *m* 144, 145
analgesic مسكن mo**sæk**kin *m* 108
and و wæ 16
animal حيوان ḥæyæ**wæn** *m* 86
ankle كعب القدم kæ'b æl-qa**dæm** *m* 137
another تاني **tæ**nī 57, 122
answer جواب gæ**wæb** *m* 13
antibiotic مضاد حيوي mo**ḍādd** **ḥæ**yæv *m* 143
antidepressant دواء ضد الاكتئاب dæ**wæ'** ḍidd æl-ikti'**æb** *m* 143
antique أنتيكة æn**tī**kæ *f* 84, 126
antique shop محل أنتيكات mæ**ḥæll** æntī**kæt** *m* 99
antiseptic مطهر mo**ṭah**hir 108
any أي æyy 16
anyone أحد **æ**ḥæd 13
anything شيء she' 18, 25, 102, 112
appendicitis إلتهاب الزائدة ilti**hæb** æz-**zæy**dæ *m* 140
appendix الزائدة æz-**zæy**dæ *f* 137
appetizer فاتح شهية [مزه] **fæ**tiḥ shæ**hiy**yæ *m* [**mæz**zæ *f*] 41, 42
apple تفاحة tof**fæ**ḥæ *f* 54, 119
appliance أداة æ**dæt** *f* 118

قاموس

appointment موعد **mæw**'id *m* 30, 131, 136, 145
apricot مشمش **mish**mish *m* 54
Arabic عربي '**a**rabī 13, 105, 127
archaeology آثار **asār** *m* 84
architect مهندس mo**hæn**dis *m* 83
area code رقم مفتاح **ra**qam mof**tāḥ** *m* 134
arm ذراع zi**rā'** *m* 137
arrival وصول wi**ṣūl** *m* 17, 65
arrive, to وصل **wa**ṣala 65, 70, 71, 130
art فن fænn *m* 84
artery شريان shir**yæn** *m* 137
art gallery معرض فنون **ma**'raḍ fo**nūn** *m* 81
artichoke خرشوف khar**shūf** *m* 42, 50
artificial صناعي ṣi**nā**'ī 38, 123
artist فنان fæ**næn** *m* 83
ashtray طفاية سجائر ṭaf**fā**yit sæ**gæ**yir *f* 27, 37
ask, to طلب **ṭa**laba 25, 60, 135
aspirin أسبرين aspi**rīn** *m* 108
asthma ربو rabw *m* 140
astringent مزيل للوجه mo**zīl** lil wægh *m* 109
at عند '**in**dæ 16
at least على الأقل '**æ**læl a**qall** 24
at once فورا **faw**ran 31
aubergine باذنجان bitin**gæn** *m* 42, 43, 50
aunt عمة '**æm**mæ *f* 93
automatic أوتوماتيك oto**mæ**tik 20, 123
autumn خريف khæ**rīf** *m* 148

B

baby طفل ṭifl *m* 24, 110
baby food غذاء الطفل gi**zæ'** aṭ-**ṭifl** *m* 110
babysitter حارسة أطفال **ḥæ**risæt aṭ**fāl** *f* 27
back *(body)* ظهر ẓahr *m* 137
back خلف khælf 30, 145
backache ألم في الظهر **æ**læm fil ẓahr *m* 140
backgammon طاولة **ṭaw**la *f* 62, 128
bacon بيكون **bæy**kon *m* 39
bad سيء **sæy**yi' 15, 95
bag كيس kīs *m* 104
baggage حقائب ḥa**qā**'ib *f/pl* 18, 21, 26, 31, 67, 74
baggage cart عربة حقائب '**a**rabit ḥa**qā**'ib *f* 18
baggage check مكتب أمانات **mæk**tæb æmæ**næt** *m* 18, 69, 74
baker's مخبز **mækh**bæz *m* 99
balcony بلكونة bæl**kō**næ *f* 23
ball *(sport)* كرة **ko**ra *f* 128
ball-point pen قلم حبر جاف **qa**læm ḥibr gæf *m* 105
banana موزة **mō**zæ *f* 54, 64
bandage رباط ro**bāṭ** *m* 108
Band-Aid بلاستر **blā**star *m* 108
bank *(finance)* بنك bænk *m* 99, 129
banknote ورقة **wa**raqa *f* 130
bar بار bār *m* 69; *(chocolate)* باكو **bæ**kō *m* 64
barber's صالون حلاقة ṣa**lōn** ḥi**læ**qa *m* 30, 99
basketball باسكيت [سلة] **bas**kēt *m* [**sæl**læ *f*] 90
bath حمام ḥæm**mæm** *m* 23, 25
bathing cap بونيه للبحر **bo**neh lil baḥr *m* 127
bathing hut كابينة لخلع الملابس kæ**bī**næ li khæl' æl-mæ**læ**bis *f* 91
bathrobe برنس **bor**nos *m* 115
bathroom حمام ḥæm**mæm** *m* 27
bath towel فوطة للحمام **fū**ṭa lil ḥæm**mæm** *f* 27
battery بطارية baṭṭā**riy**ya *f* 75, 78, 118, 120, 124
bazaar سوق [بازار] sūq *m* [ba**zār** *m*] 81, 99
be, to 159, 160
beach شاطىء **shā**ṭi' *m* 91
bean لوبية **lob**yæ *f* 52
beard ذقن zæqn *m* 31
beautiful جميل gæ**mīl** 15, 84
beauty salon صالون تجميل ṣa**lōn** tæg**mīl** *m* 30, 99
bed سرير si**rīr** *m* 24, 144
bedpan قصرية qaṣ**riy**yæ *f* 144
beef (لحم) بقري (læḥm) **ba**qarī *m* 47
beefsteak بوفتيك bof**tek** *m* 47
beer بيرة **bī**ra *f* 41, 57
before قبل qabl 16, 29; سابق **sæ**biq 152

DICTIONARY قاموس

begin, to بدأ **bædæ'æ** 80, 88, 89
behind وراء **warā'** 16, 77
Beirut بيروت **bæyrūt** *f* 65
bell *(electric)* جرس **garas** *m* 144
bellboy خادم فندق **khædim fondoq** *m* 26
belly-dancer رقصة شرقية **raqṣæ sharqiyya** *f* 89
below تحت **tæḥt** 16, 63
belt حزام **ḥizæm** *m* 116
berth سرير **sirīr** *m* 72, 73
better أحسن **æḥsæn** 15, 25, 102, 113
between بين **bēn** 16
beverage مشروب **mæshrūb** *m* 57, 58, 60
bicycle [بسكليتة] عجلة **'ægælæ** *f* [bisiklēttæ *f*] 74
big كبير **kæbir** 15, 25, 102
bill حساب **ḥisæb** *m* 31, 61, 103; *(banknote)* ورقة **waraqa** *f* 130
binoculars نظارة معظمة **naẓẓāra mo'aẓẓama** *f* 122
bird طير **ṭīr** *m* 86
birth ميلاد **mīlæd** *m* 25
birthday عيد ميلاد **'īd mīlæd** *m* 151, 152
biscuit *(Br.)* بسكوت **bæskot** *m* 64
bite *(insect)* قرصة **qarṣa** *f* 107, 139
bitter مُر **morr** 60
black أسود **æswæd** 112, 117
bladder مثانة **mæsænæ** *f* 137
blade موس **mūs** *m* 109
blanket بطانية **baṭṭaniyya** *f* 27
bleach إزالة لون **izælit lōn** *f* 30
bleed, to نظف **næzæfæ** 138, 145
blind *(window)* ستارة معدنية **sitāra mæ'dæniyyæ** *f* 29
blister كيس ماء **kīs mæ'** *m* 139
blood دم **dæmm** *m* 140, 142
blood pressure ضغط دم **ḍagṭ dæmm** *m* 140
blood transfusion نقل دم **naql dæmm** *m* 144
blouse [قميص حريمي] بلوزة **blōsæ** *f* [qæmīṣ ḥærīmī *m*] 115
blow-dry تنشيف **tænshīf** *m* 30
blue أزرق **æzraq** 112
blusher بودرة للتجميل **bodra lil tægmīl** *f* 109

boarding house بنسيون **bænsyōn** *m* 19, 22
boat مركب **mærkib** *m* 68
body جسم **gism** *m* 137
boil خراج **khorāg** *m* 139
bone عظم **'aẓm** *m* 137
book كتاب **kitæb** *m* 13, 105
booking office مكتب حجز **mæktæb ḥægz** *m* 19, 69
bookshop مكتبة **mæktæbæ** *f* 99, 105
boot بوت **būt** *m* 117
born, to be وُلد **wulidæ** 149
bottle زجاجة **zogægæ** *f* 18, 57, 58, 59
bottle-opener فتاحة زجاجات **fættæḥit zogægæt** *f* 128
bottom تحت **tæḥt** 145
bowels أحشاء **æḥshæ'** *f/pl* 137
box علبة **'ilba** *f* 119
boxing بوكس **bōx** *m* 90
boy ولد **wælæd** *m* 111
boyfriend صديق **ṣadīq** *m* 93
bra سوتيانة **sutyænæ** *f* 115
bracelet غويشة **gwēshæ** *f* 120
braces *(suspenders)* حمالات **ḥæmmælæt** *f/pl* 115
brain مخ **mokhkh** *m* 47
brakes فرامل **farāmil** *f/pl* 78
brake fluid زيت فرامل **zēt farāmil** *m* 75
brandy كونياك **konyæk** *m* 58
brassware مصنوعات نحاس أصفر **maṣnū'āt niḥæs aṣfar** *f/pl* 126
bread خبز **khobz** *m* 37, 39, 53, 64, 119
break, to كسر **kasara** 29, 118, 122, 138, 145
break down, to عَطل **'aṭala** 78
breakdown عُطل **'oṭl** *m* 78
breakdown van سيارة نجدة **sæyyārit nægdæ** *f* 78
breakfast فطار **fiṭār** *m* 24, 34, 39
breast ثدي **sædy** *m* 137; صدر **ṣidr** *m* 47, 49
breathe, to تنفس **tænæffæsæ** 140
bridge [جسر] كوبري **kobrī** *m* [zhisr *m*] 86
briefs سليب **slib** *m* 115
bring, to أحضر **aḥḍara** 14
British بريطاني **briṭānī** 93

broken مكسور maksūr 29, 118, 122, 138, 145
brooch بروش brōsh *m* 120
brother أخ ækh *m* 93
brown بني bonnī 112
bruise رضة raḍḍa *f* 139
brush فرشة forshæ *f* 110
buckle توكة tōkæ *f* 116
build, to بَنى bænǣ 83
building مبنى mæbnǣ *m* 81, 83
bulb لمبة lamba *f* 28, 75, 118
burn حرق ḥarq *m* 139
burn out, to *(bulb)* حرق ḥaraqa 28
bus أوتوبيس otobīs *m* 18, 19, 65, 66, 67, 80
business شغل shogl *m* 17
business district حي أعمال تجارية ḥæyy æ'æmǣl togǣriyyæ *m* 81
business trip رحلة شغل rihlæt shogl *f* 93
bus stop محطة أوتوبيس maḥaṭṭit otobīs *f* 66, 67
busy مشغول mæshgūl 96
but لكن lækin 16, 96
butane gas أنبوبة غاز anbūbit gǣz *f* 32
butcher's جزار [لحام] gazzār *m* [læhḥǣm *m*] 99
butter زبدة zibdæ *f* 37, 39, 64, 119
button زرار zorār *m* 29, 116
buy, to اشترى ishtara 67, 71, 101, 122

C

cabana كابينة لخلع ملابس kæbīnæ li khæl' mælǣbis *f* 91
cabin *(ship)* كابينة kæbīnæ *f* 68
cable تلغراف tiligrāf *m* 133
cable release مفتاح التصوير العالي moftǣḥ æt-taṣwīr æl-'ǣlī *m* 124
café قهوة qahwa *f* 33
Cairo القاهرة æl-qāhira *f* 65, 134
cake كيك kēk *m* 38, 55, 64
cake snop محل حلويات mæḥæll ḥælæwiyyǣt *m* 99
calculator آلة حاسبة ælæ ḥæsbæ *f* 106
calendar نتيجة nætīgæ *f* 105
call *(phone)* مكالمة mokælmæ *f* 134, 135
call, to *(give name)* سمى sæmmǣ 13; *(phone)* إتصل ittaṣala 135; *(summon)* طلب ṭalaba 79, 155
camel جمل gæmæl *m* 74
camel-hair وبر جمل wabar gæmæl *m* 113
camera كاميرا kǣmira *f* 123, 124
camera shop محل كاميرات mæḥæll kæmirāt *m* 99
camp, to عسكر 'askara 32
campbed سرير سفر sirīr safar *m* 32
camping معسكر mo'askar *m* 32
can *(of olives)* علبة 'ilbæ *f* 119
can *(to be able)* ممكن momkin 14
Canadian كندي kænædī 93, 155
canal قنال qanǣl *m* 86
cancel, to ألغى ælgā 65
candy بونبوني bonbōnī *m* 125
can opener فتاحة علب fættǣḥit 'ilæb *f* 128
cap كاسكيتة kæskittæ *f* 115
capital *(finance)* رأس المال ræ's æl-mǣl *m* 131
car سيارة sæyyāra *f* 19, 20, 26, 32, 75, 76, 78
carat قيراط qīrāṭ *m* 120
caravan كاراڤان karavan *m* 32
caraway كمون kæmūn *m* 52
carbon paper ورق كربون waraq karbōn *m* 105
carburet(t)or كاربيراتور karbīratōr *m* 78
card كارت kært *m* 78
card game كوتشينه kotshīnæ *f* 128
car hire تأجير سيارات tæ'gīr sæyyārāt *m* 19, 20
car park موقف سيارات mawqif sæyyārāt *m* 77
carpet سجادة sæggǣdæ *f* 126
car rental تأجير سيارات tæ'gīr sæyyārāt *m* 19, 20
carrot جزر gazar *m* 50
carry, to حمل ḥæmælæ 21
cartridge *(camera)* كارتردج kartridzh *m* 123
case *(cigarettes)* علبة 'ilba *f* 120; *(camera)* شنطة shanṭa *f* 124
cash, to صرف ṣarafa 130, 133
cash desk خزينة khæzīnæ *f* 104
cassette كاسيت kæsset *m* 127
castle قصر qaṣr *m* 81

catacomb سرداب موتى sir**dæb mæw**tæ *m* 81
catalogue كتالوج kætæl**ōg** *m* 83
Catholic كاثوليكي kæsol**ī**kī 85
caution إحترس iḥtæris 155
cemetery مدافن mæ**dæ**fin *m/pl* 81
centimetre سنتيمتر santi**metr** *m* 114
centre وسط wasṭ *m* 19, 21
century قرن qarn *m* 149
ceramics فخار fokh**khār** *m* 84, 126
certificate شهادة shi**hæ**dæ *f* 144
chain *(jewellery)* سلسلة sil**si**læ *f* 120
chair كرسي **kor**sī *m* 32
change *(money)* فكه **fæk**kæ *f* 77, 130; باقي **bā**qī *m* 61
change, to غير **gay**yara 60, 65, 66, 70, 75, 122; *(money)* حول **ḥæw**wælæ 18, 129
chapel كنيسة kæ**nī**sæ *f* 81
charcoal فحم fæḥm *m* 32
charge حساب ḥi**sæb** *m* 20, 28, 32, 77, 90, 135
charge, to حسب **ḥæ**sæbæ 24, 130
chauffeur سائق **sæ**'iq *m* 20
cheap رخيص ra**khīṣ** 15, 24, 25, 102
check شيك shīk *m* 131; *(restaurant)* حساب ḥi**sæb** *m* 61
check, to [على] كشف **kæ**shæfæ ['ælæ] 75, 122; *(luggage)* سجل **sæ**gælæ 74
check in, to *(airport)* تسجل tæ**sæg**gælæ 65
check-in *(airport)* تسجيل tæs**gīl** *m* 65
check out, to رحل **ra**ḥælæ 31
checkup *(medical)* كشف kæshf *m* 142
cheese جبنة **gib**næ *f* 41, 44, 64, 119
chemist's [فرماسية] أجزخانه ægzæ**khæ**næ *f* [færmæ**si**yyæ *f*] 99, 107
cheque شيك shīk *m* 131
chess *(set)* شطرنج sha**ṭa**rang *m* 128
chest صدر ṣadr *m* 137, 140
chewing gum [لبانة] مستيكه mæs**tī**kæ *f* [li**bæ**næ *f*] 125
chicken [فروج] فرخة **fær**khæ *f* [far**rūzh** *m*] 41, 49, 64
child طفل ṭifl *m* 24, 60, 82, 93, 111
children's doctor دكتور أطفال dok**tōr** aṭ**fāl** *m* 136
chips بطاطس محمرة ba**ṭā**ṭis mo**ḥam**mara *m/pl* 64; *(Am.)* شبس shebs *m/pl* 64
chocolate شوكولاته shoko**lā**ta *f* 39, 64, 119, 125
chop [كوستاليته] رياش ri**yæsh** *m* [kostæ**let**tæ *f*] 47
church كنيسة kæ**nī**sæ *f* 81, 85
cigar سيجار si**gār** *m* 125
cigarette سيجارة si**gā**ra *f* 18, 95, 125
cigarette case علبة سجاير **'il**bit sæ**gæ**yi... *f* 120
cigarette holder [مبسم] فم سجاير fomm sæ**gæ**yir *m* [**mæb**sæm *m*] 125
cigarette lighter ولاعة wæl**læ**'æ *f* 120
cine camera كاميرا سينما **kæ**mira **sī**nimæ *f* 123
cinema سينما **sī**nimæ *f* 87, 96
cinnamon قرفة **qir**fæ *f* 52
citadel قلعة **qal**'æ *f* 81
city بلد **bæ**læd *f* 81
city centre وسط البلد wasṭ æl-**bæ**læd *m* 81
city wall سور المدينة sūr æl-mæ**dī**næ *m* 81
classical كلاسيك **klæ**sik 127
clean نظيف na**ẓīf** 60
clean, to نظف **naẓ**ẓafa 29, 76
cleansing cream كريم للتنظيف krem lil tan**ẓīf** *m* 109
clock ساعة **sæ**'æ *f* 120, 153
close *(near)* قريب qa**rīb** 16, 19, 32, 85
close, to قفل **qæ**fælæ 12, 82, 98, 107, 1...
closed مقفول mæq**fūl** 15, 98
cloth قماش qo**mæsh** *m* 117
clothes ملابس mæ**læ**bis *f/pl* 29, 115
clothing ملبس **mæl**bæs *m* 111
clothing store محل ملابس mæ**ḥæll** mæ**læ**bis *m* 99
club نادي **næ**dī *m* 90; مضرب **ma**ḍrab *m* 90
coach *(bus)* أوتوبيس oto**bīs** *m* 66
coat بالطو bal**ṭō** *m* 88, 115
coffee قهوة **qah**wa *f* 39, 62
coffee service طقم قهوة ṭaqm **qah**wa *m* 126
coin عملة **'om**læ *f* 84; *(small change)* فكة **fæk**kæ *f* 130, 134

old بارد **bæ**rid 15, 25, 39, 41, 60; *(weather)* برد bærd 94
old *(illness)* زكام zo**kæ**m *m* 107
ollar ياقة **yæ**qa *f* 116
ollective taxi تاكسي مشترك **tæ**ksī mosh**ta**rak *m* 21, 67
olour لون lōn *m* 111, 123, 124
olour chart دفتر للألوان **daf**tar lil æl**wæ**n *m* 30
olourfast لون ثابت lōn **sæ**bit 112
olour rinse صبغة خفيفة **ṣab**ga khæfīfæ *f* 30
omb مشط mishṭ *m* 110
ome, to أتى æ**tæ** 36, 92, 95, 136
ommission عمولة 'o**mū**læ *f* 130
ompact disc إسطوانة كومباكت isṭiwāna kom**pakt** *f* 127
mpartment مقصورة maq**ṣū**ra *f* 73
mpass برجل **bær**gæl *m* 128
mplaint شكوى **shæk**wæ *f* 60
ncert حفلة موسيقية **ḥæf**læ mosī**qiy**yæ *f* 89
ncert hall قاعة موسيقى **qā**'æt mosīqa *f* 81, 89
ndom كابوت إنجليزي kæb**būt** ingi**lī**zī *m* 108
nfirm, to أكد **æk**kædæ 65
nfirmation تأكيد tæ'**kīd** *m* 23
ngratulations تهاني tæ**hæ**nī *f/pl* 151
nnection *(train)* مواصلة mo**wā**ṣla *f* 65, 70
nstipation إمساك im**sæk** *m* 140
nsulate قنصلية qonṣo**ley**yæ *f* 155
ntact lens عدسة لاصقة **'æ**dæsæ **lā**ṣiqa *f* 122
ntagious معدي **mu**'dī 142
ntraceptive عازل **'æ**zil *m* 108
ntract عقد 'aqd *m* 131
nvent دير dīr *m* 81
okie بيتي فور bi**tī** fōr *m/pl* 64
pper نحاس ni**ḥæs** *m* 126
pperware مصنوعات نحاس maṣnū'**āt** ni**ḥæs** *f/pl* 126
optic قبطي **qop**ṭī 84
ral مرجان mor**gæn** *m* 121
rkscrew بريمة لفتح الزجاجات bær**rī**mæ li fæth æz-zogæ**gæt** *f* 128
rn *(Am.)* ذرة **do**ra *m* 50

corner ركن rokn *m* 36; *(street)* ناصية **nā**ṣiya *f* 21, 77
corn plaster بلاستر للكالو **blās**tar lil **kal**lō *m* 108
cosmetics أدوات تجميل ædæ**wæt** tæg**mīl** *f/pl* 109
cost سعر si'r *m* 131
cot سرير أطفال si**rīr** aṭ**fāl** *m* 24
cotton قطن qoṭn *m* 112, 113
cotton wool قطن طبي qoṭn **ṭib**bī *m* 108
cough سعال so'**æl** *m* 107, 141
cough, to سعل **sa**'ala 142
cough drops أقراص للسعال aq**rāṣ** lil so'**æl** *m/pl* 108
counter شباك shib**bæk** *m* 132, 133
country بلد **bæ**læd *f* 92
countryside ريف rīf *m* 85
cousin ابن عم ibn 'æmm *m* 93; بنت عم bint 'æmm *f* 93
crab كابوريا kæ**bor**yæ *f* 46
cracker بسكوت مالح bæs**kōt** **mæ**liḥ *m* 64
cramp تقلص ta**qal**loṣ *m* 141
crayon قلم ألوان **qa**læm æl**wæn** *m* 105
cream كريم krem *m* 109; كريمة **krē**mæ *f* 55
crease resistant غير محتاج لمكوى gēr miḥ**tæg** li **mæk**wæ 112
credit card كارت مصرفي kært maṣ**ra**fī *m* 20, 31, 61, 103, 130
crib سرير أطفال si**rīr** aṭ**fāl** *m* 24
crisps شبس shebs *m/pl* 64
crossroads تقاطع ta**qā**ṭo' *m* 77
cruise جولة **gæw**læ *f* 68
cucumber خيار khi**yār** *m* 50
cuff link زرار قمصان zo**rār** qom**ṣān** *m* 120
cup فنجان fin**gæn** *m* 37, 62
currency عملة 'om**læ** *f* 129
currency exchange office مكتب تحويل **mæk**tæb tæḥ**wīl** *m* 18, 129
current تيار tay**yār** *m* 91
curtain ستارة si**tā**ra *f* 28
curve *(road)* منحنى mon**ḥæ**næ *m* 79
customs جمرك **gom**rok *m* 17, 103
customs declaration إستمارة جمرك isti**mā**rit **gom**rok *f* 132
cut *(wound)* قطع qaṭ' *m* 139

cut, to *(hair)* قص **qaṣṣa** 30
cuticle remover مزيل لجلد الأظافر **mozīl** li gild aẓāfir *m* 109
cutlery فضية للأكل **faḍḍiyyæ** lil ækl *f* 120
cystitis إلتهاب المثانة **iltihæb** æl-mæsænæ *m* 141

D

dagger خنجر **khangar** *m* 126
dairy محل ألبان **mæḥæll** æl**bæn** *m* 99
dam سد sæd *m* 81
Damascus دمشق di**mishq** *f* 70
dance, to رقص **raqaṣa** 89
dancing رقص raqṣ *m* 96
danger خطر **khaṭar** *m* 155
dangerous خطير **khaṭīr** 91
dark ضلمه **ḍal**ma 25; *(colour)* غامق **gæ**miq 57, 102, 111, 112, 125
date *(day)* تاريخ **tæ**rīkh *m* 25, 152; *(appointment)* موعد **mæw**'id *m* 95; *(fruit)* بلح **bæ**læḥ *m* 54
daughter بنت **bint** *f* 93, 138
day يوم yōm *m* 17, 20, 24, 32, 80, 90, 94, 143, 152
daylight ضوء النهار ḍo' æn-na**hār** *m* 123
decaffeinated بدون كافيين bidūn kæfæ**yīn** 39
decision قرار qa**rār** *m* 25, 103
deck *(ship)* ظهر الباخرة ẓahr æl-**bæ**khira *m* 68
deck chair كرسي بلاج قماش **korsī** blæzh qo**mæsh** *m* 91
declare, to *(customs)* أعْلَن **æ'**lænæ 17, 18
deep عميق 'æ**mīq** 142
degree *(temperature)* درجة **da**raga *f* 140
delay تأخير tæ'**khīr** *m* 71
delicious عظيم 'a**ẓīm** 61
deliver, to وصل **waṣṣ**ala 103
delivery تسليم tæs**līm** *m* 103
dentist طبيب أسنان ṭa**bīb** æs**næn** *m* 99, 145
denture طقم ṭaqm *m* 145
deodorant مزيل لرائحة العرق mo**zīl** li ra'i**ḥæt** æl-'æraq *m* 109
department قسم qism *m* 84, 101, 111
department store محل تجاري mæ**ḥæll** to**gæ**rī *m* 99
departure رحيل ræ**ḥīl** *m* 65
deposit ضمان ḍa**mān** *m* 20
desert صحراء **ṣa**ḥarā' *f* 86
dessert تحالي tæ**ḥæ**lī *m* 38, 41, 55
develop, to حمض **ḥam**maḍa 123
diabetic السكر æs-**sok**kar 140
diabetic مريض السكر ma**rīḍ** æs-**sok**kar *m* 38
dial, to إتصل it**ta**ṣala 134
dialling code رقم مفتاح **ra**qam mof**tæḥ** *m* 134
diaper تغييرة الطفل tægyī**rāt** aṭ-**ṭifl** *f* 110
diarrhoea إسهال is**hæl** *m* 140
dictionary قاموس qā**mūs** *m* 105
diesel ديزل **dī**zel *m* 75
diet رجيم ri**zhīm** *m* 38
difficult صعب ṣa'b 15
difficulty صعوبة ṣo'**ū**ba *f* 28, 103, 140
digital رقمي **ra**qamī 121
dine, to تعشى tæ'**æsh**shæ 94
dining car عربة طعام '**a**rabit ṭa'**ām** *f* 71
dining room صالة طعام **ṣā**lit ṭa'**ām** *f* 27
dinner عشاء 'æ**shæ'** *m* 34
direct مباشر mo**bæ**shir 65
direct to, وصف **wa**ṣafa 14
direction إتجاه itti**gæh** *m* 76
disabled عاجز '**æ**giz *m* 83
disc film فيلم ديسك film disk *m* 123
discotheque مرقص [ديسكو] **mar**qaṣ *m* [**dis**kō *m*] 89
discount تخفيض takh**fīḍ** *m* 131
disease مرض **ma**raḍ *m* 141
dish أكلة **æ**klæ *f* 37, 38, 41; طبق **ṭa**baq *m* 41
disinfectant مطهر mo**ṭah**hir *m* 108
dislocated مخلوع mækh**lū'** 139
dizzy بدوخه bi **dō**khæ 140
doctor دكتور dok**tōr** *m* 79, 136, 144, 155
doll عروسه 'a**rū**sa *f* 128
dollar دولار dō**lār** *m* 18, 103, 129
donkey حمار ḥo**mār** *m* 74
double bed سرير كبير si**rīr** kæ**bīr** *m* 23
double room غرفة لشخصين **gor**fa li shakh**ṣēn** *f* 19, 23
down/downstairs تحت **tæḥt** 16

downtown وسط البلد waṣt æl-**bæ**læd 81
dozen دسته **dæs**tæ *f* 148
drawing paper ورق رسم **wa**raq ræsm *m* 105
drawing pin دبوس رسم dæb**būs** ræsm *m* 105
dress فستان fos**tæn** *m* 115
dressing gown روب rōb *m* 115
dressmaker خياط khay**yāṭ** *m* 99
drink مشروب mæsh**rūb** *m* 41, 60, 94
drink, to شرب **sha**raba 37, 38
drinking water ماء شرب mæ' shorb *m* 32
drip, to *(tap)* سرب **sæ**riba 28
drive, to ساق **sæ**qa 21, 76
driving licence رخصة قيادة **rokh**ṣit qi**yæ**dæ *f* 20, 79
drugstore أجزخانه [فرماسية] æqzæ**khæ**næ *f* [færmæ**siy**yæ *f*] 99, 107
dry جاف gæf 30, 110; *(wine)* سك sek 58
dry cleaner's محل تنظيف ملابس mæ**ḥæll** tan**ẓīf** mæ**læ**bis *m* 29, 99
duck بط baṭṭ *m* 49
dummy بزازة bæz**zæ**zæ *f* 110
during أثناء æs**næ'** 16, 148
duty *(customs)* رسوم ri**sūm** *m/pl* 17
duty-free shop سوق حرة sūq **ḥor**ra *f* 19
dye صبغة **ṣab**ga *f* 30, 110
dysentery دوسنتاريا dusin**tæ**riæ *f* 141

E

each كل koll 149
ear أذن **o**zon *f* 137
earache ألم في الأذن **æ**læm fil **o**zon *m* 141
ear drops قطرة للأذن **qaṭ**ra lil **o**zon *f* 108
early مبكر mo**bæk**kir 16, 31
earring حلق **ḥæ**læq *m* 120
east شرق sharq *m* 77
easy سهل sæhl 15
eat, to أكل **æ**kælæ 37, 38, 144
egg بيضة **bē**ḍa *f* 39, 41, 44, 119
eggplant باذنجان bitin**gæn** *m* 50
Egyptian مصرى **mas**rī 18
elastic مطاط maṭ**ṭāṭ** 108
elastic bandage رباط مطاط ro**bāṭ** maṭ**ṭāṭ** *m* 108
Elastoplast بلاستر **blās**tar *m* 108
electric كهربائي kahra**bā'**ī 118
electrician كهربائي kahra**bā'**ī *m* 99
electricity كهرباء kahra**bā'** *f* 32
electronic إليكتروني elek**trō**nī 128
elevator مصعد **maṣ**'ad *m* 27, 101
embassy سفارة si**fā**ra *f* 155
emergency طوارىء ṭa**wā**ri' *m/pl* 155
emergency exit مخرج طوارىء **makh**rag ṭa**wā**ri' *m* 27
empty فاضي **fā**ḍī 15
end آخر **æ**khir *m* 150; نهاية ni**hæ**yæ *f* 71
engine *(car)* موتور mō**tōr** *m* 78
English إنجليزي ingi**lī**zī 13, 80, 83, 85, 93, 105, 106, 125, 136
enjoy, to عجب **'æ**gæbæ 61
enjoy oneself, to انبسط in**ba**saṭa 96
enlarge, to كبر **kæb**bæra 124
enough يكفي **yæk**fī 16, 119
enquiries إستعلامات isti'læ**mæt** *f/pl* 70
entrance دخول do**khūl** *m* 69, 82, 100
envelope ظرف ẓarf *m* 27, 105
equipment أدوات ædæ**wæt** *f/pl* 127
eraser أستيكه [ممحاه] æs**tī**kæ *f* [mim**ḥæh** *f*] 105
escalator سلم كهربائي **sel**lem kahra**bā'**ī *m* 101
estimate *(cost)* سعر تقريبي si'r taq**rī**bī *m* 131
evening مساء mæ**sæ'** *m* 11, 88, 94, 96, 152, 153; سهرة **sæh**ra *f* 95, 96
evening dress لبس سهرة libs **sæh**ra *m* 89; *(woman's)* فستان للسهرة fos**tæn** lil **sæh**ra *m* 115
everything كل شيء koll she' 31, 61
examine, to فحص **fa**ḥasa 139
excavations تنقيب عن آثار tan**qīb** 'æn a**sār** *m* 86
exchange, to غير **gay**yara 104
exchange rate سعر تحويل si'r tæḥ**wīl** *m* 18, 130
excluding بدون bi**dūn** 24
excursion جولة سياحية **gæw**læ siyæ**ḥiy**yæ *f* 80
excuse, to سامح **sæ**mæḥæ 11

exhaust pipe ماسورة عادم [شكمان] mæsūrit 'ædim *f* [shækmæn *m*] 78
exhibition معرض ma'raḍ *m* 81
exit خروج khorūg *m* 69, 100
expect, to إنتظر intaẓara 130
expenses مصاريف maṣārīf *m/pl* 131
expensive غالي gæli 15, 19, 24, 102
exposure *(photography)* صورة ṣūra *f* 123
exposure counter عداد الصور 'æddæd aṣ-ṣowar *m* 124
express *(mail)* مستعجل mostæ'gil 133
expression تعبير tæ'bīr *m* 11
expressway أوتوستراد ōtōstrād *m* 76
external خارج khærig 108
extra *(additional)* زيادة ziyædæ 24, 27
eye عين 'æyn *f* 137, 138
eyebrow pencil قلم كحل qalæm koḥl *m* 109
eye drops قطرة للعيون qaṭra lil 'oyūn *f* 108
eyeliner قلم للعيون qalæm lil 'oyūn *m* 109
eye shadow ظل للعيون ẓill lil 'oyūn *m* 109
eyesight نظر naẓar *m* 122
eye specialist دكتور عيون doktōr 'oyūn *m* 136

F

fabric *(cloth)* قماش qomæsh *m* 112
face وجه wægh *m* 137
face pack شد للوجه shædd lil wægh *m* 30
face powder بودرة للوجه bodra lil wægh *f* 109
factory مصنع maṣna' *m* 81
fair أرض معرض arḍ ma'riḍ *f* 81
fall *(autumn)* خريف khærīf *m* 148
fall, to سقط saqaṭa 138
family أسرة osra *f* 93, 144
fan مروحة marwaḥa *f* 28
fan belt سير مروحة sīr marwaḥa *m* 76
far بعيد bæ'īd 16, 101
fare ثمن tæmæn *m* 66, 70
farm عزبة 'izbæ *f* 86
fat *(food)* دهن dohn *m* 38
father والد wælid *m* 93
faucet حنفية ḥænæfiyyæ *f* 28
fee *(doctor)* أتعاب æt'æb *f/pl* 144
feeding bottle زجاجة أكل zogægit ækl 110
feel, to *(physical state)* شعر sha'ara 14
felt-tip pen قلم فوتر qalæm fotr *m* 106
ferry معدية mæ'diyyæ *f* 68
fever حرارة ḥarāra *f* 140
few قليل qalīl 16; *(a)* بعض ba'ḍ 16, 17, 24
field حقل ḥaql *m* 86
fig تين tīn *m* 54
file *(tool)* مبرد mabrad *m* 109
filigree مشغولات mæshgūlæt *f/pl* 126
fill in, to ملأ mælæ'æ 25, 130, 144
filling *(tooth)* حشو سنة ḥæshw sinnæ *m* 145
filling station محطة بنزين maḥaṭṭit bænzīn *f* 75
film فيلم film *m* 87, 123, 124
film winder مفتاح لف الفيلم moftæḥ læff æl-film *m* 124
filter فلتر filtar *m* 124, 125
filter-tipped بفلتر bi filtar 125
find, to وجد wægædæ 12, 76, 101
fine *(ok)* كويس kwæyyis 12, 25, 92
fine arts الفنون الجميلة æl-fonūn æl-gæmīlæ *m/pl* 84
finger أصبع asba' *m* 137
finish, to أنتهى intæhæ 88
fire حريق ḥæriq *m* 155
first أول æwwæl 66, 70, 92, 148
first-aid kit علبة إسعافات أولية 'ilbit is'æfæt æwwæliyyæ *f* 108
first class درجة أولى daraga ūlæ *f* 72
first name إسم ism *m* 25
fish سمك sæmæk *m* 41, 46
fishing صيد السمك ṣēd æs-sæmæk *m*
fishmonger's محل سمك mæḥæll sæmæk *m* 99
fitting room كابينة قياس kæbīnæt qiyæ *f* 114
fix, to صلح ṣallaḥa 75; *(treat)* عالج 'ælægæ 145
flash *(photography)* فلاش flæsh *m* 124
flash attachment تثبيت الفلاش tasbīt æl-flæsh *m* 124
flashlight بطارية جيب baṭṭāriyyit gēb *f* 1

flat *(apartment)* شقة shaqa *f* 22
flat tyre عجلة مفرقعة 'ægælæ mofarqa'a *f* 75, 78
flight رحلة riḥlæ *f* 65
floor طابق ṭābiq *m* 27
floor show عرض فني 'arḍ fænnī *m* 89
florist's محل زهور mæḥæll zohūr *m* 99
flour دقيق dæqīq *m* 38
flower وردة wærdæ *f* 86
flu أنفلونزا infilwænzæ *f* 141
fluid سائل sǣ'il *m* 122
folk art فن شعبي fænn shæ'bī *m* 84
folk music موسيقى شعبية mosīqa shæ'biyyæ *f* 127
follow, to تبع tæbæ'æ 77
food أكل ækl *m* 38, 60
food poisoning تسمم غذائي tæsæmmom gizǣ'ī *m* 141
foot قدم qadæm *m* 137
football كرة قدم korat qadæm *f* 90
foot cream كريم للقدم krem lil qadæm *m* 109
for لـ li 16; خلال khilǣl 143
foreign أجنبي ægnæbī 57
forget, to نسي næsiyæ 60
fork شوكة shōkæ *f* 37, 60
form *(document)* إستمارة istimāra *f* 130, 133, 144
fortnight أسبوعين osbū'ēn *m/dl* 152
fortress حصن ḥiṣn *m* 81
foundation cream كريم أساسي krem æsǣsī *m* 109
fountain نافورة nāfūra *f* 81
fountain pen قلم حبر qalæm ḥibr *m* 105
fowl طيور ṭoyūr *m/pl* 49
frame *(glasses)* شنبر shambar *m* 122
free *(vacant)* خالي khǣlīy 15; فاضي fāḍī 73, 96
French فرنسي fransī 41
French bean فاصوليا خضراء fǣṣolyæ khaḍra' *f* 50
french fries بطاطس محمرة baṭāṭis moḥammara *m/pl* 64
fresh طازة ṭāza 53, 54, 60
Friday (يوم) الجمعة (yōm) æl-gom'æ *m* 29, 82, 152
fried مقلي maqlī 39, 46, 48, 51
friend صديق ṣadīq *m* 95
from من min 16, 92
front أمام æmǣm *m* 71, 75, 145
fruit فاكهة fǣkihæ *f* 41, 54
fruit juice عصير فاكهة 'aṣīr fǣkihæ *m* 38 39
fruit salad سلطة فواكه salaṭit fæwǣkih *f* 55
frying pan طاسة ṭāsa *f* 128
full مليان mælyǣn 15
furrier's محل فرو mæḥæll farw *m* 99

G

game لعبة li'bæ *f* 128; *(food)* صيد (لحم) (læḥm) ṣēd *m* 41, 49
garage جاراج gærāzh *m* 26, 78
gardens حدائق ḥædǣ'iq *f/pl* 81
garlic ثوم tōm *m* 52
garment ملبس mælbæs *m* 126
gas جاز gǣz *m* 155
gasoline بنزين bænzīn *m* 75, 78
gastritis حموضة في المعدة ḥomūḍa fil mi'dæ *f* 141
gauze شاش shǣsh *m* 108
gem حجر كريم ḥagar kærīm *m* 120
general عام 'ǣm 27, 101, 136
general delivery مكتب تسليم الخطابات mæktæb tæslīm æl-khiṭābāt *m* 133
general practitioner دكتور عام doktōr 'ǣm *m* 136
genitals أعضاء التناسل a'ḍā' æt-tænǣsol *f/pl* 137
gentleman رجل ragol *m* 111
genuine طبيعي ṭabī'ī 117
geology جيولوجيا zhiyolozhyæ *f* 84
get, to *(find)* وجد wægædæ 12, 19, 21, 31; *(call)* طلب ṭalaba 136, 155; *(obtain)* حصل ḥaṣala 90, 107
get off, to نزل næzælæ 67
get to, to ذهب إلى dæhæbæ ilæ 19
get up, to نهض nahaḍa 144
gherkin مخلل mikhælil *m* 64
gift *(present)* هدية hideyyæ *f* 17
gin جين zhin *m* 58
girl بنت bint *f* 111
girlfriend صديقة ṣadīqa *f* 93, 95
give, to أعطى a'ṭā 14, 63, 64, 75, 122, 130, 131, 135
gland غدة goddæ *f* 137

glass زجاج zog**æ**g *m* 121, 126; *(drinking)* كباية kobb**æ**yæ *f* 37, 58, 59, 60
glasses [عوينات] نظارة naẓẓ**ā**ra *f* ['owæyn**æ**t *f/pl*] 122
glove [كف] جوانتي gow**æ**ntī *m* [kæff *m*] 115
glue صمغ ṣamg *m* 105
go, to ذهب z**æ**hæbæ 96
go away, to مشى **mæ**sh**æ** 155
gold ذهب z**æ**hæb *m* 120, 121
golden ذهبي z**æ**hæbī 112
gold-plated مذهب moz**æ**hhæb 121
golf جولف gōlf *m* 90
golf course أرض جولف arḍ gōlf *f* 90
good كويس **kwæyy**is 15, 36, 101, 102
good-bye مع السلامة **mæ**'æs sæ**læ**mæ 12
goods بضائع baḍ**ā**i' *f/pl* 17
goose أوز wizz *m* 49
go out, to خرج **kharagæ** 96
gram جرام grām *m* 119
grammar نحو næḥw *m* 158
grammar book كتاب نحو kit**æ**b næḥw *m* 106
grape عنب 'inæb *m* 54, 64
grapefruit جريب فروت grēb frūt *m* 39, 54
gray رمادي ram**ā**dī 112
graze سلخ sælkh *m* 139
greasy دهني **doh**nī 30, 110
great *(excellent)* عظيم 'a**ẓī**m 95
green أخضر **akh**ḍar 112
green bean فاصوليا خضراء fæṣoly**æ** khaḍra' *f* 50
greengrocer's محل الخضار mæ**ḥæ**ll æl-khoḍ**ā**r *m* 99
greeting تحية tæ**ḥiy**yæ *f* 11, 151
grey رمادى ram**ā**dī 112
grilled مشوي **mæsh**wı 41, 46, 48, 51
grocer's محل بقالة mæ**ḥæ**ll biq**ā**læ *m* 99
group مجموعة mæg**mū**'æ *f* 83
guide مرشد **mor**shid *m* 80
guidebook دليل سياحي dæ**līl** si**yæ**ḥī *m* 83, 105, 106
gum *(teeth)* لثة **lis**æ *f* 145
gynaecologist دكتور أمراض نساء **dok**tōr amr**ā**ḍ nis**æ**' *m* 136

H
hair شعر sha'r *m* 30, 110
hairbrush فرشة للشعر **for**shæ lil sha'r 110
haircut قص الشعر qaṣṣ ash-**sha'r** *m* 30
hairdresser's صالون حلاقة ṣal**ō**n ḥil**æ**qa *m* 27, 30, 99
hair dryer سيشوار sish**wā**r *m* 118
hairgrip بنسه **bin**sæ *f* 110
hair lotion مقوى للشعر mo**qaw**wī lil sha'r *m* 110
hair slide دبوس شعر dæb**būs** sha'r *m* 110
hair remover مزيل للشعر mo**zīl** lil sha'r *m* 109
hairspray سبراي للشعر sbray lil sha'r *m* 30, 110
half نصف niṣf 80, 119, 148
hall porter عامل فندق '**æ**mil **fon**doq *m* 26.
ham جامبون **zham**bon *m* 39, 47, 119
hammer شاكوش sh**æ**k**ū**sh *m* 128
hand يد yæd *f* 137
handbag *(purse)* شنطة يد **shan**ṭit yæd *f* 115, 155
hand-blown يدوي **yæ**dæwī 126
hand cream كريم لليد krem lil yæd *m* 109
handicrafts صناعات يدوية ṣin**ā**'**āt** yædæ**wiy**yæ *f/pl* 84, 126
handkerchief منديل mæn**dīl** *m* 126
handmade شغل يد **sho**gl yæd 112
hanger علاقة 'æl**læ**qa *f* 27
happy سعيد sæ'**īd** 151
harbour ميناء **mī**n**æ**' *f* 68, 81
hard ناشف **n**æshif 122
hardware store محل أدوات منزلية mæ**ḥæ**ll ædæ**wæt** mænzi**liy**yæ *m* 99
hat برنيطة barn**ī**ṭa *f* 115
have, to 160
hazelnut بندق **bon**doq *m* 63
he هو **how**æ 138, 161
head رأس ra's *f* 137
headache صداع ṣod**ā**' *m* 141
headphones سماعات للرأس sæm**mæ**'**æ**t lil ra's *f/pl* 118
head waiter متر mitr *m* 60

health صحة ṣiḥḥa *f* 58
health insurance تأمين صحي tæ'**mīn** ṣiḥḥī *m* 144
heart قلب qalb *m* 137
heart attack نوبة قلبية **næw**bæ qal**biy**yæ *f* 140
heating تدفئة tæd**fi**'æ *f* 23, 28
heavy ثقيل tæ**qīl** 15, 102
heel كعب kæ'b *m* 117
height إرتفاع irti**fæ**' *m* 85
helicopter هليكوبتر hili**kob**tar *f* 74
hello أهلا **æh**læn 11; *(phone)* آلو **æ**lo 135
help نجدة **næg**dæ *f* 155
help! النجدة æn-**næg**dæ 155
help, to ساعد **sæ**'ædæ 14, 21, 74, 101, 134; *(oneself)* أخذ بنفسه **æ**khædæ bi **naf**so 119
her ها... ...hæ, 138, 160
herbs أعشاب æ'**shæb** *f/pl* 52
here هنا **ho**næ 16, 17, 21
hieroglyphics هيروغليفية hiro**glifiy**yæ *f* 84
high عالي '**æ**lī 140
hill تل tæll *m* 86
hire تاجير tæ**gīr** *m* 20, 74
hire, to أجر **ag**gara 19, 20, 74, 90, 91, 127
his ـه ... ...oh 138, 159
history تاريخ tæ**rīkh** *m* 84
hitchhiking أوتوستوب ōtō**stop** *m* 74
hole ثقب soqb *m* 29
holiday أجازة æ**gæ**zæ *f* 17, 150, 152
home منزل **mæn**zil *m* 96
honey عسل '**æ**sæl *m* 39
hope, to تمنى tæ**mæn**næ 96
horseback riding ركوب الخيل ro**kūb** æl-**khēl** *m* 90
horse-cab عربة خيل '**a**rabit khēl *f* 74
horse racing سباق الخيل si**bæq** æl-**khēl** *m* 90
hospital مستشفى mos**tæsh**fæ *f* 99, 144
hot ساخن **sæ**khin 15, 25, 39; *(weather)* حار ḥarr 94
hotel فندق **fon**doq *m* 19, 21, 22
hotel reservation حجز فندق ḥægz **fon**doq *m* 19
hot-water bottle قربة ماء ساخن **qir**bit mæ' **sæ**khin *f* 27
hour ساعة **sæ**'æ *f* 80, 90, 153
house بيت bēt *m* 83, 86
how كيف **kæy**fæ 12, 76, 118
how far كم المسافة kæm æl-mæ**sæ**fæ 12, 76, 85
how long كم من الوقت kæm min æl-**waqt** 12, 24, 73, 76, 114
how many كم kæm 12
how much *(service)* كم kæm 12, 24; (item) بكم bi**kæm** 12, 102
hungry جعان gæ'**æn** 14
hunting صيد ṣēd *m* 91
hurry *(to be in a)* أستعجل istæ'**æ**gælæ 21, 37
hurt, to ألم **æ**læmæ 139, 140, 145
husband زوج zæwg *m* 93
hydrofoil هيدروفيل hidro**fil** *m* 68

I

I أنا **æ**næ 160
ice cream جيلاتي [أيس كريم] zhi**læ**tī *m* [æys krem *m*] 41, 55, 64
ice cube تلج tælg *m* 27, 59
ill مريض ma**rīḍ** 140, 155
illness مرض **ma**raḍ *m* 140
important مهم mo**himm** 14
imported مستورد mos**tæw**rad 112
in في fī 16, 20, 24, 31
include, to حسب **ḥæ**sæbæ 24
included محسوب mæḥ**sūb** 20, 31, 61, 80
indigestion عسر هضم 'osr haḍm *m* 141
inexpensive رخيص ra**khīṣ** 36, 123
infected ملوث mu**læw**was 139
infection تلوث tæ**læw**wos *m* 141
inflammation إلتهاب ilti**hæb** *m* 141
inflation تضخم ta**ḍakh**khom *m* 131
inflation rate نسبة التضخم **nis**bæt æt-ta**ḍakh**khom *f* 131
influenza انفلونزا infil**wæn**zæ *f* 141
information استعلامات isti'læ**mæt** *f/pl* 69
injection حقن ḥaqn *m* 144
injured مصاب mo**ṣāb** 79, 138
injury إصابة i**ṣā**bæ *f* 138
ink حبر ḥibr *m* 106

inn إستراحة istirāḥa *f* 86
inquiries إستعلامات isti'læmæt *f/pl* 70
insect bite قرص حشرة qarṣ ḥashara *m* 107, 139
insect repellent دهان ضد الحشرات dæhæn ḍidd æl-ḥasharāt *m* 108
insecticide قاتل للحشرات qātil lil ḥasharāt *m* 108
inside في الداخل fiddækhil 16
instead of بدل bædæl 38
insurance تأمين tæ'mīn *m* 20, 144
insurance company شركة تأمين shirkæt tæ'mīn *f* 79
interest *(bank)* فائدة fæydæ *f* 131
interested, to be إهتم ihtæmmæ 84
interesting مهم mohimm 84
international أجنبي ægnæbī 133; خارجي khærigī 134
interpreter مترجم motærgim *m* 131
intersection تقاطع taqāṭo' *m* 77
introduce, to قدم qaddæmæ 92
introduction *(social)* تعارف ta'ārof *m* 92; *(commercial)* خطاب توصية khiṭāb tawṣiya *m* 130
investment إستثمار istismār *m* 131
invitation عزومة 'ozūmæ *f* 94
invite, to عزم 'æzæmæ 94
invoice فاتورة fātūra *f* 131
iodine صبغة يود ṣabgit yūd *f* 108
Irish إيرلندي irlændī 93
iron *(laundry)* مكوة mækwæ *f* 118
iron, to كوى kæwæ 29
ironmonger's محل أدوات منزلية mæḥæll ædæwæt mænziliyyæ *m* 99
Islam إسلام islæm *m* 84
Islamic إسلامي islæmī 84
its ...ـه ...oh 160
ivory عاج 'æg 121

J

jacket جاكيت zhækēt *f* 115
jam مربى mirabba *f* 39, 119
jam, to زنق zænæqa 28, 124
jar برطمان barṭamān *m* 119
jaundice إلتهاب الكبد iltihæb æl-kæbid *m* 141
jaw فك fækk *m* 137
jeans بنطلون جينز banṭalōn zhinz *m* 115
jewel حجر كريم ḥagar kærīm *m* 120
jeweller's محل مجوهرات mæḥæll mogæwharāt *m* 100, 120
jewellery مجوهرات mogawharāt *f/pl* 126
jewellery box علبة جواهر 'ilbit gæwæhir *f* 120
joint مفصل mafṣal *m* 137
journey رحلة riḥlæ *f* 66
juice عصير 'aṣīr *m* 59
just *(only)* فقط faqaṭ 101

K

kaftan قفطان qofṭān *m* 126
keep, to إحتفظ iḥtafiẓa 61
ketchup كتشوب ketshob *m* 37
key مفتاح moftæḥ *m* 27
kidney كلية kilyæ *f* 47, 137
kilo(gram) كيلو kīlō *m* 119
kilometre كيلومتر kīlometr *m* 20, 79
kind لطيف laṭīf 95
kind *(type)* صنف ṣanf *m* 46, 47
knee ركبة rokbæ *f* 137
knife سكينة sikkīnæ *f* 37, 60
know, to عرف 'arafa 17, 24, 114

L

label تيكيت tikit *m* 106
lace دانتيلا dæntillæ *f* 113
lady سيدة sæyyidæ *f* 111
lake بحيرة boḥæyra *f* 86
lamb (لحم) ضاني (læḥm) ḍānī *m* 47
lamp مصباح miṣbāḥ *m* 29, 118, 126
landmark مكان إلتقاء mækæn iltiqā' *m* 86
landscape منظر manẓar *m* 92
large كبير kæbīr 20, 102, 114, 117
last أخير ækhīr 15, 66, 70; ماضي māḍī 149, 152
last name لقب laqab *m* 25
late متأخر mit'akhkhar 15
later بعدين bæ'dēn 135
laugh, to ضحك ḍaḥika 95
laundry *(place)* محل غسيل ومكوة mæḥæll gæsīl wæ mækwæ *m* 29, 100; *(clothes)* غسيل gæsīl *m* 29
laundry service خدمة غسيل ومكوة khidmit gæsīl wæ mækwæ *f* 23

laxative ملين molæyyin *m* 108
leap year سنة كبيسة sænæ kæbīsæ *f* 149
leather جلد gild *m* 113, 117
leather goods مصنوعات جلدية maṣnū'āt gildiyyæ *f/pl* 126
leave, to ترك taraka 20, 74; *(depart)* رحل raḥala 31, 95; *(train)* قام qāmæ 70, 71, 153; *(deposit)* وضع waḍa'a 26
left شمال shimæl 21, 63, 71, 77
left-luggage office مكتب أمانات mæktæb æmænæt *m* 18, 69, 74
leg ساق sæq *f* 137, 138
lemon ليمون læmūn *m* 37, 39
lemon juice عصير ليمون 'aṣīr læmūn *m* 59
lens عدسة 'ædæsæ *f* 122, 124
lentil عدس 'æds *m* 45, 52
less أقل aqall 16, 119
letter خطاب khiṭāb *m* 28, 132
letter box صندوق خطابات sondūq khiṭābāt *m* 132
letter of credit خطاب ضمان khiṭāb ḍamān *m* 130
lettuce خس khass *m* 43, 50
library مكتبة عمومية mæktæbæ 'omūmiyyæ *f* 81
licence *(permit)* رخصة rokhṣa *f* 20, 79
lie down, to تمدد tæmæddædæ 142
life belt حزام نجاة ḥizæm nægæt *m* 68
life boat مركب نجاة mærkib nægæt *m* 68
lifeguard حارس ḥæris *m* 91
lift مصعد maṣ'ad *m* 27, 101
ligament رباط ribāṭ *m* 137
light خفيف khæfīf 15, 55, 58, 102, 127; *(colour)* فاتح fætiḥ 57, 102, 111, 112
light ضوء ḍo' *m* 123; *(installation)* نور nūr *m* 28; *(cigarette)* ولاعة wællæ'æ *f* 95
lighter ولاعة wællæ'æ *f* 125
light meter مقياس الضوء miqyæs aḍ-ḍo' *m* 124
like مثل misl 111
like, to حب ḥæbbæ 60, 96; *(want)* أراد arāda14, 20, 23, 111; (take pleasure) أعجب æ'gæbæ 25, 92, 103, 111
line خط khaṭṭ *m* 66
linen *(cloth)* [تيل] كتان kittæn *m* [tīl *m*] 113
lip شفة shiffæ *f* 137
lipsalve كريم شفايف krem shæfæyif *m* 109
lipstick أحمر للشفايف aḥmar lil shæfæyif *m* 109
liqueur ليكر liqers *m* 58
listen, to سمع sæmi'æ 127
litre لتر litr *m* 75, 119
little *(a)* [قليل] شوية shwæyæ [qalīl] 16, 30
live, to عاش 'æshæ 83
liver كبد kibd *m* 137; *(food)* كبدة kibdæ *f* 47, 49
lobster كركند kærækænd *m* 42, 46
local محلى mæḥællī 37, 41, 43, 134
London لندن landan *f* 134
long طويل ṭawīl 114, 115
look, to تفرج tafarraga 101, 122
look for, to بحث عن bæḥæsæ 'æn 14
look at *(examine)* فحص faḥaṣa 139
look out! إحترس iḥtæris 155
loose *(clothes)* واسع wæsi' 114
lose, to فقد fæqadæ 122, 145, 155; *(oneself)* تاه tæhæ 14
loss خسارة khosāra *f* 131
lost تهت toht 14, 155
lost and found/lost property office مكتب مفقودات mæktæb mæfqūdæt *m* 69, 155
lot *(a)* كثير kitīr 16
lotion لوسيون losyōn *m* 109
love, to حب ḥæbbæ 95
lovely جميل gæmīl 94
low واطي wāṭi' 140
low season خارج الموسم khærig æl-mūsim 148
luck حظ ḥazz *m* 151
luggage حقائب ḥaqā'ib *f/pl* 18, 21, 26, 31, 67, 74
luggage trolley عربة حقائب 'arabit ḥaqā'ib *f* 18, 74
lump *(bump)* ورم waram *m* 139
lunch غذاء gædæ' *m* 34, 80, 94
lung رئة ri'æ *f* 137
Luxor الأقصر æl-loqṣor *f* 68

M

machine ماكينة mækænæ *f* 113
magazine مجلة mægællæ *f* 106
maid خادمة غرفة khædimæt gorfa *f* 26
mail خطابات khiṭābāt *f/pl* 28, 133
mail, to أرسل arsælæ 28
mailbox صندوق خطابات ṣondūq khiṭābāt *m* 132
main رئيسي ra'īsī 80, 101
make, to عمل 'æmælæ 131
make up, to *(prepare)* جهز gæhhæzæ 28, 73
man رجل ragol *m* 111
manager مدير modīr *m* 26
manicure مانيكير mænikūr *m* 30
many كثير kitīr 16
map خريطة kharīṭa *f* 19, 76, 106
market سوق sūq *m* 81, 100
marmalade مربة برتقال mirabbit bortoqāl *f* 39
married متزوج motæzawwig 93
mass *(church)* صلاة ṣalāh *f* 85
match كبريت kæbrīt *m* 125; *(sport)* مباراة mobārā *f* 90
match, to *(colour)* ناسب næsæbæ 111
mattress مرتبة mærtæbæ *f* 32
may *(can)* ممكن momkin 14
meal وجبة wægbæ *f* 24, 34, 143
mean, to عنى 'ænæ 13, 25
measles حصبة ḥaṣba *f* 141
measure, to قاس qāsæ 114
meat لحم læḥm *m* 41, 47, 60
meatball كفتة koftæ *f* 47
mechanic ميكانيكي mikænīkī *m* 78
mechanical pencil قلم رصاص معدني qalæm roṣāṣ mæ'dænī *m* 120
medical طبي ṭibbī 144
medical certificate شهادة طبية shihædæ ṭibbiyyæ *f* 144
medicine طب ṭibb *m* 84; *(drug)* دواء dæwæ' *m* 143
meet, to قابل qābælæ 96
melon شمام shæmmæm *m* 42, 54
Memphis ممفيس mæmfis *f* 73
mend, to رف ræffæ 29; صلح ṣallaḥa 75
menthol *(cigarettes)* بالنعناع bil næ'næ' 125

menu وجبة wægbæ *f* 37, 38; *(printed)* كارت kært *m* 37, 40, 41
message رسالة risælæ *f* 28, 135
metre متر metr *m* 114
middle وسط wasaṭ 72, 150
midnight منتصف الليل montaṣaf æl-lēl *m* 153
mild خفيف khæfīf 125
mileage كيلومترات kīlometrāt *f/pl* 20
milk [حليب] لبن læbæn *m* [ḥælīb *m*] 39, 59, 119
million مليون milyōn *m* 147
minaret مئذنة mi'zænæ *f* 86
mineral water ماء معدنية mæ' mæ'dæniyyæ *f* 59
minister *(religion)* قسيس qissīs *m* 85
mint نعناع næ'næ' *m* 52
mint tea شاي بنعناع shæy bi næ'næ' *m* 62
minute دقيقة daqīqa *f* 21, 153
mirror مرايا miræyæ *f* 114, 122
Miss آنسة ænisæ *f* 11
missing ناقص nāqiṣ 18, 29, 60
mistake خطأ khaṭa' *m* 31, 60, 61, 103
moccasin ماكاسان mækæsæn *m* 117
moisturizing cream كريم مرطب krem moraṭṭib *m* 109
moment لحظة laḥẓa *f* 13
monastery دير dīr *m* 81
Monday (يوم) الأثنين (yōm) æl-itnēn *m* 152
money نقود noqūd *f/pl* 130
money order حوالة بريدية ḥiwælæ bæridiyyæ *f* 133
month شهر shahr *m* 17, 141, 149
monument نصب تذكاري naṣb tizkærı *m* 81
moon قمر qamar *m* 94
moped دراجة بخارية darrāga bokhæriyyæ *f* 74
more أكثر aktar 16
morning صباح ṣabāḥ *m* 31, 152, 153
mosque مسجد mæsgid *m* 81, 85
mosquito net ناموسية næmūsiyyæ *f* 32
mother والدة wælidæ *f* 93
motorbike موتوسيكل mōtōsikl *m* 74
motorway أوتوستراد ōtōstrād *m* 76
mountain جبل gæbæl *m* 85

moustache شنب shæ**næb** *m* 31
mouth فم fæmm *m* 137
mouthwash غسيل للفم **gæsīl** lil fæmm *m* 108
move, to حرك **ḥ**arraka 139
movie فيلم film *m* 87
movie camera كاميرا سينما **kǣ**mira **sī**nimæ *f* 123
movies سينما **sī**nimæ *f* 87, 96
Mr. سيد **sæ**yyid *m* 11
Mrs. سيدة sæ**yyi**dæ *f* 11
much كثير ki**tīr** 16
muscle عضل **'a**ḍal *m* 137
museum متحف **mæ**tḥæf *m* 82
music موسيقى mo**sī**qa *f* 84, 127
must *(have to)* لا بد أن **lǣ** bodd æn 23, 31; يجب أن **yæ**gib æn 95
mustard مستردة mos**tar**da *f* 37, 119
my ... ي ... ī 93, 160

N

nail *(human)* ظفر **ẓ**afr *m* 109
nail brush فرشة للأظافر **for**shæ lil a**ẓā**fir *f* 109
nail clippers قصافة للأظافر qaṣ**ṣā**fa lil a**ẓā**fir *f* 109
nail file مبرد أظافر **mab**rad a**ẓā**fir *m* 109
nail polish مونوكير mono**kīr** *m* 109
nail polish remover مزيل للمونوكير mo**zīl** lil mono**kīr** *m* 109
nail scissors مقص للأظافر ma**qaṣṣ** lil a**ẓā**fir *m* 109
name إسم ism *m* 23, 79, 86, 92; *(surname)* لقب la**qab** *m* 25
napkin فوطة **fū**ṭa *f* 37
nappy تغييرة الطفل tæ**gyī**ra aṭ-**ṭifl** *f* 110
narrow ضيق **ḍæ**yyaq 117
nationality جنسية gin**se**yya *f* 25, 92
natural طبيعي ta**bī'**ī 84
natural history تاريخ طبيعي tæ**rīkh** ṭa**bī'**ī *m* 84
nauseous بقيء bi qi' 140
near قريب qa**rīb** 16, 77; قريب من qa**rīb** min 19, 32, 85
nearest أقرب **aq**rab 75, 78, 99
neck رقبة **ra**qabæ *f* 47, 137; *(nape)* قفا qa**fǣ** *m* 30

necklace عقد 'oqd *m* 120
necessary ضروري **ḍa**rūrī 89
need, to إحتاج iḥ**tǣ**gæ 29, 91, 136
needle إبرة **ib**ræ *f* 27
negative نيجاتيف nigæ**tīf** *m* 124
nephew إبن أخ ibn ækh *m* 93
nerve عصب **'a**ṣab *m* 137
nervous عصبي **'a**ṣabī 137
nervous system جهاز عصبي gi**hǣz** **'a**ṣabī *m* 137
never أبداً æ**bæ**dæn 16
new جديد gæ**dīd** 15, 117
newspaper جريدة gæ**rī**dæ *f* 105, 106
newsstand كشك جرائد koshk ga**rā'**id *m* 19, 69, 100, 105
next قادم **qā**dim 15, 21, 66, 149, 152
next to بجانب bi**gǣ**nib 16, 77
nice *(beautiful)* جميل gæ**mīl** 94
niece بنت أخ bint ækh *f* 93
night ليلة **læy**læ *f* 24; lēl ليل *m* 152
nightclub ملهى ليلي **mæl**hæ **læy**lī *m* 33, 89
night cream كريم للنوم krem lil nōm *m* 109
nightdress قميص نوم qa**mīṣ** nōm *m* 115
no لا læ 11
noisy دوشة **dæw**shæ 25
nonalcoholic بدون كحول bi**dūn** ko**ḥol** 59
none ولا واحد wæ**læ** **wǣ**ḥid 16
noodle شعرية shi'**riy**yæ *f* 45
noon ظهر ẓohr *m* 31, 153
normal عادي **'ǣ**dī 30
north شمال shæ**mǣl** *m* 77
nose أنف ænf *f* 138
nosebleed نزيف أنفي næ**zīf** **æn**fī *m* 141
not لا **lǣ** 13, 161; ليس **læy**sæ 16, 29
note *(banknote)* ورقة **wa**raqa *f* 130
notebook مفكرة mo**fæk**kira *f* 106
note paper ورق للكتابة **wa**raq lil ki**tǣ**bæ *f* 106
nothing لا شيء **lǣ** she' 16, 55
notify, to بلغ **bæl**læ**g**æ 144
now الآن æl'**æn** 16, 95
number رقم **ra**qam *m* 26, 65, 66, 134, 135
nurse ممرضة mo**ma**riḍa *f* 144
nuts مكسرات mikassa**rāt** *f/pl* 63

DICTIONARY قاموس

O

oasis واحة wæḥæ *f* 86
occupied مشغول mæsh**gūl** 15
o'clock الساعة æs-**sæ**'æ 73, 153
office مكتب **mæk**tæb *m* 18, 69, 100, 129, 132, 155
oil زيت zēt *m* 37, 75, 110
oily *(greasy)* دهني **doh**nī 30, 110
old عجوز 'æ**gūz** 15; قديم qæ**dīm** 15
old town مدينة قديمة mæ**dī**næ qa**dī**mæ *f* 82
olive زيتونة zæ**tū**næ *f* 42, 64
omelet عجة '**ig**gæ *f* 43, 44
on على 'æ**læ** 16
one-way ticket ذهاب zi**hæb** *m* 65, 72
on foot سيراً sæy**ran** 76
onion بصل **ba**ṣal *m* 50
only فقط **fa**qaṭ 16, 24, 80
onyx عقيق 'æ**qīq** *m* 121
open مفتوح mæf**tūḥ** 15, 82, 98
open, to فتح **fæ**tæḥæ 12, 82, 98, 107, 130, 132
opera أوبرا **ō**brā *f* 89
opera house دار الأوبرا dār æl-**ō**brā *f* 89
operation عملية 'æmæ**liy**yæ *f* 144
opposite أمام æ**mæm** 77
optician نظاراتي naẓā**rā**tī *m* 100
or أو æw 16
orange برتقالة borto**qā**læ *f* 39, 54, 64
orange *(colour)* برتقالي borto**qā**lī 112
orange juice عصير برتقال 'a**ṣīr** borto**qāl** *m* 59
orchestra فرقة **fir**qa *f* 89
order *(goods, meal)* طلب **ṭa**lab *m* 41, 103
order, to طلب **ṭa**laba 60, 103
oriental شرقي **shar**qī 41, 126
Orthodox أرثوذكس orto**doks** 85
other آخر **a**khar 74, 102
our ...نا ... **næ** 160
outlet *(electric)* فيشة الكهرباء **fī**shet æl-kahraba' *f* 27
outside في الخارج fil **khæ**rig 16, 36
oval بيضاوي bay**ḍā**wī 102
overheat, to *(engine)* سخن **sæ**khænæ 78
overnight *(stay)* الليلة æl-**læy**læ 24
owe, to يجب الدفع **yæ**gib æd-**dæf'** 144

P

pacifier بزازة bæz**zæ**zæ *f* 110
packet باكو **bæ**kō *m* 119; علبة **'il**ba *f* 125
page *(hotel)* خادم فندق **khæ**dim **fondo**[q] *m* 26
pain ألم **æ**læm *m* 140, 144
painkiller مهدئ mo**hæd**di' *m* 139
paint, to رسم **ræ**sæmæ 83
paintbox علبة ألوان **'il**bit æl**wæn** *f* 106
painter رسام ræs**sæm** *m* 83
painting رسم ræsm *m* 84
pair زوج zōg *m* 148
pajamas بيجامة bi**zhæ**mæ *f* 116
palace قصر qaṣr *m* 82
panties سليب slib *m* 115
pants *(trousers)* بنطلون ban**ṭa**lōn *m* 11[5]
panty girdle كورسيه kor**sey** *m* 115
panty hose شراب حريمي طويل shor**rāb** ḥæ**rī**mī ṭa**wīl** *m* 115
paper ورق **wa**raq *m* 106
paperback كتاب جيب ki**tæb** gēb *m* 106
paperclip مشبك كليبس **mæsh**bæk klibs *m* 106
paper napkin فوطة ورق **fū**ṭa **wa**raq *f* 10[6]
parcel طرد ṭard *m* 132
pardon عفواً **'af**wæn 11
parents والدين **wæ**lidæyn *m/dl* 93
park حديقة ḥæ**dī**qa *f* 82
park, to ركن [صف] **ræ**kænæ [**ṣaf**fa] 26, 77
parking ركن rækn *m* 77
parking meter عداد 'æd**dæd** *m* 77
parliament برلمان barlæ**mæn** *m* 82
party *(social gathering)* حفلة **ḥæf**læ *f* 95
pass *(permit)* إشتراك ishti**rāk** *m* 67
passport جواز سفر gæ**wæz** **sa**far *m* 17, 25, 26, 155
passport photo صورة لجواز سفر **ṣū**ra li gæ**wæz** **sa**far *f* 123
pass through, to مرّ **mar**ra 17
pasta مكرونة maka**rō**na *f* 41, 52
paste *(glue)* صمغ ṣamg *m* 106
pastries حلويات ḥalæwiy**yæt** *f/pl* 41, 55, 64
pastry shop محل حلويات mæ**ḥæll** ḥælæwiy**yæt** *m* 100

patch, to *(clothes)* رقع **raqa**'a 29
path سكة **sikkæ** *f* 86
patient مريض **marīḍ** *m* 144
pattern شكل shækl *m* 111
pay, to دفع **dæfæ**'æ 31, 61, 103
payment دفع dæf' *m* 131
pea بسله bisillæ *f* 45. 50
peach [دره] خوخ khōkh *m* [**darra** *m*] 54
peanut فول سوداني fūl sū**dæ**nī *m* 63
pear [أجاص] كمثرى kom**mitræ** *f* [ag**gāṣ** *m*] 54
pearl لولى **lūlī** *m* 121
peg *(tent)* وتد خيمة **wætæd khē**mæ *m* 32
pencil قلم رصاص **qalæm roṣāṣ** *m* 106
pencil sharpener براية bærr**æ**yæ *f* 106
pendant قلادة qil**æ**dæ *f* 120
penicillin بنسلين bensi**līn** *m* 143
penknife مطواة **maṭwa** *f* 128
pensioner معاش mæ'**æsh** *m* 83
people ناس næs *m/pl* 92
pepper فلفل **fil**fil *m* 37, 39, 52
per cent في المائة fil **mī**yæ 148
percentage نسبة **nis**bæ *f* 131
performance *(theatre)* عرض 'arḍ *m* 88
perfume [عطر] بارفان pær**fan** *m* ['iṭr *m*] 109
perhaps ربما rob**bæ**mæ 16
period *(monthly)* عادة شهرية **'æ**dæ shæhri**yy**æ *f* 141
period pains ألم العادة الشهرية **æ**læm æl-'**æ**dæ æsh-shæh**riyy**æ *m* 141
permanent wave برماننت barma**nant** *m* 30
permit ترخيص tar**khīṣ** *m* 91
person شخص shakhṣ *m* 32
personal شخصي **shakh**ṣī 17
personal/person-to-person call مكالمة شخصية mo**kæl**mæ shakh**ṣiyy**æ *f* 134
petrol بنزين bæn**zīn** *m* 75, 78
pewter معدن **mæ**'dæn *m* 121
photo صورة **ṣū**ra *f* 83, 124
photocopy فوتوكوبي foto**kō**pī *f* 131
photograph, to أخذ صور æ**kh**ædæ **ṣo**war 83
photographer مصور mo**ṣaw**wir *m* 100
photography تصوير taṣ**wīr** *m* 123
phrase جملة **gom**læ *f* 13

picnic أكلة خفيفة **æk**læ khæ**fī**fæ *f* 63
picture صورة **ṣū**ra *f* 83
piece قطعة **qiṭ**'a *f* 18, 119
pigeon حمام ḥæ**mæm** *m* 49
pill حبة **ḥæb**bæ *f* 143; *(contraceptive)* حبوب منع الحمل ḥo**būb** mæn' æl-**ḥæml** *f/pl* 141
pillow مخدة mæ**khæd**dæ *f* 27
pin دبوس dæb**būs** *m* 110, 121
pineapple أناناس ænæ**næs** *m* 54
pink وردي **wær**dī 112
pipe بايب payp *m* 125
place مكان mæ**kæn** *m* 25, 76, 91
place of birth مكان الميلاد mæ**kæn** æl-mī**læd** *m* 25
plain سهل sæhl *m* 86
plane طائرة ṭā'ira *f* 65
plantation مزرعة mæz**ræ**'æ *f* 86
plaster *(cast)* جبس gibs *m* 139
plate طبق **ṭa**baq *m* 37, 60, 63
platform *(station)* رصيف ra**ṣīf** *m* 69, 71, 72
play *(theatre)* مسرحية mæsræ**ḥiy**yæ *f* 87
play, to لعب **læ**'bæ 90, 93; *(music)* عزف **'æ**zæfæ 89
playing card كوتشينه kot**shī**næ *f* 106, 128
please من فضلك min **faḍ**lak 11
plimsolls جزمة كاوتش **gæz**mæ **kæ**witsh *f* 127
plug *(electric)* كوبس kobs *m* 29, 118
plum برقوق bær**qūq** *m* 54
pneumonia إلتهاب رئوي ilti**hæb** ri'æwī *m* 141
pocket جيب gēb *m* 116
pocket calculator آلة حاسبة للجيب **æ**læ **ḥæs**bæ lil gēb *f* 106
point, to *(show)* حدد **ḥæd**dædæ 13
poison سم simm *m* 108, 155
poisoning تسمم tæ**sæm**mom *m* 141
police بوليس bō**līs** *m* 79, 155
police station [شرطة] قسم بوليس qism bō**līs** *m* [**shor**ṭa *f*] 100, 155
pond بركة **bir**kæ *f* 86
pop music موسيقى غربية mo**sī**qa gar**biy**yæ *f* 127
port ميناء **mī**nā' *f* 68; *(wine)* بورتو **borto** *m* 59

porter [عتال] شيال **shæyyæl** *m* ['ættæl *m*] 18, 26, 74
portion مقدار **miqdār** *m* 38, 55, 60
Port Saïd بور سعيد **bōr sæ'īd** *f* 70, 72
post *(letters)* خطاب **khiṭāb** *m* 28, 133
post, to أرسل **arsælæ** 28
postage طابع **ṭābi'** 132
postage stamp طابع **ṭābi'** *m* 28, 132
postcard كارت بوستال **kært bostæl** *m* 106, 132
poste restante مكتب تسليم الخطابات **mæktæb tæslīm æl-khiṭābāt** *m* 133
post office [بوستة] مكتب بريد **mæktæb bærīd** *m* [**bōstæ** *f*] 100, 132
potato بطاطس **baṭāṭis** *m* 50
pottery خزف **khæzæf** *m* 84
poultry طيور **ṭoyūr** *m/pl* 41, 49
pound *(money)* جنيه **ginēh** *m* 18, 103, 129; *(weight)* نصف كيلو **niṣf kīlō** *m* 119
pound sterling جنيه أسترليني **ginēh istirlīnī** *m* 129
powder بودرة **bodra** *f* 109
prawn [أراديس] جمبري **gæmbærī** *m* ['arādis *m*] 42, 46
prefer, to فضل **faḍḍala** 55
preference تفضيل **tafḍīl** *m* 102
pregnant حامل **ḥæmil** 141
premium *(gasoline)* سوبر **sōbar** 75
prepare, to جهز **gæhhazæ** 107
prescribe, to كتب **kætæbæ** 143
prescription روشتة **roshettæ** *f* 107, 143
present *(gift)* هدية **hideyyæ** *f* 17
press, to *(iron)* كوى **kæwæ** 29
press stud كبسون **kæbsūn** *m* 116
pressure ضغط **ḍagt** *m* 75
pretty حلوة **ḥilwæ** 84
price ثمن **tæmæn** *m* 24
priest قسيس **qissīs** *m* 85
print *(photo)* صورة **ṣūra** *f* 124
private خاص **khāṣṣ** 24, 80
profession مهنة **mihnæ** *f* 25
profit [ربح] مكسب **mæksæb** *m* [ribḥ *m*] 131
programme برنامج **birnæmig** *m* 88
pronunciation نطق **noṭq** *m* 6, 95
propelling pencil قلم رصاص معدني **qalæm roṣāṣ mæ'dænī** *m* 121
Protestant بروتستانت **brotistant** 85
provide, to أوجد **æwgædæ** 131
public holiday أجازة **ægæzæ** *f* 150
pullover بلوفر **bolōvar** *m* 115
puppet show عرض للعرائس **'arḍ lil 'ærā'is** *m* 87
puncture عجلة مفرقعة **'ægælæ mofarqa'a** *f* 75
purchase شراء **shirā'** *m* 131
put, to وضع **waḍa'a** 24
pyjamas بيجاما **bizhæmæ** *f* 116
pyramid هرم **haram** *m* 82

Q

quality نوع **no'** *m* 104, 113
quantity كمية **kimeyyæ** *f* 16, 104
quarter ربع **rob'** *m* 148; *(part of town)* حي **ḥæyy** *m* 81, 82
question سؤال **so'æl** *m* 12
quick سريع **særi'** 15
quickly بسرعة **bisor'æ** 79, 136, 155
quiet هادىء **hædi'** 23, 25

R

rabbi حاخام **ḥækhæm** *m* 85
rabbit أرنب **ærnæb** *m* 49
race course/track أرض سباق الخيل **arḍ sibæq æl-khēl** *m* 90
racket *(sport)* مضرب **maḍrab** *m* 90
radiator *(car)* رادياتور **rādyætōr** *m* 78
radio *(set)* راديو **radyō** *m* 23, 28, 118
railway سكة حديد **sikkæ ḥædīd** *f* 69
railway station محطة قطار **maḥaṭṭit qiṭār** *f* 21, 69
rain مطر **maṭar** *m* 94
rain, to مطرت **maṭarat** 94
raincoat بالطو مطر **balṭō maṭar** *m* 116
raisin زبيب **zibīb** *m* 54
rangefinder ضابط مسافة **ḍābiṭ mæsæfæ** *m* 124
rash طفح جلدي **ṭafḥ gildī** *m* 139
rate *(price)* سعر **si'r** *m* 20; *(inflation)* نسبة **nisbæ** *f* 131
razor ماكينة حلاقة **mækinæt ḥilæqa** *f* 109
razor blade موس حلاقة **mūs ḥilæqa** *m* 109
reading-lamp لمبة للقراءة **lamba lil qirā'æ** *f* 21

ready جاهز **gæ**hiz 37, 103, 117, 122, 124, 145
real حقيقي ḥaqīqī 120
rear خلف khælf *m* 75
receipt إيصال īṣ**āl** *m* 103, 104, 144
reception إستقبال istiq**bæl** *m* 23
receptionist موظف استقبال mowa**ẓẓ**af istiq**bæl** *m* 26
recommend, to نصح naṣaḥa 22, 36, 37, 80, 87, 136, 145
record *(disc)* أسطوانة isṭi**wā**na *f* 127
record player بيك أب bīk ab *m* 118
rectangular مستطيل mosta**ṭīl** 102
red أحمر a**ḥ**mar 58, 112
reduction تخفيض takh**fīḍ** *m* 24, 83
refund إسترداد istir**dæd** *m* 104
regards تحيات tæḥi**yæt** *f/pl* 151
register, to *(luggage)* سجل **sæg**gælæ 74
registered mail بريد مسجل bærīd mo**sæg**gæl *m* 133
registration تسجيل tas**gīl** *m* 25
registration form إستمارة isti**mā**ra *f* 25, 26
regular *(petrol)* عادي **'æ**dī 75
religion دين dīn *m* 84
religious service خدمات دينية **khid**mæ dī**niy**yæ *f* 85
rent, to أجّر **ag**gara 19, 20, 74, 90, 91, 127
rental تأجير tæ'**gīr** *m* 20, 74
repair تصليح taṣ**līḥ** *m* 124
repair, to صلح **ṣal**laḥa 29, 117, 118, 120, 122, 124
repeat, to كرر kar**ra**ra 13
reservation حجز ḥægz *m* 23, 65, 72
reservations office مكتب الحجز **mæk**tæb æl-**ḥægz** *m* 19, 69
reserve, to حجز **ḥæ**gæzæ 19, 23, 36, 72, 88
restaurant مطعم **maṭ**'am *m* 19, 33, 36, 69
return, to *(give back)* أرجع ær**gæ**'æ 104; *(go back)* رجع **ræ**gæ'æ 77
return ticket ذهاب وإياب zi**hæb** wæ i**yæb** *m* 65, 72
rheumatism روماتيزم ro**mæ**tī**sm** *m* 141
rib ضلع ḍil' *m* 138
ribbon شريط shi**rīṭ** *m* 106
rice أرز roz *m* 41, 52
riding ركوب الخيل ro**kūb** æl-**khēl** *m* 90
right يمين yæ**mīn** 21, 63; *(correct)* صح ṣaḥḥ 15; صحيح ṣa**ḥīḥ** 72, 76
ring *(finger)* خاتم **khæ**tim *m* 121
ring, to *(phone)* إتصل it**ta**ṣala 134
river نهر nahr *m* 86
road طريق ṭa**rīq** *m* 76, 77, 86
road assistance نجدة **næg**dæ *f* 78
road map خريطة للطرق kha**rī**ṭa lil **ṭo**roq *f* 106
roast beef رزبيف roz**bīf** *m* 42, 47
roll *(bread)* خبز صغير khobz ṣa**gīr** *m* 39
roller skates عجل تزحلق **'æ**gæl tæ**zæḥ**loq *f/pl* 128
roll film بوبينه bo**bī**næ *f* 123
room غرفة **gor**fa *f* 19, 23, 24, 25, 28; *(space)* مكان mæ**kæn** *m* 32
room number رقم غرفة raqam **gor**fa *m* 26
room service خدمة في الغرفة **khid**mæ fil **gor**fa *f* 23
rope حبل ḥæbl *m* 128
round مستدير mostæ**dīr** 102
round *(golf)* دورة **daw**ra *f* 90
roundtrip ticket ذهاب وإياب zi**hæb** wæ i**yæb** 65, 72
rowing تجديف tæg**dīf** *m* 90
royal ملكي **mæ**lækī 82
rubber *(material)* كاوتش **kæ**witsh *m* 117; *(eraser)* [ممحاة] أستيكة æs**tī**kæ *f* [mim**ḥæ**h *f*] 106
ruins أطلال aṭ**lāl** *m/pl* 82
ruler *(for measuring)* مسطرة **mas**ṭara *f* 106

S

safe *(not dangerous)* أمان æ**mæn** 91
safe خزنة **khæz**næ *f* 26
safety pin دبوس مشبك dæb**būs** **mæsh**bæk *m* 110
sailing boat مركب شراعية **mær**kib shirā'**iy**yæ *f* 91
salad سلطة **sa**laṭa *f* 41, 43
sale بيع bē' *m* 131; *(bargains)* أوكازيون okaz**yōn** *m* 101
salt ملح mælḥ *m* 38, 39

DICTIONARY قاموس

salty مالح **mæ**liḥ 60
same نفس næfs 117
sand رمل raml *m* 91
sand dune تل رملي tæll **ram**lī *m* 86
sandal صندل **ṣan**dal *m* 117, 126
sandwich ساندويتش sænd**witsh** *m* 63, 64
sanitary towel/napkin فوطة ورق طبي fūṭit waraq ṭibbī *f* 108
Saturday (يوم) السبت (yōm) æs-**sæbt** *m* 152
sauce صلصة **ṣal**ṣa *f* 46
saucepan حلة **ḥæl**læ *f* 128
sausage سجق [مقانق] so**goq** *m* [maqāniq *m*] 42, 47, 64
scarf ايشارب i**sharb** *m* 116
scissors مقص ma**qaṣṣ** *m* 109, 128
scooter سكوتر **skō**ter *m* 74
screwdriver مفك mi**fækk** *m* 128
scuba-diving غطس عميق **gaṭs** 'æ**mīq** *m* 127
sculptor نحات næḥ**ḥæt** *m* 83
sculpture نحت **næḥt** *m* 84
sea بحر **baḥr** *m* 86
seafood أسماك æs**mæk** *f/pl* 41, 46
season موسم **mū**sim *m* 148
seasoning بهارات bohā**rāt** *f/pl* 38, 52
seat مكان mæ**kæn** *m* 72, 73, 88; *(ticket)* تذكرة tæz**ka**ra *f* 88
second ثاني **tæ**nī 148
second ثانية **sæn**yæ *f* 153
second class درجة ثانية **da**raga **tæn**yæ *f* 70, 72
second-hand مستعمل mos**tæ'**mæl 100
second hand عقرب ثواني **'æq**ræb sæ**wæ**nī *m* 121
second-hand shop محل أدوات مستعملة mæ**ḥæll** ædæ**wæt** mos**tæ'**mælæ *m* 100
secretary سكرتيرة seker**tē**ræ *f* 27, 131
section قسم **qism** *m* 105
see, to رأى **ra'**ā 25, 120; شاهد **shæ**hædæ 87, 90; *(examine)* كشف **kæ**shæfæ 136
sell, to باع **bæ'**æ 101
send, to أرسل **ar**sælæ 26, 78, 103, 132, 133
sentence جملة **gom**læ *f* 13
serious خطر **kha**ṭar 142
service خدمة **khid**mæ *f* 24, 61, 99, 101; *(religion)* صلاة ṣa**lāh** *f* 85
serviette فوطة **fū**ṭa *f* 37
set menu وجبة كاملة **wæg**bæ **kæm**læ *f* 37
setting lotion سائل لتثبيت الشعر **sæ'**il li tæs**bīt** æsh-**sha'r** *m* 30
sew, to خيط **khay**yaṭa 29
shade *(colour)* درجة **da**raga *f* 111
shampoo شامبو **sham**bo *m* 30, 110
share *(finance)* سهم **sæhm** *m* 131
shave, to حلق ذقن **ḥa**laqa zaqn 31
shaver ماكينة حلاقة mæ**ki**nat ḥi**læ**qa *f* 27, 118
shaving cream كريم للحلاقة **krēm** lil ḥi**læ**qa *m* 110
she هي **hi**yæ 138, 161
sherry شري **she**rī *m* 59
ship سفينة sæ**fī**næ *f* 68
shirt قميص qa**mīṣ** *m* 116
shivery برعشة bi **ræ'**shæ 140
shoe جزمة [حذاء] **gæz**mæ *f* [ḥi**zæ'** *m*] 117
shoelace رباط أحذية ro**bāṭ** æḥ**ziy**yæ *m* 117
shoemaker's جزمجي gæz**mæ**gī *m* 100
shoe polish ورنيش wær**nīsh** *m* 117
shoe shop محل جزم [أحذية] mæ**ḥæll** gizæm *m* [æḥ**ziy**yæ *m*] 100
shop محل mæ**ḥæll** *m* 99
shopping مشتريات moshtara'**yæt** *f/pl* 97
shopping area حي تجاري **ḥæyy** to**gæ**rī *m* 82, 101
shopping centre مركز تجاري **mær**kæz to**gæ**rī *m* 100
shop window فترينة vit**rī**næ *f* 101, 111
short قصير qa**ṣīr** 30, 114, 115
shorts شورت **short** *m* 116
shoulder كتف **kitf** *m* 47, 138
show عرض **'arḍ** *m* 88
show, to أرى **a**ra 13, 14, 76, 101, 104, 118, 123
shower دش **dōsh** *m* 23, 32
shrimp جمبري [أراديس] gæm**bæ**rī *m* [a**rā**dis *m*] 42, 46

shrink, to كش **kæsh**æ 29, 113
shut مقفول mæqfūl 15
shutter *(window)* شيش shīsh *m* 29; *(camera)* منظم فتحة العدسة monazzim fæthit æl-'ædæsæ *m* 124
sick *(ill)* مريض marīḍ 140, 155
sickness *(illness)* مرض **mara**ḍ *m* 140
side جانب **gǣ**nib *m* 30
sideboards/burns سوالف sæ**wǣ**lif *m/pl* 31
sightseeing زيارة سياحية zi**yā**ra siyǣ**ḥiy**yæ *f* 80
sightseeing tour جولة سياحية **gæw**læ siyǣ**ḥiy**yæ *f* 80
sign, to وقع **waq**qa'a 26, 130
signature توقيع tawqī' *m* 25
silk حرير ḥæ**rīr** *m* 113
silver *(colour)* فضي **fad**ḍi 112
silver فضة **fad**ḍa *f* 120, 121
silver-plated مفضض mo**fad**ḍad 121
simple سهل sæhl 123
since منذ **mon**zo 16, 150
sing, to غنى **gæn**nǣ 89
single *(not married)* عازب **'ǣ**zib 93
(ticket) ذهاب zi**hǣb** 65, 72
single cabin كابينة لشخص kæ**bī**næ li shakhṣ *f* 68
single room غرفة لشخص **gor**fæ li shakhs *f* 19, 23
sister أخت okht *f* 93
sit down, to جلس **gæ**læsæ 95
size مقاس ma**qās** *m* 114, 117, 123
skin جلد gild *m* 138
skirt جيب zhūb *f* 116
sky سماء sæ**mǣ'** *f* 94
sleep, to نام **nǣ**mæ 144
sleeping bag حقيبة للنوم ḥa**qī**bæ lil nōm *f* 32
sleeping car عربة نوم **'a**rabit nōm *f* 71, 72, 73
sleeping pill دواء منوم dæ**wǣ'** mo**næw**wim *m* 143
sleeve كم komm *m* 115
slide *(photo)* سليد slæyd *m* 123
slip كومبينزون kombi**nē**son *m* 116
slipper شبشب **shib**shib *m* 117
slow بطيء ba**ṭī'** 15; *(clock)* مؤخرة mo'**ǣkh**khira 153
slowly ببطىء bi**boṭ'** 13, 21, 135
small صغير ṣa**gīr** 15, 20, 25, 38, 60, 102, 114, 117
small change فكه **fæk**kæ *f* 130
smoke, to دخن **dæ**khkhænæ 95
smoked مدخن mo**dæ**khkhæn 46
smoker *(compartment)* تدخين tæd**khīn** *m* 73
snack أكلة خفيفة **æk**læ khæ**fī**fæ *f* 41, 63
snack bar مطعم سناك **ma**ṭ'am snǣk *m* 69
snap fastener كبسون kæb**sūn** *m* 116
sneakers جزمة كاوتش **gæz**mæ kǣ**witsh** *f* 127
snorkelling غطس **ga**ṭs *m* 91, 127
soap صابون ṣā**būn** *m* 27, 110
soccer كرة قدم korat qa**dæm** *f* 90
sock شراب [كلسات] shor**rāb** *m* [kæl**sǣt** *f/pl*] 116
socket *(outlet)* فيشة الكهرباء **fī**shet æl-kahraba' *f* 27
soda صودا **ṣō**da *f* 59
soft لين **læy**yin 122
soft drink مشروب mæsh**rūb** *m* 59, 64
sole نعل næ'l *m* 117; *(fish)* سمك موسى sæmæk **mū**sæ *m* 46
soloist عازف **'ǣ**zif *m* 89
some من الـ min æl 16
someone أحد **æ**ḥæd 95
something شيء she' *m* 29, 55, 107, 111, 138
son إبن ibn *m* 93
song أغنية og**ni**yæ *f* 127
soon قريباً qa**rī**bæn 16
sore *(painful)* مؤلم **mo'**lim 145
sorry أسف **a**sef 11
sort *(kind)* صنف ṣanf *m* 44, 119
sound-and-light show عرض الصوت والضوء 'arḍ aṣ-ṣōt wæl ḍō *m* 87
soup شوربة **shor**ba *f* 41, 45
south جنوب gæ**nūb** *m* 77
souvenir تذكار tiz**kār** *m* 126
souvenir shop محل هدايا تذكارية mæ**ḥæll** hæ**dǣ**yæ tizkǣ**riy**yæ *m* 100
spare tyre عجلة طوارىء **'æ**gælæt ta**wā**rī' *f* 75
spark(ing) plug بوجيه **bo**zhī *m* 76
speak, to كلم **kæl**læmæ 13, 135, 136

speaker *(loudspeaker)* سماعة sæm**mæ**'æ *f* 118
special خاص khāṣṣ 20, 38
special delivery بريد مستعجل bærīd mos**tæ**'gil *m* 133
specialist أخصائي akh**ṣā**'ī *m* 142
specimen *(medical)* عينة 'æ**yi**næ *f* 142
spectacle case جراب للنظارة gi**ræb** lil naẓ**ẓā**ra *m* 122
spectacles [عوينات] نظارة naẓ**ẓā**ra *f* ['owæy**næt** *f/pl*] 122
spend, to صرف ṣarafæ 102
Sphinx أبو الهول æ**būl** hōl *m* 82
spice بهار bo**hār** *m* 52
spine عامود فقري 'æ**mūd faq**rī *m* 138
sponge سفنجة sæ**fin**gæ *f* 110
spoon ملعقة mæl'aqa *f* 37, 60
sport رياضة ri**yā**ḍa *f* 90
sporting goods shop محل أدوات رياضية mæ**ḥæll** ædæ**wæt** riya**ḍiy**ya *m* 100
spring *(season)* ربيع ra**bī'** *m* 148
square مربع morabba' 102
square *(open space)* ميدان mī**dæn** *m* 82
squash club نادي أسكواش **næ**dī skwāsh *m* 90
stadium أستاد is**tæd** *m* 82
staff موظفين mu**waẓ**ẓafīn *m/pl* 26
stain بقعة **boq**'a *f* 29
stamp *(postage)* طابع **ṭā**bi' *m* 28, 125, 132
star نجم nigm *m* 94
start, to بدأ **bæ**dæ'æ 80, 88, 89; *(car)* قام **qā**ma 78
starter *(appetizer)* [مزه] فاتح شهية **fæ**tiḥ shæh**hiy**yæ *m* [**mæz**zæ *f*] 41, 42
station محطة ma**ḥaṭ**ṭa *f* 73; *(railway)* محطة قطار ma**ḥaṭ**ṭit qi**ṭār** *f* 19, 21, 69
stationer's محل أدوات كتابية mæ**ḥæll** ædæ**wæt** kitæ**biy**yæ *m* 100, 105
statue تمثال tim**sæl** *m* 82
stay إقامة iqā**mæ** *f* 31, 92
stay, to بقى ba**qā** 17, 24, 26; *(reside)* سكن sækænæ 93
steal, to سرق **sa**raqa 155
steamer باخرة **bæ**khira *f* 68
stew طاجن **ṭā**gin *m* 41
stiff neck ألم في العنق æ**læm** fil '**o**noq *m* 141
sting قرصة **qar**ṣa *f* 139
sting, to قرص **qa**raṣa 138
stitch, to *(clothes)* خيط **khay**yaṭa 29, 117
stock *(in shop)* بضاعة bo**ḍā**'a *f* 104
stocking شراب حريمي shor**rāb** ḥa**rī**mī *m* 116
stomach معدة **mi**'dæ *f* 138
stomach ache ألم في المعدة æ**læm** fil **mi**'dæ *m* 141
stools براز bo**rāz** *m* 142
stop, to وقف **wa**qafa 21, 66, 68, 70, 73
stop thief! أمسك حرامي **æm**sik ḥa**rā**mī 155
store *(shop)* محل mæ**ḥæll** *m* 99
straight ahead على طول '**a**læ ṭūl 21
strange غريب ga**rīb** 84
strawberry فراولة fa**raw**la *f* 54
street شارع **shæ**ri' *m* 25
streetcar ترام **trām** *f* 66
street map خريطة للبلد kha**rī**ṭa lil **bæ**læd *f* 19, 106
string دوبار dō**bār** *m* 106
strong قوي **qa**wī 125
student طالب **ṭā**lib *m* 83, 93
study, to درس **dæ**rasæ 93
subway *(rail)* مترو **mi**tro *m* 67
suede شاموا **shæm**wa *f* 113, 117
Suez السويس æs-su**wēs** *f* 70
sufficient كافي **kæ**fiy 70
sugar سكر **sok**kar *m* 38
suit *(man)* بدلة **bæd**læ *f*; *(woman)* بدلة حريمي **bæd**læ ḥæ**rī**mī *f* 116
suitcase حقيبة ḥa**qī**bæ *f* 18
summer صيف ṣēf *m* 148
sun شمس shæms *f* 94
sunburn ضربة شمس **ḍar**bit shæms *f* 107
Sunday (يوم) الأحد (yōm) æl-**æ**ḥæd 82, 152
sunglasses نظارة شمس naẓ**ẓā**rit shæms *f* 122
sunshade *(beach)* شمسية shæm**siy**yæ *f* 91
sunstroke ضربة شمس **ḍar**bit shæms *f* 141
sun-tan cream كريم للشمس krem lil shæms *m* 110
sun-tan oil زيت للشمس zēt lil shæms *m* 110
super *(petrol)* سوبار sō**bar** 75

supermarket سوبر ماركت **sōbar markit** *m* 100
suppository لبوس **libūs** *m* 108
surcharge رسم إضافي ræsm **idāfī** *m* 70
surgery *(consulting room)* عيادة دكتور 'iyædæt doktōr *f* 136
surname لقب laqab *m* 25
suspender belt حزام مشبك ḥizæm mæshbæk *m* 116
suspenders *(Am.)* حمالات ḥæmmælæt *f/pl* 116
swallow, to بلع bælæ'æ 143
sweater بلوفر bolōvar *m* 116
sweatshirt سويت شيرت swit shert *m* 116
sweet *(food)* حلو ḥilw 58, 60
sweet *(candy)* بونبوني bonbōnī *m* 125
sweet corn ذرة **dora** *f* 50
sweetener سكر صناعي sokkar ṣinā'ī *m* 38
swell, to ورم **warama** 139
swelling ورم **waram** *m* 139
swim, to سبح **sæbæḥæ** 91
swimming سباحة sibæḥæ *f* 90, 91
swimming pool حمام سباحة ḥæmmæm sibæḥæ *m* 91
swimming trunks مايوه mæyō *m* 128
swimsuit مايوه mæyō *m* 128
switch *(light)* مفتاح النور moftāḥ æn-nūr *m* 29
switchboard operator عامل تليفون 'æmil tilifōn *m* 26
symptom أعراض a'rāḍ *m/pl* 140
synagogue معبد يهودي mæ'bæd yæhūdī *m* 85
synthetic صناعي ṣinā'ī 112

T
table [طاولة] ترابيزه tarabēza *f* [ṭawla *f*] 36; *(list)* جدول gædwæl *m* 156
tablet قرص qorṣ *m* 108
tailor's [خياط] ترزي tærzī *m* [khayyāṭ *m*] 100
take, to أخذ ækhædæ 18, 21, 25, 66, 68, 103, 135, 143
take away, to *(carry)* أخذ معه ækhædæ mæ'æho 64, 103
talcum powder بودرة تلك bodrat tælk *f* 110
tampon تامبون طبي tæmbōn ṭibbī *m* 108
tap *(water)* حنفية ḥænæfiyyæ *f* 28
taxi تاكسي tæksī *m* 18, 19, 21, 31
tea شاي shæy *m* 39, 62, 119
team فريق færīq *m* 90
tear, to مزق mæzzæqa 139
taspoon ملعقة صغيرة mæl'aqa ṣagīra *f* 143
telegram تلغراف tiligrāf *m* 133
telegraph office مكتب تلغراف mæktæb tiligrāf *m* 100
telephone تليفون tilifōn *m* 28, 78, 79, 134
telephone, to إتصل ittaṣala134
telephone booth كابينة تليفون kæbinet tilifōn *f* 134
telephone call مكالمة mokælmæ *f* 134, 135
telephone directory دليل تليفون dælīl tilifōn *m* 134
telephone number رقم تليفون raqam tilifōn *m* 134, 135
telephoto lens عدسة مكبرة 'ædæsæ mokæbbira *f* 124
television *(set)* تليفزيون tilivisyōn *m* 23, 28, 118
telex تلكس telex *m* 133
telex, to أرسل تلكس ærsælæ telex 133
tell, to قال qāla 14, 67, 76, 135
temperature درجة حرارة daragit ḥærāræ *f* 91, 140
temple معبد mæ'bæd *m* 82
temporary مؤقت mowaqqat 145
tendon وتر watar *m* 138
tennis تنس tēnis *m* 90
tennis court ملعب تنس mæl'æb tēnis *m* 90
tent خيمة khēmæ *f* 32
tent peg وتد خيمة wætæd khēmæ *m* 32
tent pole عامود خيمة 'æmūd khēmæ *m* 32
terrace تراس tirās *m* 36
tetanus تيتانوس tītænōs *m* 139
than من min 16
thank, to شكر shakara 11
thank you شكراً shokran 11
that هذا hæzæ 13, 101
the الـ æl 8, 158

theatre مسرح **mæsraḥ** *m* 82, 87
theft سرقة **sirqa** *f* 155
their هم... ...hom 160
then بعدين bæ'**dēn** 16
there هناك hon**æk** 15, 16
thermometer ترمومتر tirmo**metr** *m* 108, 144
these هذه h**æ**zihi 63
they هم hom 15, 161
thief حرامي ḥar**āmī** *m* 155
thigh فخذ fækhd *m* 138
thin خفيف khæ**fīf** 113
think, to *(opinion)* رأى ra'**ā** 92; *(believe)* ظن **ẓan**na 61, 73, 94
this هذا **hæ**zæ 12, 13, 101
those هذه h**æ**zihi 63
thread خيط khēṭ *m* 27
throat زور zōr *m* 138, 141
throat lozenge قرص للزور qorṣ lil zōr *m* 108
through من خلال min khil**æl** 16
thumb أصبع إبهام **aṣ**ba' ib**hæm** *m* 138
Thursday (يوم) الخميس (yōm) æl-khæ**mīs** *m* 30, 152
ticket تذكرة tæz**ka**ra *f* 65, 67, 72, 88, 90
ticket office شباك تذاكر shib**bæk** tæ**zæ**kir *m* 69
tie كرافتة kara**vat**ta *f* 116
tie pin دبوس كرافته dæb**būs** kara**vat**ta 121
tight *(clothes)* ضيق **ḍæy**yæq 114
tights شراب حريمي طويل shor**rāb** hæ**rī**mī ṭa**wīl** *m* 116
time وقت waqt *m* 70; *(clock)* ساعة **sæ**'æ *f* 153; *(occasion)* مرة **mar**ra *f* 95, 143, 148
timetable جدول مواعيد **gæd**wæl mæwæ'**īd** *m 71*
tin *(can)* علبة 'ilbæ *f* 119
tin-opener فتاحة علب fæt**tæ**ḥit 'ilæb *f* 128
tint تلوين tæl**wīn** *m* 110
tinted ملون molæw**wæn** 122
tire عجلة 'æ**gæ**læ *f* 75, 76
tired تعبان tæ'**bæn** 14
tissue *(handkerchief)* منديل ورق mæn**dīl** waraq *m* 110

to *(direction)* إلى ilæ 16, 18, 21
toast توست tost *m* 39
tobacco دخان dok**hæn** *m* 125
tobacconist's محل سجائر [محل دخان] mæ**ḥæll** sæ**gæ**yir *m* [mæ**ḥæll** dok**hæ**n *m*] 100, 125
today اليوم æl-**yōm** 29, 94, 152
toe أصبع القدم **aṣ**ba' æl-qa**dæm** *m* 138
toilet *(lavatory)* تواليت tæwæ**līt** *m* 24, 32, 38, 69
toilet paper ورق تواليت **wa**raq tæwæ**līt** *m* 110
toiletries أدوات تجميل ædæ**wæt** tæg**mī**l *f/pl* 109
toilet water كولونيا ko**lon**yæ *f* 110
tomato طماطم [بندورة] ṭa**mā**ṭim *m* [bana**dū**ra *f*] 50, 119
tomb قبر qabr *m* 82
tomorrow غدا **gæ**dæn 29, 94, 152
tongue لسان li**sæn** *m* 47, 138
tonight الليلة æl-**læy**læ 87, 88, 96, 152; هذا المساء **hæ**zæl mæ**sæ**' 89
tonsils لوز **li**wæz *f/pl* 138
too كثير ki**tīr** 16, 19, 24, 25; *(also)* أيضاً **ay**ḍan 16
tool عدة '**id**dæ *f* 128
tooth سنة **sin**næ *f* 145
toothache ألم في أسنان **æ**læm fī æs**næn** *m* 145
toothbrush فرشة أسنان **for**shæt æs**næn** *f* 110, 118
toothpaste معجون أسنان mæ'**gūn** æs**næn** *m* 110
torch (flashlight) بطارية جيب baṭ**ṭā**riyyi gēb *f* 118
torn ممزق mo**mæz**zaq 139
tour جولة **gæw**læ *f* 68, 80
tourist office مكتب سياحة **mæk**tæb si**yæ**ḥæ *m* 80
tourist tax رسوم سياحية ri**sūm** siyæ**ḥiy**yæ *m/pl* 24
towards إلى ilæ 16
towel فوطة **fū**ṭa *f* 27, 108
towelling قماش فوطة qo**mæsh** **fū**ṭa *m* 113
tower برج borg *m* 82
town بلد **bæ**læd *f* 19, 21, 76, 89, 106
town hall مبنى المحافظة **mæb**næ æl-mo**ḥā**faẓa *m* 82

tow truck سيارة نجده **sæyyārit nægdæ** *f* 78
toy لعبة **li'bæ** *f* 128
toy shop محل لعب **mæḥæll li'æb** *m* 100
track سكة **sikkæ** *f* 86
tracksuit ترننج **trēning** *m* 128
traffic مرور **morūr** *m* 77
traffic light إشارة مرور **ishārat morūr** *f* 77
trailer كاراڤان **karavan** *m* 32
train قطار **qiṭār** *m* 69, 70, 71, 72, 73
tram ترام **træm** *f* 66
tranquillizer دواء مهدىء **dæwæ' mohæddi'** *m* 143
transfer *(bank)* تحويل **tæḥwīl** *m* 131
transformer محول [ترانس] **mohæwwil** *m* [trāns *m*] 118
translate, to ترجم **tærgæmæ** 13
travel, to سافر **sæfæræ** 93
travel agency مكتب سياحة **mæktæb siyæḥæ** *m* 100
travel guide دليل سياحي **dælīl siyæḥī** *m* 106
traveller's cheque شيك سياحي **shīk siyæḥī** *m* 18, 61, 103, 130
travelling bag شنطة **shanṭa** *f* 18
travel sickness دوار سفر **dowār safar** *m* 107
treatment علاج **'ilæg** *m* 143
tree شجرة **shagara** *f* 86
trip رحلة **riḥlæ** *f* 66, 93, 151
trousers بنطلون **banṭalōn** *m* 116
try, to حاول **ḥæwælæ** 135; *(taste)* تذوق **tazawwaqa** 58
try on, to قاس **qāsæ** 114
T-shirt تي شيرت **tī shert** *m* 116
tube أنبوبة **anbūbæ** *f* 119
Tuesday (يوم) الثلاثاء **(yōm) æt-tælæt** *m* 152
tuna تونة **tūna** *f* 43
tunny تونة **tūna** *f* 43
turkey ديك رومي [حباش] **dīk rūmī** *m* [ḥæbæsh *m*] 49
turn, to *(change direction)* إتجه **ittægaha** 21, 77
tweezers ملقاط **molqāṭ** *m* 110
twin bed سريرين **sirīrēn** *m/dl* 23
typewriter آلة كاتبة **ælæ kætbæ** *f* 27, 106
typing paper ورق للآلة الكاتبة **waraq lil ælæl kætbæ** *m* 106
tyre عجلة **'ægælæ** *f* 75, 76, 78

U

ugly قبيح **qabīḥ** 15
umbrella شمسية **shæmsiyyæ** *f* 91, 116
uncle عم **'æmm** *m* 93
unconscious مغمى عليه **mogmæ 'ælēh** 138
under تحت **tæḥt** 16
underground *(railway)* مترو **mitro** *m* 67
underpants سليب **slib** *m* 116
undershirt فانيله **fænillæ** *f* 116
understand, to فهم **fæhæmæ** 13
undress, to خلع **khælæ'æ** 142
university جامعة **gæmi'æ** *f* 82
until حتى **ḥættæ** 16
up فوق **foq** 16, 26
upset stomach عسر هضم **'osr haḍm** *m* 107
upstairs فوق **foq** 16
urgent عاجل **'ægil** 14, 145
urine بول **bōl** *m* 142
use إستعمال **isti'mæl** *m* 17
use, to إستعمل **istæ'æmælæ** 78, 134
useful مفيد **mofīd** 16
usual معتاد **mo'tæd** 143

V

vacancy *(room)* غرفة خالية **gorfa khælyæ** *f* 23
vacant خالي **khælīy** 15, 22
vacation أجازة **ægæzæ** *f* 152
vaccinate, to تطعم **tæṭa'ama** 139
vaginal infection تلوث في المهبل **tælæwwos fil mihbal** *m* 140
valley وادي **wædī** *m* 86
value قيمة **qīmæ** *f* 131
veal (لحم) بتلو **(læḥm) bitillo** *m* 47
vegetable خضار **khoḍār** *m/pl* 41, 50
vegetable store خضري **khoḍarī** *m* 100
vegetarian بدون لحم **bidūn læḥm** 38
vein عرق **'irq** *m* 138
venereal disease مرض تناسلي **maraḍ tænæsolī** *m* 141
very جداً **giddæn** 16, 31, 95
vest فانلة **fænillæ** *f* 116; *(Am.)* صيديري **ṣidērī** *m* 116

veterinarian طبيب بيطري **ṭabīb bīṭarī** *m* 100
video camera كاميرا ڤيديو **kǣmira vīdyō** *f* 123
video cassette كاسيت ڤيديو kæsset vīdyō *m* 123
video recorder جهاز ڤيديو gihǣz vīdyō *m* 118
view منظر manẓar *m* 23, 25
village قرية **qar**yæ *f* 76, 86
vinegar خل khæll *m* 38
vineyard مزارع كروم mæzǣri' korūm *m m/pl* 86
visit زيارة ziyāra *f* 92
visit, to زار **zā**ra 85, 95
visiting hours مواعيد الزيارة mæwǣ'īd æz-ziyāra *m/pl* 144
vitamin pills أقراص ڤيتامين aqrāṣ vitæmīn *m/pl* 108
volleyball ڤولي [الكرة الطائرة] **vō**lī *m* [æl-kora aṭ-ṭā'ira *f*] 90
voltage ڤولت الكهرباء volt æl-kahraba' *m* 27, 118
vomit, to قاء **qā**'a 140

W

waistcoat صيديري ṣidērī *m* 116
wait, to إنتظر intaẓara 21, 95, 107
waiter جرسون garsōn *m* 26
waiting room صالة إنتظار ṣālit intiẓār *f* 69
waitress جرسونة garsōna *f* 26
wake, to أيقظ æyqaẓa 27, 73
walk, to مشى mæshǣ 85
walking سير sæyer *m* 74
wall حائط ḥā'iṭ *m* 120
wall clock ساعة حائط sǣ'it ḥā'iṭ *f* 120
wallet محفظة mahfaza *f* 155
walnut عين جمل 'æyn gæmæl *f* 63
want, to *(wish)* أراد arādæ 13
warm *(weather)* حر ḥarr 94
wash, to غسل gæsælæ 29
wash basin حوض ḥōḍ *m* 28
watch ساعة sǣ'æ *f* 120, 121
watchmaker's محل ساعات mæḥæll sǣ'ǣt *m* 100, 120
watchstrap جلدة ساعة gildit sǣ'æ *f* 121
water ماء mǣ' *m* 23, 24, 28, 39, 59, 75, 91
water carrier برميل ماء bærmīl mǣ' *m* 32
water flask زمزمية zæmzæmiyyæ *f* 32
watermelon بطيخ baṭṭīkh *m* 54
water pipe شيشة [نرجيلة] shīshæ *f* [nærgīlæ *f*] 62, 126
waterproof ضد الماء ḍidd æl-mǣ' 121
water-skis أدوات إنزلاق على الماء ædæwǣt inzilǣq 'ælæl mǣ' *f/pl* 91
wave موج mæwg *m* 91
way طريق ṭarīq *m* 76
we نحن næḥno 161
weather جو gæww *m* 94
weather forecast تنبؤات جوية tænæbbo'ǣt gæwwiyyæ *f/pl* 94
wedding ring دبلة زواج diblit zæwǣg *f* 121
Wednesday (يوم) الأربعاء (yōm) æl-arba'a *m* 152
week أسبوع osbū' *m* 17, 20, 24, 80, 152
weekend نهاية الأسبوع nihǣyæt æl-osbū' *f* 20, 152
well *(water)* بئر bi'r *m* 86
well *(healthy)* كويس kwæyyis 12
west غرب garb *m* 77
what ما mǣ 12, 18, 26; ماذا mǣzæ 12, 14
wheel عجلة 'ægælæ *f* 78
when متى mætæ 12, 83
where أين æynæ 12, 83
which أي æyy 12, 66
white أبيض abyaḍ 58, 112
who من mæn 12, 83
whole بالكامل bil kǣmil 143
why لماذا limǣzæ 12, 95
wick شريط ولاعة shirīṭ wællǣ'æ *m* 125
wide واسع wǣsi' 117
wide-angle lens عدسة معظمة 'ædæsæ mo'aẓẓama *f* 124
wife زوجة zæwgæ *f* 124
wig باروكة barūka *f* 110
wind ريح rīḥ *f* 94
window شباك shibbǣk *m* 28, 36, 72; *(shop)* ڤترينة vitrīnæ *f* 101, 111
windscreen/shield زجاج أمامي zogǣg æmǣmī *m* 76
windsurfing تزحلق شراعي tæzæḥloq shirā'ī *m* 91

wine نبيت nibīt *m* 41, 57, 58, 60
wine list لستة النبيت listit æn-nibīt *f* 58
winter شتاء shitǣ' *m* 148
wiper مساحة massǣḥæ *f* 76
with *(thing)* بـ bi 16, 23; *(person)* مع mæ'æ 16, 93
withdraw, to *(bank)* سحب sæḥæbæ 130
without بدون bidūn 16, 55
woman سيدة sæyyidæ *f* 111
wonderful ممتاز momtǣz 96
wood خشب khæshæb *m* 126; *(forest)* غابة gāba *f* 86
wool صوف ṣūf *m* 112, 113
word كلمة kelmæ *f* 13, 133
work, to *(function)* عمل 'æmilæ 28, 118
working day يوم عمل yom æmæl *m* 152
worse أسوأ æswæ' 15
wound جرح gærḥ *m* 139
wrap, to غلف gællæfæ 104
write, to كتب kætæbæ 70, 102, 161
writing pad بلوك نوت blōk nōt *m* 106
writing paper ورق خطابات waraq khiṭābāt *m* 27
wrong غلط galaṭ 15, 135

X

X-ray *(photo)* أشعة æshi'æ *f* 139

Y

year سنة sænæ *f* 149
yellow أصفر aṣfar 112
yes نعم næ'æm 11
yesterday أمس æms 152
yet بعد bæ'd 16, 17
yoghurt زبادي zæbǣdī *m* 39, 64
you انتَ، انتِ، أنتم intæ, inti, intom 161
young شاب shǣbb 15
your ...كَ، ...كِ، ...كم ,...kæ, ...ki, kom 160
youth hostel بيت شباب bēt shæbǣb *m* 22

Z

zip(per) سوستة sostæ *f* 116
zoo حديقة حيوان ḥædīqat ḥæyæwǣn
zoology علم الحيوان 'ilm æl-ḥæyæwǣn *m* 84

DICTIONARY قاموس

فهرس عربي

PORTUGAL
SPAIN
ITALY
GREECE
TURKEY
TUNISIA
Mediterranean Sea
MOROCCO
SYRIA
LEBANON
IRAN
IRAQ
JORDAN
Persian Gulf
KUWAIT
BAHRAIN
QATAR
ALGERIA
LIBYA
EGYPT
SAUDI ARABIA
MAURITANIA
MALI
NIGER
Red Sea
YEMEN
SENEGAMBIA
CHAD
SUDAN
Gulf of Aden
CENTR. AFR. REP.
ETHIOPIA
ATLANTIC OCEAN
ZAIRE
KENYA
OCEAN

TURKEY
Aleppo
Cyprus
Crete
SYRIA
IRAQ
LEBANON
Beirut
Damascus
Baghdad
MEDITERRANEAN SEA
Amman
Jerusalem
Alexandria
Mersa Matruh
Port Said
JORDAN
Cairo
El-Alamein
Suez
Giza
El-Fayyoum
SAUDI ARABIA
Hurghada
Assiut
Nile
EGYPT
Luxor
Red Sea
Esna
Edfu
Aswan
Medina
Lake Nasser
Abu Simbel
Jeddah
Mecca